MORE PRAISE FOR THREE D.

"Ian Jenkins, MD proves it takes a team to build a family in his entertaining new book *Three Dads and a Baby*."

—Jerry Nunn, GoPride.com

"In the field of memoirs on polyamory, Ian Jenkins's new book *Three Dads and Baby* stands out. Not only does it turn the usual gender expectations of hetero and bisexuality by focusing on three gay men raising their child(ren) together, *Three Dads and a Baby* is packed with research and information that takes this book beyond the personal into a broader application that is useful to a wide range of people in chosen families. . . . This charming book is required reading for laypeople to legal scholars and anyone else who is interested in getting lots of information about expanded families in an entertainingly smart style."

—Elisabeth "Eli" Sheff, PhD, CSE, Expert witness, relationship coach, educator & consultant, CEO, Sheff Consulting

"With wisdom and a wonderful wit, Dr. Ian Jenkins takes us on pioneering cultural journey. What is a Family? If sheer effort is any measure, *Three Dads and a Baby*, reveals a Herculean tale by three loving partners to conquer every barrier to bring life into the world. It breaks new ground in revealing the supremely normal existence of this throuple and their two beautiful children, Piper and Parker. It is an instruction guide for how to be relentless in the pursuit of of joy and yes—dirty diapers, bottles, and no sleep. This is a great read for anyone needing the inspiration to embrace new life and family."

—Elizabeth Birch, American attorney and former corporate executive chair to the board of directors of the National Gay and Lesbian Task Force

three
dads
and a
baby

three dads and a baby

ADVENTURES IN
MODERN PARENTING

ian jenkins, md

CLEiS
PRESS

Published in the United States by Cleis Press, an imprint of Start Midnight, LLC, 221 River Street, 9th Floor, Hoboken, New Jersey 07030.

Printed in the United States.
Cover design: Jennifer Do
Cover photograph: Shutterstock
Text design: Frank Wiedemann
First Edition.
10 9 8 7 6 5 4 3 2 1

Trade paper ISBN: 978-1-62778-310-1
E-book ISBN: 978-1-62778-522-8

Jenkins family crest reprinted with permission from William Greer Albergotti III, MD.

Disclosures: Some names and identifying details were changed to protect personal privacy. The comments, anecdotes, and events are as accurate as my memory and notes taken at the time allow.

To my children, Piper Joy and Parker Lewis.
You taught me a child's riotous gigglestorm
is our most precious resource.

TABLE OF CONTENTS

1   **CHAPTER 1:**   Neonatal Life Destruction Syndrome

5   **CHAPTER 2:**   The Offer

11   **CHAPTER 3:**   Sixteen, Beer, Pickup Truck

17   **CHAPTER 4:**   The Oven

21   **CHAPTER 5:**   Why Three?

29   **CHAPTER 6:**   Negotiations

37   **CHAPTER 7:**   Are the Kids Alright?

43   **CHAPTER 8:**   Implantation

51   **CHAPTER 9:**   Mom Wanted

55   **CHAPTER 10:**   Hell. With Lawyers.

61   **CHAPTER 11:**   Regrouping. With Lawyers.

67   **CHAPTER 12:**   Three Men and a Legal Landscape

73   **CHAPTER 13:**   Choice and Fate

79   **CHAPTER 14:**   Ian and Alan

87   **CHAPTER 15:**   Zika

93   **CHAPTER 16:**   The Chapter on Masturbation

99   **CHAPTER 17:**   The Fuckery of Dr. Collins

105   **CHAPTER 18:**   Escape to Blumberg

109   **CHAPTER 19:**   The Swimmers

113   **CHAPTER 20:**   The Meggs

119   **CHAPTER 21:**   Making Babies

127   **CHAPTER 22:**   The Blueberry Convergence

133   **CHAPTER 23:**   Our Scandalous Poly Lifestyle

137	**CHAPTER 24:**	Coming Out Poly
143	**CHAPTER 25:**	Blood
149	**CHAPTER 26:**	What's in a Name?
155	**CHAPTER 27:**	Leave
161	**CHAPTER 28:**	Dread & Precedent
167	**CHAPTER 29:**	A Few Good Men
175	**CHAPTER 30:**	The Colander
179	**CHAPTER 31:**	The Shower
185	**CHAPTER 32:**	The Nursery
189	**CHAPTER 33:**	Breech
194	**CHAPTER 34:**	The Fuckery of Dr. Collins, Part Deux
201	**CHAPTER 35:**	The Racket
207	**CHAPTER 36:**	Emergency
213	**CHAPTER 37:**	Glamping
219	**CHAPTER 38:**	The Push
225	**CHAPTER 39:**	NICU
233	**CHAPTER 40:**	Home
239	**CHAPTER 41:**	The Milk Angel
245	**CHAPTER 42:**	Piper's Diapers: Meditations on Poop and Disney
249	**CHAPTER 43:**	#Blessed
253	**CHAPTER 44:**	Love
257	**CHAPTER 45:**	Afterword
257	Acknowledgments	
265	Endnotes	

CHAPTER 1

NEONATE LIFE DESTRUCTION SYNDROME

W e'd heard crazy stories from all sorts of friends and relatives about how a baby would explode our lives. "You think you're tired at work?" one said. "Wait till baby." Another told us he couldn't possibly bother with canvas grocery bags: "It's just way too much to think about after a baby." One couple didn't eat at a restaurant for a full year after their baby was born, despite living fifteen minutes from their parents, who had successfully raised three children to adulthood. We had friends who never flushed a toilet after 8:00 p.m. to avoid waking their kids. But Neonate Life Destruction Syndrome was *not* going to happen to us.

Even when she was just six days old, everything had come together. No one was exhausted. We had her routines sorted out; baby was kicking ass and taking milk. She wasn't quite ready for a STEM career or the United States Senate, but she did seem ready for college (drinking, sleeping all day, partying all night). We'd had twenty visitors. We'd watched two movies at home. And we'd posted all her adventures on social media, from her first moments to napping with our dogs. I'd already gotten a dozen very serious replies to my toileting post: "Any reason I can't dangle a poopy baby over a bidet? Asking for a friend." I hadn't taken leave from my career as a hospital doctor. I'd even polished off several work presentations, hosted a webinar on hospital safety, and chaired two hospital committee meetings.

So we felt ready to take her out into the world. Why not shopping? We needed both staples and treats, as every healthy family runs on a mixture of organic vegetables and chocolate. In our first humbling parenting experience, we'd lost track of what day it was and arrived at Costco midday on Saturday. But baby slept through it all, snuggled to my partner Jeremy's chest with a baby-porting gadget called a ring sling. One admiring shopper went out of her way to thank my partner for doing his part. "Used to be the men made the women do all the work. More and more men are contributing. The times sure are a-changing!"

Jeremy, ever the gracious pastor's son, smiled and thanked her. After she walked on, he said, "Lady, you don't know the half of it!" The woman hadn't realized it, but she'd just met a true modern family. *Three* fathers had accompanied our bundle of joy to the store that day. Alan and I had been partnered for fourteen years, and Jeremy had joined us five years ago, making us a polyamorous triad, or "throuple." Our baby's genetic mom had come with us to the store and smiled watching people try to guess at the relationships that bound the four of us. And earlier that day, we'd fed baby some colostrum from her amazing surrogate, who'd been pumping precious breast milk for us since the birth. She'd done all the hard work for us, and we were having an amazing week precisely because none of us had to go through the trials of childbirth or breastfeeding.

All told, it took three fathers and two women to make our beloved little one. We know, right there, some people have some strong opinions about our decision to raise children despite knowing nothing else about us. According to the American Library Association's records of book suppression, the children's book *Heather Has Two Mommies* was the ninth most challenged book in the 1990s.[1] America has changed a lot since then, but imagine what the reception would be for *Heather Has Three Polyamorous Daddies and Two Mommies*!

We're not an ordinary family. But do we have crazy lives, wild parties, unstable relationships, lots of drama, and concerned families? No, not even remotely. We work, we clean the house, we ask each other what we should have for dinner, we pay taxes, we Netflix. Nothing to see here.

But was becoming *poly parents* an adventure?

Oh yes.

CHAPTER 2

THE OFFER

Twenty-seven months earlier . . .

I downed a carefully selected appetizer with my two boyfriends at a Memorial Day party. I had to save calories for the cake Jeremy had assembled out of red, white, and blue layers so the slices looked like American flags. He'd wandered away for a margarita refill, and when he returned, he leaned in and whispered, "Hey . . . do we want to have kids?"

His friends Stephanie and Julie had offered him embryos to adopt. They'd done two cycles of IVF with a sperm donor, and now they had three beautiful kids—plus two frozen embryos left over. They didn't have room for any more children in their family, but they didn't want to discard the embryos. Would we be interested?

We would. We needed to think long and hard about it, but we were intrigued. We agreed to drink more margaritas and discuss it at home.

In our eight pre-Jeremy years, Alan brought up having kids a dozen times. Once he said he'd be a great father, and I could be, too, with supervision. We knew he was right, but we never took the first step. Then Jeremy entered the picture: a zookeeper and nurturer by trade. With a third voice at the table, our conversations about parenting began to change. It says quite a lot about my second partner that Julie picked him to raise two of her children.

But Julie wasn't the first to tell us we should have kids. For years, our good friend Neha had been nudging us toward parenthood. We'd known her and her husband, Fred, since we moved to San Diego. Alan and Neha had worked together as psychiatrists on a children's unit, and Fred had rotated through the hospital medicine unit where I worked. Neha had impeccable taste and a knack for telling us that we'd disappointed her in way that felt like a compliment because she knew we were capable of much more. Our two biggest crimes: (1) hosting parties inside rather than using our deck with views of sparkly San Diego and Tijuana, and (2) "failing to get on the baby train."

"I'm worried," she once said over hors d'oeuvres at her place, "that you're going to put it off until it's too late. Which would be a most regrettable error."

Then we talked about the barriers. It may sound odd, but in our day-to-day lives, being in a gay throuple felt entirely normal. We lived in California. All of our friends and coworkers embraced us, so we didn't think of it as a barrier. Our problem was biological: none of us had a uterus. When Neha would ask why we hadn't had kids, I'd joke that we'd been trying desperately but seemed to be infertile.

We'd heard mixed things about adoption, the obvious solution, from our next-door neighbors. They'd had home interviews to get listed as adoptive parents. To make their home kid safe, they'd installed a retractable, heavy-duty pool cover, one an adult could walk across. They were lovely people, but they still got turned down. What would happen when our interviewer saw our uncovered death trap of a pool— co-owned by three unmarried gay guys? We didn't think we had a snowball's chance in hell of being accepted and didn't like the idea of some agency coming to our house to pass judgment on our fitness as parents in the first place.

At this point, Fred and Neha's two youngest kids burst out of their room in tears accusing each other of stealing toys and other crimes that seem unforgivable to children and meaningless to adults.

"Hush! Stop this nonsense and apologize to each other. Now shoo!" said Neha. "Don't make any decisions on the basis of our children's current behavior," she added after they'd exchanged insincere apologies. "I'm told this disgraceful behavior will eventually come to an end."

"When they're twenty?" Fred asked.

"Do not frighten them," she replied, as if we couldn't hear. "This is a delicate situation." Fred laughed and asked about IVF.

Alan said it sounded terrible. He'd heard figures of $8,000 each for the egg donor and agency, plus legal fees, test costs, and other hassles,[2] and the huge whopper—surrogacy. According to our Google searches, surrogacy costs were preposterous. One site said that fees ran from $90,000 to $130,000 or more in high-demand states like California.[3] Other sites said to expect between $165,000 and *$240,000*. That's right—a quarter of a million dollars to *make* a baby. Then you have to raise it. I assume that any quarter-million-dollar baby would expect to go to a private school and receive one-on-one coaching in equestrian sports. The kind where you wear a velvet helmet and ride your own horse.

Alan is many things, but perhaps first and foremost, he is an excellent internet shopper, and he had already done his research on bargain surrogacy. You could get a surrogate for far less in Africa, Asia, or India, he explained, but not without other hassles. In the famous case of "Baby Gammy," an Australian couple had a child by a Thai surrogate. The kid had Down syndrome—and the parents returned home without her. The media made it sound like the couple had dumped an abnormal baby on an impoverished surrogate. But a court later found that contrary to the scandalous headlines, they hadn't abandoned baby Gammy—civil unrest had forced them to flee Thailand while Gammy was too sick to travel. Plus, the surrogate had wanted to keep their baby.[4]

"I need another drink just hearing about that," said Neha, waving an empty glass in Fred's direction. He refilled it. Fred makes killer cocktails. That night we were having French 75s—gin, lemon juice, simple syrup, champagne. If Fred and Neha invite you to dinner, you should go.

Alan wasn't done with his stories about foreign surrogacy. Another Thai surrogate had refused to relinquish a baby she bore for a gay couple, saying she disagreed with their sexual orientation.[5] With multiple messy surrogacy cases making headlines, Thailand banned international surrogacy, creating legal nightmares for couples who already had pregnant surrogates. Several other Asian countries, some of which had previously lacked any surrogacy regulations at all, also imposed new laws. Many couples turned to Cambodian surrogates, only to find themselves in limbo when the country jailed an Australian nurse who ran a surrogacy clinic, stopped issuing visas to surrogate-born babies, and froze payments to surrogates. About fifty babies got stuck in Cambodia.[6,7] Mexico made more sense for us—we can see Tijuana from our house. But gay couples had ended up with their babies stuck there, too, when Mexico followed the Asian nations and also clamped down on surrogacy businesses.[8]

Surrogacy in the United States isn't simple, either, due to a complex patchwork of state regulations.[9] Louisiana punishes anyone entering into a paid surrogacy contract with civil and criminal penalties. At the time, New York and Michigan considered all surrogacy contracts void and compensated surrogacy agreements criminal (New York legalized surrogacy in 2020). In Arizona and Indiana, contracts are considered unenforceable, but some courts will grant prebirth parentage orders to intended parents. Seven states create significant legal hurdles for intended parents, and many others require additional steps (like amendments to birth certificates). Only ten states and the District of Columbia make it easy, reliably issuing prebirth orders to name both parents on the child's birth certificate.

Being gay adds even more challenges. In Louisiana, assisted reproduction is permitted, but only for heterosexual married couples. In Idaho and Tennessee, a gay couple would have to take their child to another state, obtain a second-parent adoption for the nongenetic parent, then return to their home state and seek recognition of the adoption, just to be named legal parents. As of late 2019, it was *unclear* if Mississippi would recognize an out-of-state second-parent adoption. And Nebraska simply *won't*. If you're the nongenetic parent to a child born by surrogacy in Nebraska, even if you're married to your same-sex partner, you remain a legal nobody. You get to worry about the consequences if your partner dies, or you get divorced, or even if you just want to take your child on a trip without the legal parent.

Consider one example of the extra challenges facing same-sex parents: a couple in Utah, known only as Jon and Noel to protect their privacy, were blocked from parenting by surrogacy *because* they're gay. Utah state law required a married couple to submit evidence that an intended "mother" is medically unfit to carry a child before surrogacy can proceed.[10] This intrusive law at least provided a path to parenting for straight couples and lesbians, but it completely shut out gay men. What was the idea behind this law? I imagined that Utah lawmakers thought long and hard about the number of penises found in various relationships, and then (I'm just guessing here) decided that zero penises = acceptable, one penis = optimal, and two penises = ick! Then, motivated by either malice or willful indifference, they wrote a law to keep gays from parenting.

Utah is a conservative state, and conservatives resent state intrusion into private affairs. Therefore, Utah legislators had no choice but to climb into bed with Jon and Noel and count their penises and weigh in on their fitness to have children. This wasn't 1950. Jon and Noel's case went to state Supreme Court in *2017*, and the Court decided in their favor in *2019*.[11] When I write that out, it sounds insane. At least the three of *us* had the good fortune specifically decided to live in California. Surrogacy might be impossible for a throuple, but better California than Utah or Louisiana, right?

Even putting aside legal concerns, if we were going to try surrogacy, we wanted to work with friends. Someone we could trust to eat right, go to appointments, take vitamins, not drink, and abstain from skydiving and heroin while pregnant. Someone who'd care about our babies, maybe remain in their lives as an aunt figure—but not try to snatch the kid. Alan had an Ethiopian friend from medical school who'd half joked about having his kids and worried about her eggs "getting old and dusty." Single, childless, and nearly forty, she knew it was soon or never. We liked the idea of beautiful, intelligent, mixed-race babies. "A little melanin is not a bad thing when you're growing up in San Diego!" Alan said. But these discussions never went beyond the "our kids would be so cool!" stage.

"Forgive me," Neha said, "but you're getting old and dusty, too! Like I said, putting this off would be a most regrettable error."

"What if they don't want to?" asked Fred. "Parenting was complicated for *us*. For them, it's crazy!"

But that was *then*, back in an era of pure hypotheticals. Things felt a lot different after margaritas, American flag cake, and an offer of two frozen embryos. Parenthood suddenly became much more plausible.

CHAPTER 3

SIXTEEN, BEER, PICKUP TRUCK

A block from our house, a dark curve in the road gives parked cars a measure of privacy and a lovely view of the San Diego skyline. Teens park there. In the afternoon they smoke weed. In the evening, judging by the litter they leave behind, they eat fast food and have sex. "That's disgusting," Alan would say when we walked our dogs past the evidence, and Jeremy would reply, "Well, at least they're using protection!" Our neighbors, the rejected adoptive parents, drive an enormous monster truck, and when they come across occupied cars at night, they pull up nose to nose, flick on their brights, and blind the teenagers until the kids lose their nerve and drive off.

Some teens had parked there in a pickup truck that Memorial Day. We really don't care about loitering or fornicating, but we *hate* littering. So, inspired by our neighbors, Jeremy drove by them slowly and used his cell phone to snap a picture of their license plate, which scared them away.

"It pisses me off," said Alan, "that we'd have to go through an expensive, crazy process to reproduce while some sixteen-year-olds are drinking beer and making oops babies in pickup trucks."

Back home we talked about all the hurdles we'd face if we adopted embryos. First, which two of us would get to be parents? Being in a throuple meant we had three salaries to defray costs, but someone would have to volunteer to be left off the birth certificate—without the rights of a legal parent. Second, would an in-vitro fertilization (IVF) clinic work with us? Hospitals are legally required to treat every patient that comes in the door, but IVF is an elective procedure. Could a clinic decide we were one parent too many? Third, how would we handle the poly thing with the kid? This last one seemed the easiest. I just didn't believe that kids who grew up with a loving, respectful, honest parental relationship would have a problem with it. Our kids would just be lucky to have an extra parent. Alan worried about all sorts of problems that could arise, like how a kid would fill out financial aid forms with three parents. We *all* worried about them getting teased, suffering over a choice we'd made. But there wasn't anything we could do about society, besides live in a tolerant community, which we already did.

Gay couples don't stumble into parenthood by accident. It's always a deliberate act, and a complicated one. Expectations differ for us, too. I've had friends with cystic fibrosis who knew they'd never be able to father children, but most straight couples expect they'll be able to have kids. And their parents often ask, "When are you giving us a grandchild?" But parents of gay kids say something else. We often hear it when we come out. Even supportive parents may tell us, "I love you the same, but I really wanted grandchildren." After she had some time to acclimate, that's what my mother said. And growing up, I'd learned the same lesson she had: gays can't have children.

In our pre-Jeremy years, Alan and I had talked about kids on numerous occasions. The same concerns kept coming up. Besides not having a uterus and related hassles, our concerns were the Earth, and happiness.

As for the Earth, the news about our precious blue planet gets more and more terrifying every year. In late 2017, fifteen *thousand* scientists from 184 countries warned that we faced calamity if we didn't change our ways.[12] Since 1970, the human population has grown by about four billion,[13] while 60 percent of the wild animals and 83 percent of the mammals vanished. Bird populations from Europe to Antarctica have declined 50 to 88 percent. Ninety-seven percent fewer bluefin tuna and 99 percent fewer blue whales in the oceans. Up to sixty times fewer insects in Puerto Rico. Twenty-five *times* as much biomass tied up in humans and livestock as in wild animals today.[14] Carbon emissions surged in 2018, accelerating global warming.[15]

What are we doing about it? We have the science. Thirteen federal agencies concluded that humans are definitely causing global warming.[16] And President Trump, who has said that the concept of global warming was created by the Chinese and has called it a "very expensive hoax,"[17] appointed Scott Pruitt to run the Environmental Protection Agency, which he'd previously sought to eliminate. Pruitt hollowed it out from the inside, slashing regulations, deriding climate science, and welcoming coal lobbyists to advise him. Over seven hundred employees left the EPA in the months following his appointment.[18] When ethics scandals finally pushed Pruitt out, a coal lobbyist replaced him.

I'm doing my part. Our xeriscaped yard only receives water from our rooftop collection system. I shower about ten minutes a week (if I stink, no one's told me yet). We have two electric vehicles, which we charge with our rooftop solar. But we know the greatest single thing any individual person can do for the planet is this: *reduce your baby emissions.* I cannot hope to offset the vast environmental impact of kids, grandkids, etc., with short showers.

As for the impact of kids on happiness, Alan and I had discussed it a bunch of times. Child rearing comes with a lot of stress.[19] A survey from *Child* magazine found babies slashed the amount of time spent with friends by about two-thirds.[20] Adults without kids are healthier, have more rewarding social lives, enjoy more recreational activities, suffer less stress, and are 75 percent more likely to report a full night of sleep, according to a poll of more than a million adults cataloged by polling platform CivicScience.[21] A review of studies on child rearing and marital satisfaction, published in 2003, found that parents had significantly lower satisfaction than nonparents.[22] Mothers of infants were a third less likely to report high satisfaction, and the more kids a couple had, the worse the effect. The effects were worse in recent years and for wealthier parents—people more accustomed to childless freedom, perhaps. People like us.

Despite this, parents are a third *more* likely to report feeling very happy. John Dick, writing at qz.com, wondered if that's because hardships might drive being childless, or maybe parents just say they're happy because they're supposed to. Or perhaps joy "doesn't just have to come from extrinsic things and fabulous social lives—it can come from the adventure of raising a family, from teaching and nurturing others, from sacrifice, and from unconditional love."[23]

Perhaps. The research on parenting and happiness is mixed, and much of it measures happiness on a single dimension, as if exhaustion and fulfillment exist on some kind of continuum. What if parents find themselves more happy, and more *unhappy*, at the same time?[24] Parenthood affects parents in different ways, some of which are personal and some of which can be predicted. We knew, for example, we could expect huge IVF costs. Other likely risks included strained partner relationships and exhaustion. As a colleague put it, "It's definitely worth it. But I never yelled at my husband before we had kids. And the sleep deprivation is dog shit."

Had Alan and I just been saying these things because the barriers to having kids seemed too high to bother scaling? Maybe. Regardless, welcoming Jeremy into our home changed things. He's a joyful person, and a nurturer. And once there were three of us, we had a special advantage for dealing with stress and exhaustion. However bad it got, two parents could always escape to a date night (or to sleep) while the third handled baby care. We had a built-in nanny. We just didn't have ovaries.

For an hour after we got home that Memorial Day, we talked about our relationship, values, and resources. I've since learned the simplest reason to have kids, which I'll share later, but at the time none of us really understood it. So we talked about our goals. We wanted our kids to enjoy rich educations and experience other cultures. We wanted them to understand just how lucky they would be compared to most people in the world today and throughout history. We would teach them empathy, by involving them in generous acts and asking them to consider others' perspectives. We would compliment our children for being compassionate and considerate, not for being beautiful or handsome. We would praise hard work, not intelligence. We wouldn't hit them.

If we had girls, we wanted them to know about female leaders, scientists, and artists, and feel free to be whomever they wanted. If we had boys, we wanted them to grow up without toxic masculinity, that American version of machismo that keeps boys and men from expressing tenderness or vulnerability. Just the idea that being nurturing is considered a *feminine* trait instead of a *desirable* trait is a tragic state of affairs. We wanted our children to know that they and everyone else had an inviolate right to bodily integrity and that intimacy was something you gave, never something you took.

By then, we decided we'd make a throuple of good dads. But we had to know one thing for sure: that we were ready to put a child's needs ahead of our own. That's a start every child deserves. So we decided not to decide. Having children was too big a decision to make in an evening. We needed to sleep on it. Before we could sleep on it, we had to walk our goldendoodles. For those of you unlucky enough not to have met a goldendoodle, they're half golden retriever and half poodle, and they're sweet, intelligent, adorable, and playful. And they don't shed. If you don't have a child by poly triad, consider getting a doodle.

We took the doodles on a looping walk through our neighborhood. Even then, the discussion didn't stop. We wanted our children to play an instrument. We wanted them to speak a second language, probably Spanish. On our walk we realized we'd been saying "our children" the whole evening. We *had* decided. We would adopt those embryos and raise them in a loving home.

I felt a mixture of excitement and trepidation. We were all on the same page about the rewards of parenting. We would teach our children our values, share their joys and adventures, thrill at their achievements. I didn't like the alternative—work, fill a house with stuff, die alone in a nursing home—but I never would have pushed the family toward parenthood myself. Alan and I had been together eight years before Jeremy, and we never seriously pursued having kids. As a throuple, we talked about children more, but again, we never took any concrete steps. Had that been for a good reason? What if this went wrong? Honestly, I'd never really liked babies. Kids, I could get behind, but what if I really didn't love the baby? What if we had a problem child? Parenthood could suck up all my free time for decades. I might have to put my hobbies on hold until I turned *sixty*.

Nearly home, we passed the curve in the road where the teens hung out. They'd been eating food from In-N-Out—a local burger joint. I picked up their trash while my partners wrangled the doodles.

"No condoms tonight," said Jeremy.

"Sixteen, beer, pickup truck," said Alan.

CHAPTER 4

THE OVEN

Before we could raise adopted embryos, of course, we needed a mom. We racked our brains for possible surrogates and even reconsidered using an agency, but in the end, Alan found us our surrogate by bringing up our search with a friend from Boston who'd recently moved near to us. He was having lunch with Delilah—the mom who told us that parental sleep deprivation was "dog shit"—and told her about our two leads.

One was a coworker of Jeremy's, who liked being pregnant and said she was open to the idea. The other was Jeremy's sister-in-law. That felt . . . a little too close. She was pretty religious, which we thought might be a factor if we came up against fetal abnormalities and the possibility of abortion. But more than that, it just felt weird to get Jeremy's sister-in-law pregnant with our child.

"I would totally do that for you!" Delilah said. "I really think we should help people if they want to become parents."

Alan hadn't been fishing for an offer and hadn't been expecting one.

"Oh wow," he just said, too surprised to discuss it in much detail, "that would be a huge gift!" They talked briefly about how big a commitment a surrogacy would be, finished lunch, and went back to seeing patients. He let the idea settle for a week, then emailed her to confirm she was serious.

She was. She just wanted to talk to her husband, Richard, about it. He soon agreed, and she fell more and more in love with the idea. She had only one condition—she only wanted to do single-embryo implantations. Nearly forty, she didn't want to take chances. We didn't want her to take chances, either. We scheduled a brunch to discuss it further.

Brunch is a big deal. Back when politicians used to openly attack gay people, accusing us of pushing our dangerous "gay agenda," a friend joked, "I'll tell you the gay agenda: cute shoes, nice vacations, brunch." He called going to brunch "gay church." So we were going to have a religious experience with Delilah and Richard—at least, as close as we got to religious experience.

Delilah and Richard are wonderful, open people, and we jumped into the whole pregnancy thing as soon as the waiter brought our mimosas.

"You really don't mind being pregnant?" Jeremy asked, removing a ten-inch spear of rosemary from his waffle stack.

"No! It sounds crazy, but I'm an easy pregnant. I mean, there's all these inconveniences. Motion puts a baby to sleep, so they wake up when you go to bed, and they can kick you all night. But it's so worth it!" Delilah turned out to be some sort of miraculous, earth-mother love goddess. "You're good people. Being parents will make you even better people. Your life and hers will be full of love, and that's just something the world needs more of, so this is just a gift I want to give you."

There's all sorts of stuff that intended parents and surrogates could disagree on. But with Delilah, we found ourselves on exactly the same wavelength. She never smoked; she ate lots of vegetables. She wouldn't drink an ounce, except "sometimes late in pregnancy, you both need a small glass of wine." We worried that a surrogate might get attached to the baby. No problem there. "And remember, I've got kids of my own," she said. "If we do this, there has to be no chance whatsoever that we end up with the baby."

Richard nodded furiously. "We've got three boys. Love them. No more."

That wasn't all. "If we come across some terrible fetal abnormality," said Delilah, "everything's up to you. Terminate, carry to term, it's your baby. We're fine with it. We get it." The good news continued. "I think it's great that we're friends. But not best friends, you know?" We did. Delilah lived a half hour away, and we didn't see her too often. We were friends, but not everyday friends, where things would feel awkward. Delilah wanted her kids to know our baby, and to stay in baby's life, but not too close—like an aunt, not a parent. That's what we wanted, too; we didn't want to tell our children that they'd been born to a stranger. We wanted to tell them that their daddies loved them, and so did their moms. We really couldn't believe our luck.

Sitting next to Richard, I felt like I had to whisper an important question. "You don't mind we're going to . . . you know, occupy your wife for a while?"

"Not at all," he said. "She's happy pregnant. It's great."

Not only did we and Delilah make a lovely match, she spoke directly and honestly. Money came up, but never awkwardly. "I really want to do this," she said, "but the whole thing about compensation feels gross. I don't think I could do it for money. But it's not an entirely comfortable process. There are risks. It also seems weird for it to be nothing." Delilah had already checked with her health insurance and uncovered a wrinkle. The surrogacy policy required forfeiture of half of any payments, to recoup health-care costs. But prenatal care for an altruistic surrogate, one who'd donated space in her oven, was free.

"Delilah," said Jeremy, "we'd have to give you something. We couldn't accept such a huge gift."

"That's right," said Alan. "If you insisted on an altruistic surrogacy, we would be so moved we'd *have* to contribute something . . . I don't know . . . how about to your favorite charities?"

Brilliant. Alan's such a fixer. We clinked out another round of mimosa toasts and grinned and laughed. We loved Delilah and Richard. We had some hurdles—she needed a surrogacy contract and approval from her ob-gyn—but we'd found our oven. And we'd also incurred our first surrogacy cost: recruitment brunch. So far this was the cheapest surrogacy in history!

"They're so cool!" Jeremy said as we left. "We love them, right?"

We sure did. We'd just begun, but we were already humbled by the generosity of our embryo donors and surrogacy volunteer. We thanked our lucky stars and whispered a little atheist prayer that our luck would hold out.

Surrogacy Costs:

Brunch:	$100.00
Total:	$100.00

CHAPTER 5

WHY THREE

M aybe I should back up and explain why I ended up in a throuple to begin with. People live poly lives for all sorts of reasons, but mine are simple: I don't get jealous, and *any* relationship I had was fated to be nontraditional. As a kid, I learned that same-sex desire was wrong and shameful long before I experienced it. Gay marriage didn't exist (gay couples didn't seem to, either). I didn't want a solitary life, or a sham heterosexual marriage, or a life in hiding, so I *had* to publicly shun sexual conventions. I picked a lifetime of nontraditional relationships before I picked a college. From one boyfriend to two, it's just a question of human nature.

Many people believe humans are naturally monogamous and naturally heterosexual. But monogamy is not "natural." Consider *The Myth of Monogamy: Fidelity and Infidelity in Animals and People* by David Barash and Judith Lipton. Most of their book outlines the evidence that nonmonogamy is the rule for both sexes of most species, even the ones we think of as monogamous, even humans. But they let culture neuter their conclusion. The rest of their book argues that we can overcome our inclinations and live monogamously anyway.[25]

In an interview, Lipton even compared our nonmonogamous tendencies to our taste for unhealthy food.[26] Obey the urge to cheat v. suppress your natural desires—little attention is given to the third option, polyamory. "The evidence is also overwhelming that many people are capable not only of 'making love to' but also of loving more than one person at the same time," the authors write. "But we are socially prohibited from doing either."[27] Maybe that should change. Maybe we should stop living in cages of our own making and instead permit ourselves to love more than one person and build overlapping relationships.

According to a commonly repeated statistic, half of American marriages end in divorce. The truth isn't that bad, but it's not great. Depending on how you measure it, and whether you include separation as well as divorce, the true marriage disruption rate is probably about 40 to 45 percent. The rate is falling, but that's partly because fewer people are getting married in the first place.[28, 29] The first time's definitely the charm: "60 to 67 percent of second marriages fail, and 70 to 73 percent of third marriages end on the rocks."[30,i] Are we supposed to take that "till death do us part" stuff seriously at a third wedding? Heck, my biological parents divorced each other *twice,* and each has divorced or separated from someone else, too. And that's just the *marriages* that end. Americans are getting married later and later, and having more relationships before they get married. Are those relationships *failures?* I thought so, until an extraordinary gentleman convinced me otherwise.

Eighteen years old, in my first week of college, I met Bernard Mayes, a delightful dean of communications who immediately pretended to hit on me. "*You're* a pretty one," he joked, caressing my hand. It would have seemed questionable had he not been pushing seventy and wielding a charming British accent. We saw each other regularly at activist events

---

i Again, this depends on the source and methods. You can *definitely* trust these numbers, which were compiled by divorce attorneys.

and became friends. Bernard had survived the bombing of London, served as an Episcopalian priest, cofounded National Public Radio, and pioneered suicide prevention hotlines. He never condescended to the youthful students he met, who had much less interesting stories to share. I'll never forget what he said about marriage as he recalled the end of his decades-long relationship with his treasured partner. Imagine an elderly, dignified professor in a conservative tweed suit, tears in his eyes, and that Monty Python accent.

"Most relationships end, but that does not mean that they *failed*. They do not fail if they brought us joy, or taught us things, or shepherded us through difficult times. They only fail if we wrong each other." I'd spent several years with my first boyfriend at the time, and I'd told Bernard that I thought we'd be together our whole lives. That may have been on Bernard's mind when he added, "We're told we are meant to be married forever, but nothing is forever. We should stay together as long as we can be *good* to each other." Relationships end, just as lives end. They can still be cherished and celebrated.

At the same time I was getting to know Bernard, I ran into Margaret Mead's writings in anthropology classes. Mead advised women to marry three times: once for passion, once for a coparent to their children, and once for companionship.[31] This makes perfect sense to me. Americans can expect to live almost eighty years, and we're very different people at different stages of our lives. So are our spouses. Marriage is no longer a business arrangement. We marry for love and companionship. Most of us expect to have a number of relationships over our lives—an average of eleven, according to a 2012 study, and it would surely be more if we weren't constrained by social and religious rules.[32] The line from that fact to polyamory is one simple, heretical question: *Why give up everything wonderful about one relationship to experience the joys of another?*

Relatively few of us have embraced polyamory, but it's probably more than you'd guess: a 2016 study found that 22 percent of single Americans had tried "consensual nonmonogamy," or CNM, at some point—more men than women, and more LGB people than heterosexuals.[33] Another estimate, from independent academic Kelly Cookson, is that 9.8 million Americans have some kind of CNM agreement with their partner.[34] In contrast to *consensual* nonmonogamy, many people have extra partners in a damaging and dishonest way: by cheating. How many? Cheaters lie, so it's hard to know. One study found that almost six times as many women admitted an affair on a computer survey than during a face-to-face interview.[35] People surely still lie on surveys, but the available data is still illuminating.

> ▸ The 1981 National Survey of Women found that 10 percent had a secondary sexual partner. The rate was lowest for married women (4 percent) and highest for cohabiting women (20 percent).[36]

> ▸ According to a 1999 survey, most college students engage in "extra-dyadic" experiences (cheating) despite social pressure to be monogamous.[37]

> ▸ About 12 percent of married men and 7 percent of married women say they have sex outside their marriage each year. Lifetime rates of infidelity increased through the early 2000s, for both men and women, and for younger and older age groups.[38]

> ▸ In a 2015 study, about one in four people admitted to cheating on their current "monogamous" partner. Those in "monogamous" relationships had the same risk of sexually transmitted infection as those in open relationships.[39]

> ▸ A 2016 sample of 655 students found that over a third had cheated in their current "monogamous" relationship.[40]

> ▸ Seventy-eight percent of men interviewed by sociologist Eric Anderson for a 2012 book admitted to affairs despite

wanting to remain faithful.[41] After reviewing studies on infidelity, and accounting for varying results (25 to 72 percent of men in recent research), he wrote in the *Washington Post*[42] that "cheating is as common as fidelity."[ii]

But people who answer sex surveys are probably not representative of the general population. Can we trust these numbers? "There are probably more scientifically worthless 'facts' on extramarital relations than on any other facet of human behavior," says Tom Smith, of the National Opinion Research Center, whose well-respected work estimates that only about 15 to 18 percent of married people have had affairs.[43] But whatever the rate, a lot of people risk the end of a marriage, public shame, losing child custody, etc., to have another partner. And whatever the rate, it's *beside the point.* What really matters is how many partnered people *want* another partner.

Here's one measure: the online "married sex survey," conducted by iVillage in 2013 and reported on Today.com, found that 32 percent of male respondents and 13 percent of female respondents would cheat if they knew they wouldn't get caught.[44] That's a lot of (unreliable) people. How many would want another sexual or romantic partner if their spouse, and society, *supported and encouraged* them? What if we could celebrate affection rather than condemning it as betrayal, and consider it human nature rather than a failure? iVillage conducted another poll in 2007, partnering with MSNBC. Over seventy thousand people completed it. And of those in monogamous relationships, 68 percent of men and 43 percent of women said they desired another person.[45]

So the big question isn't "Why would anyone consider a polyamorous relationship?" "Why do we uphold lifelong, monogamous marriage as a societal ideal, no matter how often we fail at it?" It might help Americans to step away from their own culture for a moment. Monogamy hasn't

ii The *Post* ran his piece the day before Valentine's Day, just in case anyone was feeling secure in their relationship.

25

been normal throughout most of human history, according to *Sex at Dawn: The Prehistoric Origins of Modern Sexuality*. Authors Christopher Ryan and Cacilda Jethá argue that until the agricultural revolution led to the concepts of property and wealth accumulation, most humans lived in cooperative nomadic communities. They shared resources and lived without a concept of property. Humans had diffuse concepts of parental responsibility, nonmonogamous relationships, and little sexual jealousy.[46]

Monogamy isn't even normal in many other areas of the world *today*. South Africa's former president Jacob Zuma married six times and currently has four wives. In Kazakhstan, polygamy has been decriminalized since 1998.[47] There are polygamy clubs in Malaysia and Indonesia, where much polygamy occurs under Islamic traditions allowing men to marry up to four women.[48, 49] A lot of this kind of polygamy involves deeply unequal societies, discrimination, and restricted options for women, and it makes me as uncomfortable as the involuntary polygamy and indoctrination found in some fundamentalist Mormon sects in the United States. But marriage can be unfair to women whether it's monogamous or polygamous, and both equal and matriarchal models of polygamy also exist.

Sex at Dawn gives a number of examples. The matrilineal Mosuo of China are said to enjoy "walking marriage," where men visit multiple women's homes. The truth, even more interesting, is that these "marriages" are discreet relationships without expectations of fidelity. The Mosuo enjoy "nearly absolute sexual freedom and autonomy for both men and women," and their language lacks words for "husband" or "wife." Mosuo men help raise the children born to women in their homes, usually of unclear paternity, rather than their biological children. Many women in rural Tibet have multiple husbands and similarly don't know which one has fathered their children.

Many other cultures embrace sexual freedoms that would surprise Westerners. The Dagara people of Burkina Faso call women "mother" and men "father," because they usually don't know who their biological father is. The Canela and Marind-anim peoples have wedding night orgies for the brides (as did ancient Romans), and the Canela marriage ceremony advises spouses not to be jealous of their partners' lovers. The Kulina have ritual hunts that end in partner swapping. At least twenty tribal cultures, from the Amazon to Polynesia, lack a concept of single paternity. Some of them believe that a fetus is made up of the accumulated semen of multiple men; mothers sleep with several men to give their babies the desirable traits of several dads.[50] And the matrilineal Trobriand people don't believe biological fathers contribute to children, who are considered part of the mother's lineage only.[51]

I had no idea that some cultures believed in multiple biological dads until I read *Sex at Dawn,* and I bet most Americans don't know about nonmonogamous traditional cultures. But if you ask me, Westerners, and particularly Americans, are polyamorous animals in social handcuffs, and they *do* know that. Understanding either their own feelings or those of others,' most people "get" my throuple immediately. They understand we're just regular people in a nonstandard relationship. "Lucky," some of them whisper. "I could have used another spouse to help with my kids," parents often, and unselfconsciously, admit. But not everyone gets it. "I just don't think it's possible to love more than one person," one told me, while preparing dinner for his three fully and equally loved children.

To each their own.

CHAPTER 6

NEGOTIATIONS

We live in a bubble—we mostly hang out with pro-choice, college-educated adults on the left coast. I don't think any of our friends or coworkers would equate a fertilized egg, or an embryo, with a baby. I don't believe that *anyone* does, actually, whatever they say about their politics. That's why no one has funerals for failed IVF embryos. But the mistake that some liberal pundits or abortion rights advocates make is to say that fertilized eggs, embryos, or even fetuses mean *nothing*. They say they're just tissue, or part of a woman's body, which doesn't capture how much a parent loves a child that could be. It ignores the recognition that a fertilized egg *is* a unique human life, whether it matures or not. It ignores the hope and love that goes into making embryos, or even the decision to have kids the old-fashioned way.

In short, it wasn't easy for Julie and Stephanie to give up their embryos.

On paper, it was an easy decision. They wanted the embryos to become children who knew their siblings and bio-mom in San Diego.

They needed some trustworthy, childless people with the means to raise them, and we fit the bill. But that didn't make it any easier to give up their children. Embryo adoption would make them legal strangers to their biological kids. If we wanted to raise them as Scientologists, abscond to Sri Lanka, or enroll them in cage fighting classes, we could. Would we? Absolutely not. Julie and Stephanie knew the kids would be at higher risk of abduction by aliens than getting mistreated by us, but the heart will have its say.

To get better acquainted, we invited Julie, Stephanie, and their kids over for a pool party at our place, complete with colorful pool noodles, splashing, four boisterous dogs, and trays of dino chicken nuggets. Suffice to say, Julie had made some remarkably cute and well-behaved kids. They entranced Jeremy, the most eager would-be father. I caught him running his hand through their five-year-old's hair. "Psst!" I whispered as she ran off. "Not an auction."

"I can't help myself," he said, mystified. "We'd be getting two just like them. It's so weird getting a preview of your kids." The kid quality did not surprise us. We knew the mom, and we'd seen the profile of the sperm donor, a handsome Latin pharmacist with a broad smile and over forty children via sperm donation (mental note: don't let the kids date anyone conceived with donor sperm, or we might get a half sibling pairing and funny-looking grandkids). We loved watching the kids laugh and play with each other. Maybe the reality differs from my memory, but when I think back on my interactions with my brothers, I'm just glad our parents didn't keep flamethrowers in the house.

So the kids were adorable. We were in. The mothers still had to process the momentous decision. First, Jeremy spoke with them several more times by phone. Then he enlisted Alan, the family's only board-certified psychiatrist, in the negotiations. Alan took Julie out to dinner to discuss donation and did two things that made all the difference. First, he listened. There's no talking someone out of their emotions, so he brought them out and validated them. Second, he didn't push them. Quite the opposite—he told the moms to back out if they needed to. "If you're not absolutely sure you want someone else to raise your kids, don't do it. And if you're not sure we're the right family to raise your kids, don't let us." They had alternatives: wait, find the resources to raise them themselves, find someone else, or discard them.

It sounds like reverse psychology, but he was just empathizing. It *would* be strange to have biological children raised in a home across town. Would the kids feel rejected? Would the mothers regret their decision? These were valid concerns. The last thing any of the five potential parents wanted would be a strained relationship or bitterness about the decision.

It took months, but the mothers agreed to move forward. It was time for a road trip to meet Dr. Collins, the reproductive medicine doctor who had done the IVF for Julie's pregnancies before she and Stephanie moved to San Diego. Dr. Collins worked for FISC, the Fertility Institute of Southern California, and FISC held Julie's two remaining embryos, cryogenically preserved in a deep freezer. Now *we* had to make a big decision. There would only be two legal parents for our kid. Should we present ourselves as poly to Dr. Collins? What if she wouldn't work with us? There had been times in my life when it was unwise, or literally unsafe, to proclaim my gayness. As a group, we decided this was another opportunity for discretion. One of us would be the secret dad.

But who? Jeremy's friend had made the offer, and Jeremy had the strongest desire to parent, so he would be a declared parent. Alan and I both had reservations about having kids, but we all agreed that, if it came to it, Alan would have an easier time being a stay-at-home dad, and I would have an easier time being a breadwinner. That was the best we could do; Alan headed off to be dad number two, and I set about winning bread. I felt relieved, honestly. I'd committed to having a child with my partners, but I didn't mind a little bit more time when I wasn't thrust into the decisions. I stayed at home to work through my trepidation about the life-changing arrival of infants, and I let Alan and Jeremy make the trek to Collins to discuss the embryo adoption and implantation process. And wow, is it ever a process.

Step one: Delilah would have a medical evaluation to make sure she was medically fit for surrogacy. I figured this would be simple, but it wasn't. Dr. Collins charged for her exam separate from the implantation cycle costs, and she did a hysterosalpingogram (an imaging study of her uterus and fallopian tubes) to look for abnormalities, even though Delilah'd had three healthy kids. After that, Delilah had FDA-mandated labs to rule out infectious diseases. We got a bill for each step.

Step two: her *husband* had to undergo an exam and lab testing, with the rationale that he might infect her with an STI down the road even if she was initially negative. Possible, I guess, but couldn't he pick up an STI at any point along the way?

Step three: *Julie* needed an exam and testing to "clear" the embryos as safe to implant. How does an evaluation for STIs done eight years after embryos were made tell you if she had an STI *then?* I have no idea. Surely her exam eight years ago mattered more? Add-ons were starting to frustrate us, and we'd just begun.

Step four: we hired lawyers to represent Jeremy and Alan on one side, and the mothers on the other, to draft an embryo adoption contract. Once the four of them signed it, Alan and Jeremy would be the legal parents of two frozen balls of cells.

Step five: we hired two more lawyers to represent Jeremy and Alan on one side, and Delilah on the other, to write a surrogacy contract. We went with highly recommended attorneys: one local, for Alan, and one from Washington, DC, for Jeremy. This contract was much more complicated. It covered psychiatric care if Delilah had pregnancy-related depression or grief over handing over the baby she would make. It covered the cost of maternity clothes, possible bed rest, and injuries. We had to agree on a supplemental life insurance policy—Alan and Jeremy fought an epic battle over that detail, because most companies didn't want to issue a large insurance policy to cover the wages of a well-paid pharmaceutical developer like

Delilah, if something went wrong. They eventually secured a $1 million policy from Lloyd's of London for two-thirds less than other offers.

Step six: Alan and Jeremy (and Delilah) needed psychiatric clearances to certify they were fit to be parents (or a surrogate). This *seemed* reasonable, especially before we asked Delilah to give up a child she'd made with her own body. But this requirement turned out to be needlessly expensive. Collins's office provided a list of potential PhD psychologists in the region who could do this work. Most of them wanted $650 for the interview—good work, if you can get it!—plus another $500 for psych testing. Basically, we'd have a healthy woman, three times a happy mother, and already interviewed by a psychologist, fill out bubble sheets to see if she was fit for surrogacy. (Sixteen, beer, pickup truck!)

What a crock of shit! No one uses bubble sheets to figure out if they can parent. This was all make-work to spend money and look official. Luckily, Alan knew these tests could only be ordered by PhD *psychologists*. And, right there on Dr. Collins's list, Alan spotted a licensed *social worker* he knew and trusted, who only wanted $350 for the interview and would not be ordering any tests. Alan's knowledge saved $800 of our money from evaporating. Welcome to surrogacy costs, I guess!

Step seven: Delilah would receive preimplantation hormone injections to prepare her uterus for an embryo, which Collins would thaw and implant. Those last three words, *thaw and implant,* were a big deal. For some reason, prescribing the standard hormones and implanting an embryo runs about $25,000 in America, for which you can get yourself a year of university or half a fancy kitchen remodel. Why? I still could not tell you.

That was all just to get pregnant. It tired me out just hearing about it, but I had the easiest job in the family. Alan and Jeremy, the two "designated parents," drove out of town to clinic appointments, led the contract negotiations, and haggled with lawyers. I only had to review drafts of the contracts they brought home and work hospital shifts to help pay for it all. It's a surreal job, being a side parent, and I had to remind myself that our kid would someday need three involved dads, not two. But as the weeks rolled by, our documents took shape, and the hypothetical pregnancy we planned, and the hypothetical baby we hoped would result, took shape in our mind.

As for the documents, I have to say that being a reproductive medicine attorney does not seem to be the hardest job in the world. They email you a standard contract and ask if you want to change the details. We could have done it ourselves, but IVF doctors won't proceed without clearance from a well-paid attorney.[iii] Yay. In the end, we made few alterations to the contracts. Julie and Stephanie requested one major change: a clause requiring their consent before any embryos could be destroyed. That made perfect sense to us.

It felt like it had taken twenty years, but finally we'd adopted embryos, signed a contract with Delilah, and confirmed she was medically fit for pregnancy. In addition, she, Alan, and Jeremy had all been declared not insane by mental health professionals. It was time to implant—after one more important decision.

Dr. Collins recommended that we have the embryos genetically tested. Thawing, hatching, testing, and refreezing would cost us $3,845, but it would tell us if an embryo had a fatal, or major, chromosomal abnormality. That could save us an even more expensive implantation cycle, but more importantly, we could avoid putting Delilah through injections and the small but real health risks of implantation, plus heartache over fetal loss or decisions about abortion, if it turned out there was a defect. It would also save us valuable time. Wasting a whole cycle on a nonviable embryo did not seem wise with a surrogate (and two dads) pushing forty. Collins warned that there was about a 50 percent risk of major genetic abnormalities.

Julie and Stephanie didn't want it done. They'd had three healthy IVF kids without testing, and they worried it could damage an embryo—

---

iii California also requires legal representation. No one ever told us. I learned this months later, drafting this book.

understandably so. While Collins said it was safe, the clinic would have to thaw and refreeze the embryos to remove cells for testing. But the moms knew we wanted to do it. We discussed it for a month. Eventually, they stated their objection, told us it was our decision, and backed away. We wrote the clinic a check and crossed our fingers.

Alan and Jeremy didn't tolerate the nail-biting wait as well as I did. I knew we had a 25 percent chance of two viable embryos, a 50 percent chance of one, and a 25 percent chance of none. I decided to expect one viable embryo and not get too attached. My partners, however, had already gotten attached—they loved the idea of two kids, kids that would be ours but would know their genetic siblings and bio-mom across town. But nature apparently only wanted us to have one kid. The testing showed one viable embryo and one with a devastating monosomy 16 (missing one copy of a chromosome). The embryo, if implanted, would almost certainly die, and if it lived, it would have severe abnormalities. Shit.

We didn't tell the moms. We figured it would be better to celebrate a pregnancy and break the bad news *then* rather than to tell them an embryo didn't make it before even rolling the dice on the other. At least we knew where we stood: we had a female embryo to implant, and a surrogate ready to go. Of course, few first-time parents feel completely ready, and we had the additional uncertainties of poly parenting to worry about. It felt like we'd ridden a long ski lift to the top of a mountain, picked a slope we'd never been down before, and paused at the top, our skis over the edge. With one push, we'd be speeding into new territory, hoping there weren't moguls around the corner. Or cliffs.

Previous costs:	$100.00
Fifteen-minute consultation with Collins:	$350.00
Exams and tests for Delilah:	$1,275.00
Exams and tests for Richard:	$530.00
Exams and tests for Julie:	$530.00

Three Dads and a Baby

Surrogacy contract	
Surrogate:	$2,750.00
Fathers:	$1,500.00
Embryo adoption contract	
Mothers:	$1,000.00
Fathers:	$500.00
Embryo testing	$3,845.00
Life insurance for Delilah:	$1,250.00
Psych clearance for Delilah:	$350.00*
Psych clearances for Alan and Jeremy:	$400.00
Embryo storage fees:	$1,200.00
Subtotal:	$15,480.00
Total:	$15,580.00

*but not $1,150!

CHAPTER 7

ARE THE KIDS ALRIGHT?

On the edge of making a kid, we'd obviously decided we could be good parents, poly or not. We had zero statistics about how kids of poly families turned out, and truly did not want our unique relationship to burden our children. We just didn't think research on other families could tell us anything about our unique circumstances. Still, many people (and courts) question the parenting ability of poly families. They want to know what the evidence says, so I feel obliged to review it. Since we were gay before we were poly, I'll start there.

Gays have been accused of being unfit parents since straights knew we existed. "What if growing up with gay parents irrevocably harms children? Can society take that chance?" our opponents would ask, although they never seemed to worry about kids born to straight parents in dire circumstances. And even though infertile couples get married all the time, the parenting question got hitched to the marriage question. "We're not homophobes," advocates of traditional marriage would say, "We're just thinking of the children."

Three Dads and a Baby

Consider some talking points from the National Organization for Marriage, a leading opponent of marriage equality. "Two men might each be a good father, but neither can be a mom," reads one. "Marriage is about bringing men and women together so that children can have both mothers and fathers," reads another.[52] I've always suspected that NOM doesn't believe its own "mom and dad" argument, since NOM never tried to ban single parenting or divorce. But I recently realized I can *prove* it, and later on, I will. For now, I'll stick to the research.

NOM's own website says that until 2012, research showed that kids with gay parents did as well as or better than kids with heterosexual parents. That changed with the publication of a study written by Mark Regnerus, of the University of Texas.[53] Writing in the online magazine *Slate,* Regnerus claimed the kids of homosexual parents have higher rates of unemployment, psychiatric disorders, infidelity, and other problems.[54] The data "may suggest that the household instability that the [study] reveals is just too common among same sex couples to take the social gamble" involved if we were to "esteem and support" gay parents.

That's the academic way to say that same-sex parents don't deserve respect or equality. But his study doesn't show that at all. To start, you would think it compared children with heterosexual parents to children with LGBTQ+ parents. It didn't. The study grouped subjects into those who said a biological parent had *ever* had a same-sex relationship, and those who did not, regardless of who raised the kids. The "same-sex" group had a lot of broken relationships in it, which is no surprise. The kids were born from 1971 to 1994, so their *parents* grew up in an era of rampant homophobia when gay marriage was universally banned. Shockingly, Regnerus *included* broken families in the "same-sex" group but *excluded* them from the heterosexual group. He really just compared outcomes from intact biological families to the outcomes of failed, fake heterosexual relationships of persecuted people. Then, after finding that discrimination harms families and kids, Regnerus concluded we should just continue discriminating.

It's almost like he had some kind of ax to grind. Would it surprise you to learn that conservative think tanks funded the study? Or that Regnerus said his faith informs his research, and that he hoped it would benefit the Catholic Church?[55] Or that conservative religious groups, from NOM to Focus on the Family to the Family Research Council, all jumped on Regnerus's conclusions to oppose LGBTQ+ parenting and marriage equality?[56,57]

At least Regnerus's study was widely recognized as deeply flawed and reliant on obviously incorrect data. One respondent claimed he weighed eighty-eight pounds with a height of seven foot eight. Another said he'd been arrested when he was one year old. An independent analysis found that only about a fifth (fifty-one of 236) of the subjects Regnerus considered "raised by" same sex-parents had actually been raised by a same-sex couple for at least a year.[58] A federal judge called the work "not worthy of serious consideration,"[59] and major sociology and medical groups rejected the study's conclusions. An audit of the journal's publication process found that reviewers had personal biases against gay marriage and failed to identify major methodological flaws in the study.[60]

As far as anyone knows, same-sex parenting works just fine. But I also wanted to know how *poly* parenting affected kids. To find out, I interviewed Elisabeth Sheff, PhD, a leading researcher in polyamory and poly families, and author of *The Polyamorists Next Door: Inside Multiple-Partner Relationships and Families.* The first thing she told me was that polyamory research is quite limited. Sheff had to recruit subjects from polyamory support groups, so she ended up with highly self-selected volunteers: generally wealthy, well-educated, white, cisgender people who were "successful" and open polyamorists. "Social privilege makes it easier to be sexually freaky," she explained. "One of these families was a quad, and they used to go to preschools, present themselves as poly, and ask, 'Can you deal with it?'—that's something you can do in the [San Francisco] bay area." So Sheff couldn't tell me what it's like to be closeted and poly in, say, rural Alabama.

Sheff faced another barrier in her studies: red tape. To protect subjects, human research is regulated by ethics review boards, which are particularly cautious around sexual taboos. Her volunteers could (conceivably) lose their jobs or custody of their children if their information became public. It took Sheff five years of regular meetings to get permission to talk to the kids, and the ethics review board at Sheff's university forbade her from keeping real names or contact information—making long-term follow-up especially challenging. Despite these limitations, Sheff had spent years studying people just like us, except that most were straight, with some bisexual women mixed in. So would our kids be okay?

"From these optimistic poly families willing to volunteer [for interviews] and wave the poly flag," said Sheff, "they're more than okay. These kids are in great shape. When they're young they don't realize other families are different, so it's taken for granted. When they do notice the difference, they view it as a deficit for their peers—how do they survive with only one to two parents?" Sheff said these kids appreciate having extra parents to help with homework and drive them to activities and social events, which is just what I hoped to hear. These parents also had excellent communication skills, developed over years of juggling multiple relationships, and the kids picked up their parents' skills. "As they grow up and move on out, they're comfortable establishing networks of supportive people, while some of their peers flail."

Were there any downsides? According to Sheff, extra parents bring "extra surveillance," which not all kids appreciated. And they had to think about how to present their families to peers. Often, they didn't have to explain their family dynamics if they didn't want to. With lots of divorced families around, most adults would just assume extra parents were just ex-partners who got along really well. Some kids would ask for accommodation when their friends came over, especially for sleepovers—it often helped if Mommy's boyfriend made himself scarce at such times. But Sheff assured me that kids navigated their parents' poly identities quite well. "They usually find accepting friends. There are enough family variants out there that lots of kids identify as some 'other' family structure, too."

I asked Sheff for some tips. Her answers reinforced the plans my throuple had already made. "Don't act ashamed. Be askable," she said. "Take the child seriously. Give age-appropriate, honest responses. Collaborate with them on keeping the relationship private if they want." A lot of the pitfalls she warned me about, however, applied only to "non-nesting" (visiting) partners: "You don't have to introduce partners to the children right away, or emphasize that the relationship is sexual. But tell the truth, especially with older kids. Let them know there's no cheating going on." Sheff gave the example of a teenager whose friends guessed that a regular visitor was a romantic partner before the child figured it out herself—that left her feeling embarrassed and lied to. Lastly, she had advice for families in less welcoming environments: "Make sure the kid doesn't out the family at the wrong time. It's like some nudity at home versus out in public. Make sure the kids know what aspects of the family they talk about outside the home."

I asked if kids of poly parents had poly relationships themselves. I figured they would, but among Dr. Sheff's sample, few did. Instead, they grew up more open and welcoming. "The young adults of these unions tend to express more gender and sexual fluidity," she said, "and care less for labels. Many had pansexual or queer identities, even if in practice they had solely monogamous heterosexual relationships." The children grew up happy and supported, with good communication skills, establishing their own healthy relationships. Sheff's final judgment? "Polyamorous families can provide healthy, loving, stable environments in which children can thrive."

Oh, I almost forgot: I promised to prove that the "kids need a mom and a dad" argument was fake. How? Polyamory. The conservative religious organizations that oppose same-sex marriage would never endorse poly parenting by two men and two women, even though their kids would have both moms and dads in abundance. If you can get NOM to stick to their "moms and dads" argument and publicly back poly families, I'll give you a thousand bucks. If you can get them to support a quad marriage, I'll double it.

CHAPTER 8

IMPLANTATION

At last, Dr. Collins's office had the psychiatric clearances, the lawyers had signed off on the surrogacy contract, and Delilah had taken her course of deep, daily hormone injections (sorry, Delilah!). The procedure itself seemed a little anticlimactic. Collins thawed our embryo and injected it into Delilah's uterus—no more trouble than a pap smear. Then the waiting began. Nine days later, she'd take a pregnancy test.

Delilah wasn't done with shots. When I heard this bit of bad news, I had to remind myself of physiology knowledge that had faded in my memory since I studied reproductive medicine in the—this is painful to write—late nineties. When women get pregnant the old-fashioned way, the ovarian follicle that releases the egg develops into the corpus luteum, or "yellow body," a temporary hormone-making structure that prevents a menstrual cycle from washing out the embryo. Delilah hadn't released an egg and didn't have a corpus luteum, so she needed injected hormones. Bummer.

As the pregnancy-testing day approached, Delilah felt great. I remembered how she'd said she was a "happy pregnant," and in truth, she was absolutely beaming. "I don't even need the pregnancy test," she said. "I've had three kids. I can feel it. I'm pregnant."

She wasn't.

It made perfect sense. Women feel pregnant because of pregnancy-related hormones, and Delilah was getting them injected. Without them, she wouldn't have even suspected she was pregnant—she'd had her test two weeks into the life of the embryo, and at that point in a natural pregnancy, she wouldn't even have missed a period. Not that it mattered. We'd lost our baby. I felt numb, drained to the point of emptiness, like an animated shell plodding through patient visits at the hospital, struggling to focus on other people's suffering. We had envisioned two happy siblings, delighting in each other and in their extended family. After the genetic tests, we'd made peace with the idea of an only child. Now, after all the conversations, contracts, medications, and preparations, we had nothing.

Actually, we had worse than nothing: we had terrible news. We had to call Jeremy and Alan's parents, my father and step mother, and my mother, one by one, repeating the story, dodging questions about what we were going to do next, wishing we could just be quiet. But that wasn't the worst of it. For Julie and Stephanie, we had a double whammy of terrible news. That burden fell to Jeremy. He called them from our bed, staring at the ceiling and anxiously fidgeting with one of our dog's floppy ears.

"It's bad news. I'll just say it. She's not pregnant." Then the predictable pause, as he listened to their optimism about the second embryo. Ugh. "But there's a problem . . ." he continued, and his voice strained as he told them how the remaining embryo had a fatal genetic error. They went from two kids to none in sixty seconds.

These were dark days for our triad. I didn't try to make sense of the failure. I don't think these things have a purpose. They happen, or they don't; it's not the universe talking to us. I did reason, though, that while we wanted a baby, the world had billions of people already, trying again would be really expensive, and babies required lots of work. To be honest, I'd been a little scared of fatherhood. We'd all acknowledged some fear, which we assumed was universal. You'd have to be foolish *not* to worry about such a monumental change. But how much worry is normal? I didn't know, and I couldn't, and I'd had some meta-worry: worrying about the appropriateness of my worrying. So together, we grieved. Privately, I felt a little bit of relief mixed in with my disappointment. As I contemplated us remaining childless, I thought maybe we would just focus on enjoying each other.

Jeremy's reaction blew my reasoning to bits. The loss devastated him. The day after, I found him staring glumly out the window. He told me all about the compromises he'd made to get to this point: "I was raised Nazarene, and in a way, it was easy being gay. No one ever expected me to date. I could just say I was waiting for 'the one.' That was the proper, Christian thing, anyway. I believed it. I thought I was going to get married and have this wonderful ceremony and my parents would love it and I'd be a dad. I gave all that up when we became a throuple. I disappointed my parents, but *I* had expectations, too. This was going to be something we really did together."

A little bit of background is in order here. Jeremy is a full, equal, 100 percent member of our family. We love him to death. He's not some "plus-one" Alan and I are dating. In fact, while Alan and I took some time figuring out our relationship and forging a partnership, we took to Jeremy like gay fishes to gay water. While Alan and I had gone on some dates with a few people before we found Jeremy, none of them felt like they could be part of our family, and while Alan joined me, he wouldn't ever have sought another partner the way I had. He always limited his shopping to Amazon.com.

Then I got introduced to Jeremy through a mutual acquaintance.[iv] We met for lunch—as the sole member of the extra boyfriend committee,

---

iv "Mutual acquaintance" being the euphemism I use for "online dating."

I'd always suss out our potential dates before introducing them to Alan. I thought Jeremy was charming, handsome, and funny. At the time, Alan and I had already been together for eight years, and Jeremy had no interest in dating a couple. I said that was no problem, we can't have too many friends, and I invited him home to dinner. We had such a great time we spent every evening together for a week. Thinking back, I can't remember anything we did besides eat and laugh and talk. Alan had finally found someone he could enthusiastically welcome to the family. Jeremy soon changed his mind about dating a couple, and not long after that, he moved in. That was five years before the baby-making adventures.

Yet there were, and are, costs for Jeremy in this relationship. He gave up the romantic wedding idea, to start. When he moved in, he took a guest room downstairs. It made sense at the time; he'd just joined the relationship, and Alan and I were already established in the master bedroom. It didn't make sense for him to replace one of us in the master then, but I have since offered to rotate out. That geography says something about our relationship, and I care about making it equitable. Jeremy started out in a guest room, feeling like a guest, left off the title to the home, and with separate finances. In the beginning, he insisted on paying rent, and we accepted, which seems crazy to us now. It took time for him to be comfortable with using family money to pay off his car loan and max out his retirement contributions. It didn't seem like family money for years.

It didn't help to be a zookeeper in a relationship with two doctors. Once, Jeremy wrote out a list of things we each contributed to the home. Under columns for Alan and me, he mentioned our medical training and incomes, and Alan having taught himself to play both the guitar and piano. Under his own, he wrote things like "childlike sense of wonder," and "able to reach things on the top shelf" (he's six five).

This is a vast undersell. First, we can't equate people's value with their income, not while (for example) some investment bankers make millions skimming money off transactions without producing anything of value for society. Second, and more importantly, *zoos cannot keep their animals alive, educate visitors, or fight extinction without zookeepers.* And Jeremy is no ordinary zookeeper. He's worked on several avian propagation projects, saving endangered species like the ʻalalā, or Hawaiian crow, a beautiful and intelligent animal that went extinct in the wild. Jeremy has hatched more ʻalalā chicks than anyone else in the world, *ever,* living or dead. Thanks in part to his work, the ʻalalā has been reintroduced to the rain forests of Hawaii.

He's also worked with the ʻakekeʻe and ʻakikiki, two critically endangered Hawaiian honeycreepers that hatch from eggs that weigh less than two M&M's. Jeremy single-handedly wrote their feeding and care protocols. He retrieved the first eggs from wild nests in the foggy, virgin rainforest of Kauai, miles from any roads or trails. To access the nests, built on spindly, moss-covered branches forty feet in the air, he climbed ladders held in place by wires. He's literally the first human being to hatch an ʻakekeʻe egg. He kept the first captive chick in an incubator and fed it bee larvae with tweezers every two hours.

It's because of things like this that when someone asks what we do and I say, "Hospital doctor," and Alan says, "Psychiatrist," they don't give two shits, and when Jeremy says he's a zookeeper, they say, "Cool!" and press him for work stories. And we'd made a lot of progress with Jeremy's place in our home. He directed the remodel of his room, then helped redesign the dining room and entryway and replaced some of our furniture. Then there's his urban farm. I built a chicken coop to his specifications and he filled it with breeds he hand-raised from chicks, which supply us with a stream of white, tan, dark-brown, green, blue, spotted, and olive eggs. Then we got bees and jars of our own honey, and a miniature rabbit farm to supply meat without the cruelty of industrial farms. Now there's no question that this is Jeremy's home, too. It wouldn't be home without him. All our friends love him, we love him, and I thought he felt secure and satisfied as a member of the family.

I was wrong. Lying there on the bed, looking like he'd been gut-punched, Jeremy recounted the sacrifices he'd made to join our family, from the big wedding to raising children. "I had all these plans," he said. "I talked to people about preschool. I thought about the values we'd teach them. We were going to have kids." He curled up around a pillow. "I really wanted to be a dad," he said quietly, and that settled it. I knew we would try again before I even talked to Alan.

First, we needed to solidify the legal status of our family. We'd have to do it to protect our baby, and we owed it to Jeremy, too. But three guys can't get married anywhere in the world. The closest thing I've heard of took place in Latin America.

In 2017, *The Guardian* reported the first "legal union" between three men in Colombia—"and possibly the world."[61] But the three men in this *"trieja"* had not had a three-way marriage. Colombia still limited marriages to two people and had only legalized gay marriage the year before. The *trieja* had just gotten a lawyer to draft an agreement and a notary to witness it.

We just wanted Jeremy and any future baby protected, so we had a lawyer create trusts containing all our assets. That way, if anyone got run over by a truck, the others would inherit their property without brutal inheritance taxes (from which married couples are automatically spared).

That just left one remaining detail: Jeremy reminded me we had a frozen, nonviable embryo, which the moms were reluctant to discard, and we were paying the storage fees. "Wait," I asked, "we're paying to store a nonviable embryo?" It didn't make sense. It *was* a difficult situation, but dragging it out didn't make it any easier. There was no chance that embryo would survive. It wouldn't just be foolish to spend $10,000 to implant it—it would be wrong. Death was certain, and one does not impose the risks of pregnancy on a surrogate for no reason.

My partners asked me not to fault the moms, and I didn't. They'd made a difficult decision to give their children up for adoption, only to lose both. It eventually took ten months (and fifty dollars for a mobile notary) to get that embryo-discard form signed, all of it with us in the awkward role of nagging them about permission to discard their last embryo. Yuck.

We did get one great piece of news: Delilah wanted to try again. She wasn't just willing—she became our cheerleader. After letting us collect ourselves, she started asking about the timeline. She prodded us to get going, and with a collective sigh, we took stock of what we had to do. We only ("only") needed to find and contract with an egg donor, collect and fertilize eggs, hope we got viable embryos, implant one, and hope it stuck. If we had nothing to show for two cycles except tragedy and an enormous bill, it would be the end of our baby-making exploits.

Prior costs:	$15,580.00
Implantation cycle:	$9,200.00
Delilah's medications:	$401.00
Trusts and wills:	$6,753.00
Mobile notary:	$50.00
Extra embryo storage payments:	$200.00
Subtotal:	$16,604.00
Total:	$32,184.00

CHAPTER 9

MOM WANTED

Shortly after our embryo failed to implant, our friend Meghan visited us. Alan told her the story of our embryo woes with a look of abject horror on his face, but the horror had more to do with the brown lump on the plate she had handed him than the story. For years, we've loved Meghan . . . much more than we love her pancakes.

Alan had been friends with Meghan since they were seven years old, but I didn't get to know her well until we visited her in Argentina in 2009. Meghan fell in love with Argentina on a vacation. Who wouldn't? Buenos Aires has a magical, decayed opulence, with grand Parisian mansions with trees bursting from cracks in the stonework. Restaurants don't even open for dinner until nine; the locals think the barest hint of spice makes food unbearable. Their only compliment for food is *suave,* which I think means "grease puddle." Their Spanish has an Italian lilt and idiosyncrasies like pronouncing the double "l" as a "zh" instead of a "y." Argentina is enrapturing—but leave it to Meghan to move there, learn an entirely new language, and open a yoga business and an in-home restaurant.

Three Dads and a Baby

During that trip in 2009, after eating an unholy amount of ice cream (*Sambayón?* Eight kinds of dulce de leche? Yes, please) and walking the mazes of ornate mausoleums in La Recoleta Cemetery, we headed to Iguazu Falls, on the border with Brazil. There are three hundred falls at Iguazu, and they put Niagara to shame. They're populated by herds of playful raccoon-like coati and gregarious, attractive Latin Americans. In our hotel room, we introduced Meghan to the music of Brandi Carlile. When Alan and I sang "Fall Apart Again," with its lyrical promise of unconditional friendship, she touched her heart and sighed. Later, she held my hand and said, "Ian, do you think that was the moment when I was no longer just Alan's friend, but *your* friend, too?" Not exactly—that was the moment I fell *in love* with her. When Meghan says stuff like that, I think all we need to do is clone her and put her in charge of all the governments in the world. She might not balance the books, but we'd never have another war.

So we were thrilled when Meghan decided to visit us in San Diego. She offered to make pancakes the first morning, and Alan eagerly accepted, thinking of fluffy white, buttery-syrupy Bisquick goodness. He showered while Meghan whipped up a batch of . . . something. She added whole-wheat flour, oats, and a heaping scoop of cocoa. Then flaxseeds. When she plopped the dark-brown batter in a pan, it just sat there. I couldn't wait to hear what Alan thought.

"Oh God! What the hell is this?" he asked, when she handed him a plate. "A cow patty?"

"Your pancakes!" said Meghan.

"They most certainly are not," said Alan, poking his cake suspiciously.

"They're actually marginally edible!" said Jeremy, after a bite. "What's in them?"

"Healthy things," said Meghan.

"Well, your . . . food pucks do not look great," said Alan. Meghan laughed and frowned simultaneously. "No? Nutrition loaf? Hippie cakes? Health bricks!"

Alan picked at his health brick while he told the story of our embryo failure, our decision to try again with donated eggs, and the complex choices involved. Most straight couples just had sex—there was no discussion about which eggs or which sperm or whether someone's gametes were too old. But we had to pick from the sperm of three dads and find a mom. We definitely wanted a friend over a stranger. That way, we'd know more about what kind of kids we'd have, and they could grow up with their genetic mom in their lives. We'd pay our donor, of course, and pay for expenses, but she'd have to risk some health problems and discomfort for us—and at the end, accept that the child would be ours, not hers.

Jeremy explained how we'd gotten an egg offer from his delightful cousin Suzanne. She wanted to *have* kids but not *raise* kids. There was just one problem: Jeremy wanted to be a father, but not with his cousin.

Meghan took this all in with a deeply serious expression on her face. She'd also thought about having kids but wasn't in a place to raise them herself—nor was there a father on the horizon. She asked how they got the eggs (a needle through the vagina into the ovaries—under anesthesia). What risks? How old is too old to be an egg donor? She got so lost in the conversation she almost burned a health brick.

Meghan reached out to a friend and her mom for advice. The next day she said she wanted to be our mom. She felt sure she could handle being a mom without being a parent—sort of an aunt figure. She wanted to see her child grow up. Instead of paying her for her eggs, she asked, would we agree to cover travel expenses once a year for her to visit the child? Absolutely we would! We knew we wanted our child to learn Spanish and have an involved genetic mom—why not use a dear friend? We even imagined our kiddo vacationing with Meghan and learning about another language and culture at the same time.

That was that. We had our mom. We still faced a big hurdle—our IVF clinic. While I'd had my doubts about being a dad, I'd always known that if I raised some kids, I wanted at least a chance to raise my own biological kids. It's a desire baked into our DNA, and for me, a practical concern as well—if I didn't at least try to father some children, my mother would murder me. But for me to have a chance at fatherhood, we'd have to call the clinic and come clean about being a throuple. Jeremy called our case coordinator, Tricia, whom we loved. "Tricia, you love the gays, right?" he asked.

"Of course I love the gays!" she said. Jeremy told her about Meghan and me, and explained that we wanted each dad to fertilize a third of the eggs we collected. She seemed fine with it. "I think Dr. Collins will be okay with it," she said. "Let me discuss it with her."

And—phew—Collins agreed to proceed and met with Jeremy to confirm the details. In addition to a contract with Meghan, we'd have to update the contract with Delilah. Legally, Alan and Jeremy would still be "the parents," which meant that I would be, at least on paper, nobody. Their sperm would be parental sperm, and their bio-kids would be their legal children—no problem. But for me to fertilize any eggs, I needed a sperm-donation contract with my own life partners, which is the same arrangement a woman would have with a stranger she wanted only gametes from, a stranger who had no right to parent or even meet the resulting child. Collins's note from the visit simply reads, "Ian will be providing sperm sample as a sperm donor without any legal rights," which is the only way Collins figured we could move forward.

We were going to need a bunch of lawyers.

Prior costs:	$32,184.00
Another ten-minute chat with Collins:	$250.00
Total:	$32,434.00

CHAPTER 10

HELL.
WITH LAWYERS.

S urrogacy comes with wallet-crushing expenses. The most painful costs are the ones that don't even directly contribute to the baby making—like our legal expenses, which seemed almost unreal. We sometimes wondered if IVF doctors cared about their patients' expenses at all, or if they just wanted to hear that their asses were covered for any upcoming medical procedures. "I'm beginning to wonder if lawyers pay kickbacks to IVF doctors to drive up these costs," Alan muttered at one point, as he studied our latest bill. "Like . . . how is this even possible?" Allow me to explain.

Alan and Jeremy had already paid for a contract with Delilah, and all three had undergone psychiatric evaluations to certify them as fit parents (take a deep breath . . . okay!). Now that we were making our own embryos, we agreed to each fertilize a third of Meghan's eggs and implant the healthiest embryo. To proceed, the three of us needed a contract with Meghan, I needed to be added to the contract with Delilah, and—according to our lawyers—we needed a sperm-donor contract between me and

Alan and Jeremy, the "intended parents." They said that was the only way forward, even though I'd really be an equal parent.

Alan and Jeremy, as always, did the legwork finding me an attorney to help me review and sign the sperm donor agreement. I'd be working with Will Halm, a Los Angeles–based attorney and gay surrogacy trailblazer. Not only does he advocate for gay parenting rights and provide reproductive law services to same-sex couples, he and his partner, Marcellin Simard, had one of the first children carried by a surrogate for a gay couple, back in the mid-1990s. The event was described in a 1998 article in the *New York Times*,[62] as well as a piece in a San Diego paper, which described their surrogate as "one of the few surrogate mothers willing to carry children for male gay couples."[63] I scheduled the call as soon as possible, because time was short. Meghan was scheduled to come donate eggs, and I was heading to a medical conference in a few days, with senior leadership from my hospital. I had no choice but to schedule the call in the middle of seeing hospitalized patients. I just hoped none of them had an emergency.

Will walked me through the document, which sounded superharsh. As a standard sperm-donor contract, it said that I had no rights to see the child, would not be a parent, could not have any say in its upbringing, and had no responsibility for it—the opposite of our plans. "If you sign this, you have to understand you will not be part of the child's life," he explained. I sighed and walked him through our whole story. No, that wasn't what we wanted . . . yes, I was going to be an equal parent, and we wanted to make sure my commitment to the child and my responsibilities were clear. Will asked a few more questions until he understood our goals and said he'd craft something with the opposing counsel and get back to me.

Presumably, Alan and Jeremy were having similar conversations about the document with their attorney. Why we had to do this separately escaped me. The attorneys wanted it that way, but I didn't know whether that actually helped us. We were one family, and we didn't need opposing counsel to make this seem like a fight.

Actually, opposing counsel would *turn* this into a fight. The next day,

I flew to Salt Lake City for my conference. That night, Jeremy called. He was not happy.

"What did you do?" he asked. His voice was flat, dead.

"I don't know what you mean," I said.

"The contract."

"Jeremy, what's wrong?" Long pause.

"Our lawyer said you refused to sign. Why would you refuse to sign?" It went downhill from there. Apparently their lawyer called, distressed and frantic, reporting that I'd torpedoed the sperm-donation contract and thrown our whole implantation timeline into question. I tried to explain my sperm-donor contract discussion with Will—that I'd done exactly what I thought my job had been. No, I didn't refuse to sign. I told the lawyer the truth and explained our goals like I'd been asked to. I was trying to put my *obligations* on that contract.

"I don't understand why you did this." Long pause. "The reason I'm *frustrated* with you . . ." he said, but he had five minutes of reasons. *The implantation could be delayed. The legal fees could go through the roof, or since they'd already gone through the roof, they really could go to the moon. You could have just signed the agreement. Why didn't you just sign it?* I could hear his voice. It wasn't frustration. It was controlled fury.

He handed the phone off to Alan. "What did you do?" he asked, and my heart sank again. Another angry partner. Another round of dizzying, accusing questions. I got tired of defending myself and told him I felt attacked by both my partners. "I'm sorry you feel that way," he replied, which felt like a physical punch. I felt my voice breaking. Alan asked me to draft a reply to the lawyers and share it with them, so I squeaked out a flat goodbye and hung up before I started sobbing. For the next half hour, I worked on an email to our legal team. After I forwarded it to my partners, I saw Alan had already sent off a reply of his own without sharing it with me. Fine.

Jeremy called. I didn't answer; I was crying. Jeremy texted. I replied that I literally couldn't talk. He said we needed more closure; I said I'd been through enough. He asked me to call again. I muted my phone and set it facedown on the dresser.

All next day, I played phone tag with my attorney. I'd call between conference sessions, and he'd be unavailable, but his office wouldn't give out his direct line. When I finally got ahold of him and said I just wanted to sign the original agreement, he did not agree. "I know your actual family plan, and I can't advise you to misrepresent it in an important legal document," he said. I reminded him about our deadline, and about my confidence in Alan and Jeremy not to steal the baby. I even tried telling him how disruptive this delay had been to our relationship and begged him to help. Will wouldn't budge: "I don't think that would be the right choice for your family. You need to be a parent, not a stranger."

My partners were, in a word, pissed.

I called that night, and they put me on speakerphone. I explained how I'd spent the day frantically trying to reach Will through his office staff, while my coworkers wondered what was wrong.

"He doesn't even have Will's number," said Jeremy.

"How can you not have his direct line?" Alan asked.

I kept trying to defend what I'd done, because I'd done my best, but Jeremy said, "Whether you feel you're in the right or not, you know I'm upset, and you should just apologize." Um, what? I got repeatedly attacked for doing my best, and *I* was supposed to apologize? *Like Alan did?* I thought. *Sorry you feel that way*? I didn't apologize. I suggested they start with the presumption their partner was doing his best instead of acting like he'd sabotaged the family plans. On the other end of the line, my partners just wanted to know how their carefully laid plans had been blown up by the supplemental parent, the literal third wheel who'd come along for the ride but laid none of the groundwork, sat out of almost all the clinic appointments, then asked for a third of the eggs to fertilize. All I'd needed to do was say yes. We hung up mad.

I stared at the blinking red digits of the alarm clock until after twelve thirty in the fucking morning. I would be up in six hours at a conference with my boss's boss. This fight had hit a six on the Richter scale of domestic disputes, but it felt even worse than it might have because I'd never been at odds with both boyfriends at once. And while I was out of town! I wasn't used to friction with either boyfriend, and now I felt like an outcast. We'd just had the biggest fight of our five-year relationship over me doing my best to follow legal instructions. How well could we handle another failed implantation, or a colicky baby at 3:00 a.m.? What if the kid actually got sick? I know it sounds corny, but through whatever stress or loneliness I ever deal with in my life, my relationship feels like a warm light, keeping me safe and guiding me. If I stop for a minute to think about it, I smile. But that night, I couldn't feel any light or warmth from home.

My chest felt like I'd been impaled on a lance. I couldn't sleep. I cried hot, heavy tears instead.

CHAPTER 11

REGROUPING.
WITH LAWYERS.

That fight remains my worst memory from our relationship. The good news is when I got home, everyone felt too tired to stay angry. We just lay on our bed and talked it through, again—yay. I still felt like I'd gotten in huge trouble for doing exactly what I'd been told; Alan and Jeremy still seemed to think I'd tried to sabotage the deal. "Wasn't I supposed to explain our situation to the attorney, who could recommend changes to my sperm-donation agreement?" I asked.

"*No*," said Alan. "We'd already softened it as much as legally possible."

"Wait!" I said. "You'd already been over it with your attorneys?"

Jeremy nodded. What I'd been shown had already been tweaked as much as California law would permit for a sperm-donor contract. Their attorneys knew it wasn't perfect but figured it was the best way to get our goals accomplished. The edits I thought it was my job to suggest? None were even possible. Now it all made sense. With the contract essentially finished, my actions looked like sabotage. "You didn't know? I'm sorry.

Really," said Jeremy, as Alan nodded. "We should have explained that better."

I *didn't* know. I certainly didn't know I was supposed to . . . I don't know, lie? Tell Will I didn't live with my partners and plan to raise the kid with them? To lighten things up, I joked that instead of Will, we could call him "Will Not." And I apologized for screwing things up, even though I'd been trying to help. And for getting defensive. It's one of my flaws; I don't take criticism well, and I tend to explain myself instead of validating people's experiences when we have disagreements. It's self-defeating; when people's feelings are hurt, winning an argument with them doesn't make anyone feel better. I've screwed up enough apologies that I more than owed my guys a pass. That's just how I'm wired. At least I'm trying to improve.

With apologies and affirmations of love exchanged, we had to figure out if we had the energy for starting over with embryos (and lawyers). I felt like shit, but I remembered how broken Jeremy felt after our first implantation failed. I knew we'd regret it if we didn't push on, and while we felt discouraged now, that would pass. Jeremy and Alan agreed, so we took stock of our situation.

We needed legal approval for our nontraditional family, and we needed it quickly. It wouldn't be easy. Jeremy's Washington, DC–based attorney, who'd already signaled great annoyance with him over Collins's detailed contract demands, formally fired him after the sperm-donation kerfuffle. She didn't refer Jeremy to other lawyers, even when he asked. Jeremy had to make a series of long phone calls describing the series of events to skeptical reproductive law attorneys, only to be told our case sounded too complicated, or to be referred to the lawyer that had just fired him, or another lawyer who couldn't take on this aspect of our case. Jeremy spent three hours on the phone that day, which left him "emotionally exhausted, nauseated, and on the edge of tears," and only a trip to Claim Jumper for cocktails and carb loading soothed him.

There was a silver lining. I'd joked about "Will Not," but the truth was that Will was entirely right. He couldn't advise me to lie on a legal document, and it didn't make any sense for one of us to sign away all rights to a child—not for us, and not for the kid. I'd torpedoed our plans, but they were bad plans, and now we might get legal documents that accurately reflected our family situation and better protected the parents and any children. *If* everything worked out, that is.

As we prepared to slog through the legal complications of presenting ourselves as a family, we realized that our contracts had not been thoughtfully prepared. For example, the contract with Delilah applied only to the two adopted embryos. For us to implant new embryos, the contract would have to be reworded, generating more legal fees. Our experienced, well-regarded attorneys could certainly have thought of the possibility of needing additional IVF cycles, but we would have to pay for the oversight. I could call or email them to complain—if I wanted to burn bridges. I didn't.

So we paid an attorney so Delilah could indicate she knew she was working with a throuple, and we paid another attorney to "represent" me so that I could add my signature, even though I'd helped shape the original contract with Alan and Jeremy. Meghan needed a lawyer to represent her for egg donation, and a psychiatric eval. But then it got truly crazy.

As none of us were married, the lawyers told us we'd need four separate attorneys for the contract with Meghan. If we were married, one attorney could just create a contract for the spouses, because spouses are assumed to be on the same page (all marriages are, of course, free of conflict). We just recoiled in surprise. We'd carefully planned our family-to-be, so what were they worried about? Perhaps two of us would want to raise children to share in their joys of growth and discovery, while the third wanted them for . . . sale on the black market? Spare organs for transplantation? Satanic rituals? It didn't make any sense. How could we be in any position to raise a child if we couldn't jointly sign a contract? Wouldn't agreeing on a single contract and *signing* it establish our intentions? Wasn't that the point of a contract? But this was nonnegotiable—we had to have four attorneys billing $500 an hour just to sign an agreement between a committed family and Alan's lifelong friend.

That was just the beginning. Our lawyer wouldn't move forward with us unless we had a separate *parenting agreement.* This document would outline our intentions with regard to the child or children that resulted from our fertility work. Again, we were mystified. What would this parenting agreement say? Our attorneys said it needed to outline the rights and responsibilities of the three parents—for example, that all of us wanted to contribute to decisions about the child's health care, upbringing, schooling, and so on, and that we were all responsible for the child as well, meaning that we had to help take care of the kids—diaper them, contribute financially, that sort of thing.

This left us utterly confused. Was the purpose of the document . . . to define the word *parent?* What could it possibly mean for us to have surrogacy contracts specifying we would all three be "parents" if that meant that any of us could walk away from a child's life? That's not parenting! I wanted to ask if their standard contract work specifying that a man and woman would be a child's parents included the notion that either or both of them could just walk away from the kid at any time. Actually, I wanted to show the lawyer the definition of the word *parent* in a dictionary.

That *still* wasn't the worst of it. Not only did we need to sit down with a *fifth* attorney for $1,800 to list platitudes about what parenting meant to us, we had to have (ohmygodohmygodohmygod) *three separate attorneys* "represent" us in our individual signings of the contract. It was necessary, they said, to protect each of our individual interests, since the three of us couldn't legally marry. Still, these three attorneys would make sure we knew what we were getting into when we signed the agreement. That way, we wouldn't be surprised by our *own words,* and an attorney could review the document *an attorney already wrote.* For this privilege, we would pay each of them at least $700 to $1,000; the individual costs varied. We apparently seemed more like warring nations negotiating peace after a decade-long war, and not a family.

At the time, we felt tremendous pressure to nod and write checks on command. We didn't want to risk offending them, or getting a reputation in the reproductive attorney community. Jeremy had already been referred out to Washington, DC, and I worried if we had to look any farther east, we might end up having our legal discussions in French. Thus, we felt unable to shop around, and California's maze of surrogacy regulations mandated their assistance. We knew we weren't the easiest clients to deal with, because our throuple threw a wrench in legal machinery designed to deal with more typical relationships. And while we had to have the lawyers' okay to proceed with our surrogacy, our surrogacy plans had a time frame. We didn't seem to have an option fighting this recommendation, but we couldn't help but notice how lucrative it would be for our lawyers. The whole parenting agreement thing was going to cost us $3,300, and it wouldn't even be a legally binding contract, just a statement of intent (Do I seem like someone who needs help expressing myself?).

If we hadn't been stunned by the absurdity of it all, we would have been furious. But we wanted our baby, so we gritted our teeth and wrote checks and moved on. Still, we couldn't help but wonder: *Who were all these lawmakers and doctors to sit in judgment of our family plan?* We were all stable, employed professionals without criminal histories or toxic habits. Between us, we have twenty-seven years of higher education. If any ordinary family had to jump through literally any hoops to make their own babies, it'd be a civil rights violation.

"Why is this so difficult?" Jeremy asked as we drove home.

"Sixteen, beer, pickup truck," said Alan.

You know what's most hilarious about this? The lawyer we settled on to manage the birth certificate for our future baby told us sperm donors don't need legal representation in the first place. That was all another expensive exercise in ass-covering. But the requirement that I get a sperm-donor attorney forced us down a road toward equal parenting. We didn't know it, but we'd end up making a little bit of history as a result.

Prior costs:	$32,434.00
Ten-minute Collins visit to say we want to make embryos:	$350.00
Psych clearance for Ian:	$200.00
Sperm-donor contract for Ian to Alan and Jeremy:	$1,500.00
Psych clearance revision for Delilah:	$150.00
Parenting agreement costs:	
Agreement drafting:	$1,800.00
Jeremy's representation for parenting agreement:	$850.00
Ian's representation for parenting agreement:	$500.00
Alan's representation for parenting agreement:	$700.00
Getting Delilah's contract rewritten to add Ian:	$500.00
Meghan's egg-donation contract:	$1,500.00
Meghan's expenses:	
Psych clearance:	$400.00
Exam and routine labs:	$475.00
Subtotal (just for permission to try to make a baby):	$8,925.00
Total:	$41,359.00

CHAPTER 12

THREE MEN AND A LEGAL LANDSCAPE

When we talked about becoming fathers, we focused on our own desires and resources. Could we parent consistently? Would having three dads burden our kids? When we read our embryo adoption contracts and surrogacy contracts, we just followed the advice of the clinic and our attorneys. In retrospect, reading *anything* about the legalities of poly parenting would have been wise. I'm just catching up on that research now. And things can certainly go wrong.

April and Shane Divilbiss lived in Memphis, Tennessee, raising Alana, April's daughter from a previous relationship, when their romantic life got complicated. April fell for Chris Littrell, and April did not want to cheat or leave Shane. Instead, Shane agreed to let Chris move in to their home and share April's affection—they had a polyfidelitious "V" (a "vee," not a triad, because the men were not romantic with each other). Then the threesome told their story on an MTV program called *Sex in the 90's: It's a Group Thing*. Alana's paternal grandmother saw the program and sought custody on the grounds that the threesome's "depravity" would "endanger the morals or health" of the girl. A judge subsequently removed Alana from April's home and gave custody to the grandparents. April Divilbiss eventually concluded the grandmother could provide a better life for her daughter than she could, and dropped the appeal. But she still believes losing her child because of her polyamory was unjust.[64]

That was 1998, in Tennessee.[65] Elisabeth Sheff, the researcher who told me about poly-parenting outcomes, also told me a much more recent and more disturbing story. Some grandparents who disapproved of their child's poly lifestyle pretended to come around long enough to get access to their grandchildren—and abducted them. According to Sheff, they'd done their homework and fled to Texas, where a family court judge gave custody to the grandparents because the poly lifestyle was an "abomination" and put the child's "immortal soul" in danger. The judge allowed the parents only brief, supervised visits, far from their home, and fighting a long-distance legal battle proved beyond their means. Their kids were legally stolen away from them.[66]

Sheff, who had interviewed the parents and offered to testify as a witness in favor of poly parenting, said this terrifying case was the worst of the custody battles she'd heard of, but far from the only one. For custody issues, poly families face an uphill battle, just like same-sex parents did before the establishment of gay marriage rights. Sheff noted two divides in the legal cases she knew of: poly families lost cases until about five years ago, when they began to win, and now the legal landscape looks like the electoral map—poly families win in liberal states and lose in conservative ones. In red states, she said, courts and child protection service workers are often biased against poly parents, and family courts have even cited the Ten Commandments in their rulings.

Concerned by these nightmare custody stories, I did some research on poly parenting. I'd always thought kids could only have two legal parents, but that's not quite true. Poly parenting is odd, yes, but tri-parenting is not, and I found tri-parent or tri-custody examples in eleven states. In Alaska, a dying woman wanted to remain a parent while a male couple adopted her child. In Delaware, Washington, and North Dakota, tri-parent families involved a woman, her husband, and the biological parent of a child from a prior relationship. Louisiana allowed a grandparent guardian to share legal parentage with the parents, and it allowed dual paternity for a woman's husband and her kid's biological father. Several cases in the US and Canada involved sperm donors and lesbian couples; in a 2013 Florida case, they were all listed on the birth certificate (of a two-year-old). In 2009, a gay, married couple in New Jersey had a child with a longtime friend and even gave media interviews about their tri-parenting arrangement. Sadly, it fell apart when she decided to move. In 2015 a judge gave the nonbiological father joint custody, saying he was a "psychological parent" but not a legal parent.[67]

But none of these stories involved a polyamorous family. They involved a family, plus a nonromantic third parent. I found *zero* examples of throuples doing what we wanted to do—be equal parents of a child from the beginning. In fact, the online resources I found (a poly blog and a checklist for poly-parenting planning from the Sexual Freedom Legal Defense and Education Fund[68]) just said that there are two slots on birth certificates for parents, and that was that. Unable to secure legal parentage by birth certificate, some poly families seek legal parenting status in other ways. Third-parent *adoption* for throuples has occurred in California, Alaska, Oregon, Massachusetts, and Washington. But results are mixed. Some Oregon throuples got third-parent adoption for kids, and others failed. In New York, a judge recognized "tri-custody," including the nonbiological mother in a male-female-female throuple, when the two women separated from the father.[69,v]

Luckily for us, California is perhaps the most surrogate-friendly state in the union. A 1993 State Supreme Court case, *Johnson vs. Calvert,*

---

v The Alliance Defending Freedom, an organization that "advocates for your right to freely live out your faith" (read: "fights gay rights") took a dim view of this case on their website. Worried that anything but "true marriage" would mean "random caregivers, moving…in and out of a child's life," the ADF "remains committed to promoting the truth that marriage is the lifelong union of one man and one woman." I guess the ADF's version of freedom is the freedom to live in their one approved relationship model.

found that the legal parents of a child born by a surrogate are those speci-fied in the surrogacy contract, making it nearly impossible for a surrogate to claim parentage of the child she bears. A 2012 law reinforced this find-ing, as did a 2017 decision by the State Supreme Court.[vi,70, 71] And in the most significant legal advance in American multiparenting, California passed a law permitting tri-parent birth certificates in 2013. The law, SB 274, allows a third parent to be added to a birth certificate if excluding the third parent would be detrimental to the child.

SB 274 was written because of a profoundly messy case in which a kid's lesbian parents had a relationship that a California Court of Appeal called "stormy from the start [and] marked by verbal and physical abuse by both women."[72] Melissa suffered from bipolar disorder and abused methamphetamines, and she accused Irene of physically abusing her. She even filed a request for a restraining order. While the couple separated, she had a child by a father, Jesus, who supported her. Then Melissa rec-onciled with Irene and disappeared with the child. Later, Melissa's new boyfriend, Jose, tried to murder Irene, and Melissa was incarcerated as an accessory to attempted murder. With the mothers out of the picture, the child ended up in foster care. Although Jesus had provided financial sup-port and sought custody, the Court of Appeal denied him parental rights, because state law did not allow children to have more than two parents. Like I said: messy. SB 274 sought to prevent "detriment" to children who would otherwise be deprived of additional parents, like Jesus, by allowing children to have three parents in special cases.[73]

Opponents worried that SB 274 "eroded traditional parental roles."[74] Yeah, no kidding—one has to erode the mythology of two-parent families to recognize the variety of caregivers that take care of some kids in the real world. Out of a terrible situation came an opportunity for nontraditional

---

vi A surrogate refused to have a "selective reduction" (abortion) of one fetus when she became pregnant with triplets, despite agreeing to reduction in her contract. By allowing lower court rulings to stand, the State Supreme Court ended her attempt to get custody of the "extra" child that resulted and rejected her claim that surrogacy itself violated the Constitution.

families. We'd have three dads and hopefully two involved mother figures to pitch in, showering our child with extra love. That's nontraditional; it used to be that men only made money and women only raised babies and did chores. If you go back far enough, men traditionally *owned* their wives. It used to be legal to rape your wife—Texas only eliminated this spousal rape exemption in *1994*, when I was in college, which is mind-boggling.

Clearly, some traditions deserve eroding, the sooner the better. Besides, in the train wreck situation that inspired SB 274, Melissa had already eroded traditional roles as much as humanly possible. She'd been charged as an accessory to the attempted murder of another parent. Limiting parenthood to two people hadn't prevented that mess, and "parental roles" weren't the issue. This was about what was best for the children.

Other opponents of SB 274 objected that more parents meant more possible conflicts. That's true, I guess, but it also means more help. No one ever recommends single parenting even though it totally eliminates conflict. Nor would denying a third parent their legal standing prevent conflict. That argument reminded me of objections to gay marriage on the basis that some people object to gay sex. Sorry to break it to you, morality police, but we gays didn't wait for legal marriage to have sex. Gay marriage bans didn't prevent one orgasm, and from the way I hear married people complain about their sexual frequency, gay marriage bans probably *facilitated* a bunch of orgasms. Likewise, depriving a third parent of legal recognition doesn't prevent conflict, it just leaves one parent powerless. And deprives a kid of their love and resources.

Only now, researching these legal issues long after the fact, did I realize how lucky we were to be in California. I mean, Alan and I deliberately moved to California, but . . . we lived in the only state to pass a law allowing tri-parent birth certificates. While several other state courts have recognized third parents in individual cases, and some states allow gamete donors to be de facto parents, California was the best place in America for our weird little family.

Beyond the multiparenting issue, it was shocking how recently

Three Dads and a Baby

California had fixed the gender issues on its birth certificates. AB 1951 removed the "mother" and "father" blanks on the certificates and replaced them with "parent." This had only gone into effect January 1 of 2016. Before that, same-sex couples had no choice but to decide which parent had to pretend to be another gender. It's not the end of the world, but I don't want any straight men telling me that's not insulting unless they've signed a form saying they were a woman.

In any case, I'm embarrassed to admit that our prepregnancy legal planning went no further than understanding that there would be two parents on the birth certificate and one of us would be left off. Beyond that, we relied on our own stability and the sanity of our families not to cause trouble. This wasn't entirely unreasonable at the time, but in retrospect, the 2016 elections have definitely changed the legal landscape for LGBTQ+ families. I had not expected that. During the celebration of the Supreme Court's *Obergefell* decision legalizing same-sex marriage in 2015, I saw the White House lit up with rainbow lights and thought we were done with antigay politics in America. We aren't.

CHAPTER 13

CHOICE
AND FATE

Jeremy is seven years younger than me and five years younger than Alan, but since we're all grown-ups with jobs and stuff, that hardly makes a difference, except for a few things. Once I made a comment about "people our age," and Jeremy replied with faux snottiness, "You must mean people *your* age."

Or this: we'd agreed to do a home workout program together, and Alan wanted Jeremy to start the on-demand video we were going to use.

"Hey Jeremy, could you get the tape started?"

"*What* are you talking about?" Jeremy asked. "The tape? What the hell is a *tape?*"

"What? The . . . DVD?" Alan said.

"Let me look," said Jeremy. "Maybe we have this on Laserdisc. Or did you mean eight-track? Ohhhh, you meant 'on-demand video' this whole time, didn't you?"

"Jesus Christ. He's a vicious little twerp tonight," Alan said.

"Sorry, Grandpa, what did you say?" asked Jeremy. "I was thinking about getting the old projector down from the attic so we could get started on our workout. Afterward, do you want to play with your Smurfs?"

"Yeah, would you get them?" said Alan. "I think they're by your fidget spinner. Unless you'd prefer Pokémon."

"I would, but the online version is better. Is your dial-up modem working?"

"These millennial twits are so rude!" said Alan.

And that last insult actually bothered Jeremy, a little. "Whoa, who you calling millennial?" he asked, setting off a fierce dispute about whether Jeremy was a millennial, which Wikipedia helpfully ended by confirming that yup, his birthdate in the early 1980s meant he was one of them. Jeremy sulked for several minutes, which is, of course, just what you'd expect from a millennial. "Well, that was a downer for everyone," he said later. "I'm a millennial, and you two guys are old and busted."

Jeremy and Alan were just teasing, and we don't really believe in millennials. The practice of dividing people into generations makes as much sense as doing it by zodiac sign. But the encounter did make me wonder about fate. You don't pick whom you fall in love with. I only met Alan because he got assigned to be my third-year medical student midway through my medicine residency. I met Jeremy via internet lottery. Chance threw us together, and our choices built our family from there.

And while most families just decide whether to have a baby or not, our choices kept coming. We had to pick a surrogate and a genetic mom, and then we had to decide who'd be a dad—and possibly what gender kid we wanted from what dad. We figured we'd make the choosing truly weird and get ancestry testing done for Meghan and the three of us. Let's meet the candidates:

Anyone who knows Alan's parents would probably describe him as half Mexican, while the truth is a little more complicated. His "Mexican" ancestry hails from a geographic area that is currently inside the United States but used to be part of Mexico. According to his genetic analysis, he's 19 percent Native American, and since "Latino" means a mix of

European and Native genes, the math fits the family history. Two conclusions: labels are for soup cans, and Alan's parents blessed him with what he calls the "hybrid vigor" of a mixed ancestry.

Jeremy, on the other hand, considered himself solidly Swedish. He's six-foot-five, with the wingspan of a full-grown pterodactyl. His arms are so long, tailors have told him they're the longest they've ever seen, and doctors have evaluated him for Marfan syndrome, a genetic disease that causes heart and eye problems and makes you lanky. Would there be pterodactyl in his ancestry? Nope. But apparently he's 0.4 percent Asian. The rest, 99.6 percent, is European—and a lot more English than Swedish.

What about me? Was I dad material? Before Lasik, I was so myopic I needed glasses to find my contacts. I've got a crazy cross/underbite from a long jaw that's worn down my front teeth. Two oral surgeons have proposed hacking a quarter inch of bone out of my jaw on both sides (no thanks, ma'am). Worse, despite a memory that allows me to crush standardized tests, I'm terrible with names and faces. Everyone says that, but there's definitely something wrong with my wiring. I have trouble with names of people I *know*. I've had trouble recognizing *friends* if I see them out of context. People have greeted me and had conversations to "catch up," and by the end I still hadn't figured who they were. I can remember in which room on which hospital floor something happened fifteen years ago, yet my whole life feels like I started watching *Game of Thrones* in season six: *Tell me again . . . who's getting killed?*

My genetic analysis provided a bunch of specifics, most of which I already knew. I can smell asparagus pee. I don't have back hair or a unibrow; I have detached earlobes. Some of it missed the mark: I am *not* sweaty; I *am* prone to baldness (but winning). I did appreciate learning that I couldn't get, or pass on to kids, hereditary iron overload, cystic fibrosis, or forty-one other major genetic diseases. That was despite being shockingly, boringly inbred: 100 percent northern and western European.

You know who else is shockingly, boringly white? Meghan. One hundred percent European, although she at least had some southern European thrown in. She made the mistake of sharing her results with me, and now I'm throwing them all in a book—*muah ha-ha!* She's also free of major genetic disease, which is good news for our progeny, but she had a "slightly increased risk" of getting blood clots. That caught my eye because her egg-retrieval medications increase the risk of clots, but "slightly increased risk" is too vague to do anything about. Let's share some of her other dark secrets: she's likely to consume more caffeine and unlikely to be a deep sleeper and has muscle composition more common in elite power athletes. Maybe Junior would get an athletic scholarship!

Oh, I left out one major finding from my analysis: I have more Neanderthal variants than 98 percent of the tested population, a population that is more white and thus more Neanderthal than average (there're almost no Neanderthal genes in Africa). That solved the mystery of my stupid underbite: I literally have a caveman jaw.

Since my mother's family hails from Germany, home to the Neander Valley, I did what any supportive son would do: I told her it was her fault. But the news of our Neanderthal heritage delighted her. "We're excellent, so those genes must be excellent, too!" I told her Neanderthal genes are associated with disease. "No, they're not," she said. "I'm in excellent health!"

"Didn't you have inflammatory arthritis, a dozen colon polyps, and atrial fibrillation so bad you had to have part of your heart's conduction system ablated?"

"Apart from that," she said. She vowed to prove the value of our Neanderthal heritage, but her research showed the opposite. She sent me an email, which I immediately shared with Alan and Jeremy to see if they'd be stunned or amused. "I found a researcher who says Neanderthal genes cause disease," she wrote, "and offered to send him some of my blood to prove just how good Neanderthal genes can be. He didn't reply."

"Go figure," said Jeremy.

"Jesus Christ," said Alan.

Looking back, what seemed like a series of difficult choices turned out to be anything but. Each choice was just a natural extension of how we live our lives together. We'd share the potential for biological parentage because we'd share in every other aspect of parenting. We picked our genetic mother the same way we picked our surrogate—by accepting an offer from a loving woman we trusted. Everything came back around to fate.

CHAPTER 14

IAN AND ALAN

Before Alan became my partner, he was my medical student. When I tell people this, it sounds very *Grey's Anatomy,* as all the trainee surgeons in that show sleep with all their supervisors, rotating faster than they take call. But the truth is a little less interesting. The real world of medicine is nothing like *Grey's Anatomy,* and in three years in training I think I heard about one resident who dated a nurse and zero who slept with supervising doctors.

Alan and I met in Boston, when he was a third-year medical student—that's when you do all your clinical rotations—and I was a second-year resident, supervising first-year residents and working underneath the attending physicians. Both students and trainee doctors do one-month rotations so we gain experience in all the specialties (in the case of students) and all the clinics, wards, and intensive care units where internal medicine patients are treated (in the case of trainee internists). And for this month, I would be supervising Alan and his costudent, Hans.

I recognized Alan as a fellow gay immediately. He was professional and reserved, yes, but the signs were there. Neatly pressed white coat and shirt, occasionally pink? Check. Gucci-brand glasses? Check. Fashionable, neatly knotted tie? Check. Neat and conscientious progress notes in cursive? Check. Striving and motivated, like all medical students, but without that asshole edge? Check. Oh—bonding immediately with the frail little old lady admitted with confusion and nicknaming her "my Golden Girl"? Double check. And he wasn't *just* gay—this is a prerequisite for me, but hardly sufficient—he was smarter than the other students. It was obvious, even though he wasn't straining to show off his medical knowledge, like half of them were. I could tell from everything he said. Months later, I would tell him he only said interesting, witty things, like he was reading lines for a high-brow sitcom.

Contrast Hans: stained lab coat with half the collar folded inside, monotonous white shirts, absent flair, sloppy handwriting, stoner vibe, no Golden Girl.

I thought Alan knew I was gay as readily as I'd figured him out, and so I assumed we were already partners in crime. We shared plenty of chuckles over a mishap that happened while Hans interviewed one of his first patients on the rotation. The ER called to tell me an HIV-positive man had to be admitted for dehydration from severe diarrhea, so we went down to see him. I prepped Hans for the interview, because students doing their first interviews always benefit from a little preparation and our patient was probably one of the gays, and I wasn't sure how comfortable Hans would be with the social history part of the interview. Back when I was in medical school in Virginia, a good number of the students would damn near swoon if there had to be a frank discussion about sexuality—and I wanted to set Hans up for success.

"So Hans, our patient is HIV-positive," I said. "How do you think that happened?"

"Drugs?" he asked. "Or sexually transmitted?"

"Yeah, most likely either IV drugs or he's gay, and knowing his primary care doctor, I'm betting on the latter. How might that affect your interview?"

"Um, what?" Which was a good thing to say, actually. Medical students often try to just guess, and it's an important skill in medicine to just say you don't know.

"Well, if he's gay, what questions might you need to ask about his sexual habits?"

"Oh," he replied, blushing already. "I guess because he could have, he could get . . . uh, the diarrhea, if it's an infection, it gets spread that way."

"Which way?" I asked.

Hans stared at us.

"His sexual behavior might have put him at risk for infection with bacterial or viral pathogens, which can be acquired from exposure to microscopic amounts of stool. Otherwise known as fecal-oral transmission," said Alan, who has a degree in microbiology.

"Oh, yeah," Hans concurred. "Pathogens get swallowed and they spread the . . . infection." I asked Hans if he felt comfortable asking our new patient about his sexual habits, and he gave me a thumbs-up.

The patient was indeed gay—a bear, actually, with a bit of a pot belly, a beard, even the archetypal plaid flannel shirt. He was as good-natured as you might expect a bear to be, and delighted to participate in training the next generation of doctors. He happily answered Hans's questions about his symptoms, medical history, medications, and family history—and then it was time for the social history, which is when we ask about the sex, drugs, and rock 'n' roll.

"So do you, are you, sexually active?" asked Hans.

"Oh yes."

"Men, women, or both?"

"Just men."

"And what . . . kind of sex?"

"Do you mean . . . anal sex? I'm versatile." Hans's face posed the question. "I top and I bottom." Still no understanding. "Insertive and receptive?" *That,* Hans had heard in class.

"And do you . . . ?" Our bear leaned forward, waiting for Hans's question. "Do you have fecal-oral sex?" And as soon as our patient recoiled, wide-eyed, Hans began to walk it back. "Oh jeez. I'm sorry. I meant to say . . . oh, this is embarrassing."

Our patient grimaced, then smiled, and then he suppressed a laugh . . . and then he lost it completely and laughed so hard he cried and doctors and nurses looked in from the row of computers behind us. Hans turned bright red, and for the first time, I saw one of Alan's most charming features: how adorable he looks when he tries not to laugh. The unstoppable force of hilarity meets the immovable object of his desire to maintain his composure, and the result includes tears, half-muffled giggles, and high-pitched protestations that he's very sorry and knows he shouldn't be laughing.

Finally, the patient collected himself and said, "No. I'm not sure that's a thing, but if it is, it's definitely not for me." Poor Hans, but if you're going to say something embarrassing to a patient, it never hurts to find one with a sense of humor.

That night I went to check on Hans's note, and Alan came along. Student notes aren't part of the formal medical record, but they're important practice. I was expecting to read a detailed summary of the patient's symptoms, medical history, exam, and labs. The assessment and plan sections usually run a page or longer, especially if the student authors are "gunners"—that is, eager to show off their medical knowledge to everyone from the doctors writing their evaluations to themselves. Hans's just contained two sentences:

1. Diarrhea: consult infectious disease service.

2. HIV infection: continue antiretroviral regimen.

"Jesus," said Alan. "That's . . . succinct."

"I know, right?" I said. "If you don't know anything about a disease, google it." See? We were chums. Actually, the word the gays use is *family,* as in, "I'm going to introduce you to this guy. You'll like him—he's family" (wink). We were family.

Our next stop was a "doc box," or physician workroom, where we reviewed results of spinal fluid tests that were coming back on a patient we'd done a lumbar puncture on earlier, for suspected meningitis. Sharing the room: a fire-haired resident from the class a year ahead of mine by the name of Jason. I'd never thought a ton about Jason—there were about sixty residents per class in my internship, I'd never worked closely with him, and I had about one hundred hours of clinical duties a week to occupy my thoughts. I knew he was cheerful, friendly, and had a slightly feminine style, and that was it.

"What do you think?" I asked Alan, as we looked at the test results. The spinal fluid had too many white cells, too much protein, and too little glucose.

"Looks like bacterial meningitis," he said. "Good thing we gave him those STAT antibiotics!"

Jason looked over our shoulders. "Awwwww mm-hmm!" he said. "Mister's got the meningitis for reeeeals, mkay?" And he turned back to his own work, shaking his head like a guest on *Jerry Springer*.

Holy shit! I thought. *Jason's gay. Supergay.* I thought about all the information I had—dress, mannerisms, speech—but it really came down to this: Jason had a little journal with him he used to keep track of patients, and he'd written "Jason!" on the front, and the dot of the exclamation point was a *heart*. Jason was family, too—right in front of us. I know this chapter makes my training program sound gayer than the theater department at a liberal arts college, but it contains every gay colleague I met in three years except one. So to have three gays alone in a doc box at 1:00 a.m. on the medicine ward? What were the odds? I wished I'd had champagne to celebrate.

I wrote a quick note—"I think he's family!"—and tapped on it so Alan would read it. He gave me a face like I'd served him sour milk. *You don't think so?* I mouthed. He shrugged.

Alan's friends at the time included an ambitious and intelligent gay fellow student, who may in fact be someone you know. That's because he's so loud I'm fairly sure you've heard him, probably asking yourself "what was *that?*" And he's so flamboyant you could see him sparkling from the international space station. This is a student who tried to convince a senior citizen with pneumonia that she should watch the Mariah Carey vehicle *Glitter*. When Alan told his friend about my comments in the doc box, the conversation went something like this:

"Alan, what's your resident like?"

"Oh, he's a jerk. Rigid and argumentative and asks tough questions on rounds."

"That bad?"

"And he had the nerve to ask about a gay-acting resident and if I thought he was family, like he was one of us."

"Waaait, what? You're talking about Ian?"

"Yeah, why?"

"Please, I heard he *is* one of us." Alan shook his head. "I swear! He's out. Promise!"

The night Alan found out I was gay, we started having sex in the call rooms between trips to the emergency room to see patients. "I hope that will favorably influence my evaluation," he said, making cute little doe eyes at me and curling up in the tiny single bed with the crisp hospital sheets and flimsy blanket.

No, that *did not* happen. I already told you, medicine is nothing like *Grey's Anatomy,* and Alan is professional and reserved. He performed admirably on his rotation, took exceptional care of his patients, never said an inappropriate word, waited until the rotation had been over a month and all evaluations had been completed, and then reasoned that the straight-acting, jerk resident was probably just trying to do his best for his patients and compensating for a deep-seated anxiety about inadvertently harming a patient.

Then he asked if I would like to "hang out" sometime, in a manner that left me completely unsure as to whether we were going on a date or just being social. He told me later he still wasn't sure if I was gay. I brought a baking stone, homemade pizza dough and other ingredients, and a bottle of wine over to his place and made him dinner, and that made it a date. And without planning it or realizing it until later (medical trainees are too busy to think of such things), we'd had our first date on Valentine's Day. That was way back in 2003.

Since then, he's substantially improved me. He's mellowed me out. Some of this would have happened with the passage of time, but he gave me some pointers. Helped me to take a breather from being a medicine gunner and enjoy an occasional episode of *Project Runway* or *RuPaul's Drag Race*. Took me to every concert I've ever attended and introduced me to pleasures ranging from the music of Radiohead to the rainforests of Maui and Kauai. Taught me to install whole bathrooms and kitchens— we've leveled subfloors, laid travertine, wired appliances, soldered copper pipe, and hung cabinets. And had we not met, I might still be wearing pleated pants and ill-fitting shirts.

In return, I keep making him dinner. And—no minor contribution—I found us our Jeremy, with whom we were about to make a baby. We just had one more roadblock.

A virus.

CHAPTER 15

ZIKA

In 2014, Brazil hosted both the World Cup and a canoe-racing tournament in Rio. Soon after, doctors in the state capital Natal started seeing patients with a pink rash, fever, bloodshot eyes, and aches. First it was a few, then dozens, then hundreds. The doctors were stumped. Tests for dengue and other viruses were negative, and doctors dubbed the fevers "*doença misteriosa*"—the mystery disease. Only after thousands of tests did virologists identify the culprit: Zika, a virus first identified in Africa and known to be making its way through the islands of the South Pacific. The canoe competition had brought athletes from Polynesia, and the World Cup brought teams and fans from . . . well, the world. Some of them likely brought Zika in their blood. At the time, finding Zika seemed like good news. Experts thought of it as a harmless illness, lasting a week and causing no complications.[75]

Then, in 2015, the babies came. Like the rush of fevers, Brazil saw an epidemic of microcephalic babies—kids with normal faces, but small heads and brains (in a cruel bit of irony, the name of the city at the epicenter, Natal, means "birth" in English, as in prenatal testing). Many of their mothers had suffered the *doença misteriosa* while pregnant. Doctors also saw a spike in cases of Guillain-Barré disease—a type of acquired paralysis. Zika hadn't always wreaked so much havoc with the nervous system. The increase in virulence compared to previous outbreaks may have been due to a mutation in a single gene, one that made it deadlier to nerve cells.[76] Whatever the cause, by January 2016, the director general of the World Health Organization warned that Zika was "spreading explosively" in the Americas, with up to four million cases in twenty countries expected by the end of the year.[77] Fearing more microcephalic babies, officials from five countries flat-out told their citizens to avoid or delay getting pregnant.[78] Experts even warned women to avoid having sex with men who'd visited these countries, as Zika could be spread by semen.

Now we were trying to schedule Meghan's egg-collection cycle, at the same time that Zika news was spooking IVF doctors across America, both North and South. Dr. Collins's office called. She wanted to do my sperm collection and discuss our management plan for Zika risk. I finally had something important to contribute to the pregnancy effort besides money.

Turns out I am not the best person to pick out onesies for an infant. Or quilt her a blanket. Or pick out the best bottle nipples for different stages of infancy. Recruiting egg donors and surrogates? That was Alan. Picking out baby clothes and designing the nursery? That's Alan and Jeremy. Filling out a baby shower registry? Jeremy. Singing Disney songs to the baby, before and after conception, in the car or the shower or the kitchen, in and not in her presence? Jeremy. Oh God, is that ever Jeremy. Honestly, my partners planned everything.

The only thing I'd be the best dad for would be . . . teaching the baby martial arts. I'd done karate for twenty years and Brazilian jujitsu for several. There was no question: if the family ever got attacked by Mad Max–style bandits, yakuza, or zombies, I'd be expected to defend us, either with my fists or my trusty katana. But let's be honest: this isn't the most useful parenting skill. I didn't feel like the MVP for any of the baby work that had yet come up.

But now we needed someone with internal medicine training to analyze professional guidelines about an infectious disease and consider the performance of different test modalities. This, I could help with. I made myself a double cappuccino, strapped myself into my office swivel chair, and googled like crazy.

I learned that about 1 to 13 percent of Zika-affected fetuses suffered microcephaly.[79] But, (1) having fetal Zika without microcephaly did not mean everything was hunky-dory; the child might end up with a badly damaged, normal-size brain; (2) we'd have to do everything in our earthly powers to keep our child from having a profound, preventable neurologic disability. Microcephaly would mean abortion. We did *not* want a Zika-affected child. Testing Meghan seemed mandatory.

There were two tests for Zika infection. PCR, or polymerase chain reaction, detects viral genetic material. PCR tells you if someone has Zika *right now*—it's only positive for a week or so. Meghan could be PCR-negative despite having been exposed to Zika, and traces of Zika could be hanging out in her eggs, just waiting to scramble our baby's brain.

Serology, the other test, looks for antibodies to Zika, not the virus itself. Serology *would* tell us if Meghan had been infected with Zika in the past, but it also had drawbacks. Zika belongs to a family of insect-borne viruses called flaviviruses. If Meghan had ever had another flavivirus, cross-reacting antibodies could give us a false positive result for Zika.

Was that possible? "Flavi-" comes from the Latin word for yellow, as the first flavivirus identified causes yellow fever. Yellow fever got its name because some victims develop liver failure, which makes you yellow. And Meghan had only ever turned yellow once, when she had a bad hair dye. She swears that strangers stopped across the street to play air guitar and yell "R-r-r-rock and r-r-r-roll!" in their Río de la Plata accents. Dengue, another flavivirus in Latin America, causes fever, headache, vomiting, and severe muscle pain, for which it earned the nickname "bone-break fever," and Meghan had never had compatible symptoms. With zero reported cases, Buenos Aires didn't have yellow fever, dengue, *or* Zika transmission. All the Zika transmission happened much farther north, near tropical Brazil. Great!

Now for a crazy coincidence. As the Zika epidemic unfolded, hospitals everywhere developed protocols for screening and testing patients with fever or rash. My hospital's response was led by the perennially cheerful, effervescent, and talented Dr. Lucia Torriani. By sheer luck, Dr. Torriani *mistakenly added me* to a group email *two days* before our meeting with Dr. Collins. I wrote her back, told her about our Argentinian egg donor, and asked her for advice. She called me instantly.

"Ian, my darling," she said in her musical Italian accent, "*Buon giorno!* I'm so delighted to learn that you're going to be a father. I must know if you'd encourage your children to attend medical school. But that's another matter. What's this about Zika?"

I told her that Meghan hailed from Buenos Aires, an area without Zika activity. I said I'd read the statements from the CDC and the Society for Maternal-Fetal Medicine about Zika testing. Here's what Dr. Scaligeri recommended doing about Zika: absolutely nothing. "Why are you contemplating testing? There's just not any risk. What would be the point? There's no transmission in her area. Even if the local authorities are missing some cases, the amount of transmission would be negligible. You don't think Argentina has ceased having babies, do you?"

We did have some points of disagreement. She didn't even recommend doing a serology, which could give us a false positive from prior dengue infection. "For any tests, he's asking totally out of guidelines. You'd be throwing your money down the rabbit's hole. Is that what they say?" But I was pretty damned sure that Meghan had never had dengue, so the negative test result would reassure everyone. I didn't press the issue. It's not easy to get thirty minutes of free, dedicated consultation from an epidemiologist, so I thanked her five times over. "No problem at all, my dear," she said. "*Ciao bello.*"

I printed out a stack of documents to prepare for our discussion with Dr. Collins. Then I tried to forget about Zika and think warmly about my . . . relationship with Alan and Jeremy, since I was supposed to produce some sperm before the Zika meeting. And I really did figure we had all the virus stuff covered. Alan had already sat down with Collins and looked at a CDC map, and Collins had assured him she had no concerns about Zika. So it had to be some little thing, and anyway, we were as well prepared as any family in San Diego could have been.

But nothing could have prepared us for the fuckery we would walk into at that meeting.

CHAPTER 16

THE CHAPTER
ON MASTURBATION

Alan and Jeremy had already trekked to FISC to do their sperm donations, so I got a bit of a rundown on the layout. They gave you a specimen cup, guided you to your masturbation cubbyhole, and left you alone for your "me time." The room had a couch with a fresh sheet thrown over it (it still looked disgusting), a vanity and sink, a nice TV, and a steel pass-through in the wall with an adjacent "I'm done" switch for private specimen handoff. The pass-through door was labeled with a fluid-filled beaker that looked like it held a half liter, but hey, no pressure.

On the counter by the sink, the staff had left a stack of 8.5x11–size comment cards. What did people write? "Dear clinic director, I just masturbated into a cup, and I'd like you to know how friendly your receptionists are!" Next to these, I found framed comments about the clinic's porn:

> Sexual excitement has been proven to improve ejaculate
> volume, sperm count, and sperm quality. This is especially
> important for men with poor sperm counts and sperm quality.

> Excitement may increase the odds of pregnancy. Thus, we have
> provided videos you may use for sexual stimulation.
> We apologize to any men who find these videos offensive.

> Do *not* hurry to collect the specimen.

"Do *not* hurry." Doctor-ese for "take your time, you'll ejaculate more." The actual sperming instructions waited nearby, framed in wood that had been absolutely wrecked by a multitude of splashes. Even though the room appeared to have been carefully cleaned, that just made every surface in sight seem as filthy as a laptop owned by a teenage boy. I didn't even want to sit. The instructions read:

Method for Semen Collection for IVF Procedures and Laboratory Testing (Follow procedure precisely to avoid semen contamination)

▸ Wash and dry hands.

▸ Open surgical scrub brush and sponge package. Open sterile towel kit (blue).

▸ Remove specimen cup from plastic wrap. Turn lid until loose. *Do Not Open.* Cap should remain in place until just before ejaculation.

▸ Rewet your hands and your genitals. Retract foreskin, if present.

▸ Use the *brush* to scrub your *hands.* Use the *sponge* to clean your *genitals.*

▸ Rinse hands and genitals thoroughly. Surgical scrub soap kills sperm.

▸ Dry hands and genitals thoroughly, using sterile towels. Water immobilizes sperm.

▸ If needed, use buzzer to ask assistant for a "collection helper kit."

▸ While ejaculating, do not touch the inside of specimen cup with any part of your body. Target the center of the bottom of the cup.

▸ Replace lid. Tighten securely. Place in collection box. Flip switch to notify nurse.

WARNING: DO NOT USE ANY FORM OF LUBRICANT DURING PROCESS

I never figured out what a "collection helper kit" was. I didn't ever figure out what they could be. I doubted that anyone made medical-grade Fleshlights.

Problem #1: Privacy. This was not a romantic or secluded setting. I eyed the flat-screen TV suspiciously . . . how many guys cranked up the sound on that? I figured you'd never know if the walls were well insulated or not and would never want to take the chance. Then it got worse—I heard everyone bustling about outside. Hey, clinic—get yourself a white noise machine!

Problem #2: I was pretty sure that everything in the room had been touched by masturbating guys. This is actually *not* a turn-on for me. I felt like I do in the hospital, convinced that every surface is trying to kill me, like when I have a patient with lice, scabies, hepatitis A, or (as has happened twice) bacteria resistant to every known antibiotic. So I went into cautious doctor mode, and that does not feel sexy.

Problem #3: This wasn't a fatal problem, but both Alan and Jeremy noticed that FISC's big pile o' porn was 100 percent straight. Two dozen DVDs, and all of them hetero. Two issues: first, the porn's in there for a reason. And second, we all got the creeping feeling that we weren't welcome. *Of course* some people seeking fertility assistance are gay, so throw 'em a bone (heh heh), and leave one gay title in the pile. You don't wait for gay clients to think about this stuff. Having no gay porn at all was like filling out paperwork and finding the relationship options were limited to "married," "single," and "divorced."

The more I thought about it, the more this bothered me. The office had just told me that sexual excitement was important for semen collection. Their little *omission* might decrease their clients' *emission*—and decrease the odds of pregnancy. We had already paid Collins's office many thousands of dollars. A little courtesy wouldn't hurt, and reducing the odds of success now seemed unforgivable. My visual stimulation was limited to my "partner": a narrow-necked specimen cup with an inside I must not touch with "any part of [my] body" (my knee? A pinkie toe?). Yay! I just needed to very calmly have an orgasm without moving.

Problem #4: Semen collection requires semisterile conditions, and I did my surgical scrub as instructed. When done, I was sparkly clean, and every trace of natural skin oil had been etched away to squeaky dryness by this super soap. Again, no lubricants were allowed—bad for the little swimmers, apparently.

Standing there, sterile, creeped out, feeling listened to, with the staff waiting for results . . . that was the moment when I decided that I wasn't going to be a biological father. Genetics aren't destiny, we didn't need a half dozen kids, and it just didn't seem to be in the cards.

Naw, I'm kidding. It was like *Jurassic Park,* when they find out the supposedly all-female dinosaurs are breeding, and a scientist muses, "Life finds a way." Wondering what range of reappearance times the office staff were used to, I placed my specimen cup in the pass-through and flipped the switch. The office's system carefully avoided any moment where a donor might feel judged by the staff's reaction to their specimen's volume . . . color . . . bouquet . . . whatever. Nice touch—everyone could pretend I hadn't just produced a sperm sample and they hadn't just accepted it. I walked out trying not to make a face that said, "Yeah, it's me, that guy that just ejaculated in a cup for you."

Then, I gave up about seventy vials of blood so I could be tested for every disease known to man. No big deal—I've got veins you could stick a Bic pen in. The tests were the FDA-mandated tissue donor labs, and they included all the major STIs plus infections like Epstein-Barr virus (an infection that most adults have and the body never gets rid of), and even HTLV, a virus found in the Caribbean, which can cause leukemia or spastic paralysis (I did *not* have HTLV—phew).

After my testing, I met Dr. Collins for the first time for a brief exam. Her expertly done highlights said "Southern California," but her age said "experience" and her expression said "serious," and I felt comfortable with her. An exam is required of sperm donors, to ensure they're healthy, but I assure you mine was a joke. She listened to my heart for five seconds, each lung for a breath, and pressed on my abdomen. Then she peeked at my genitals (yup, genitals present, no weeping ulcers), and that was it. I'm not faulting her—the exam was legally required, and since I didn't actually need a physical exam, it didn't bother me to receive a cursory one—but it was obviously just a formality. And a money-drainer. This was the *sixth* exam my family had paid for. (Sixteen, beer, pickup.)

After that, I joined Alan, Jeremy, Dr. Collins, our surrogacy coordinator, and . . . some unidentified woman we'd never seen before and were not expecting, to discuss Zika risk management.

CHAPTER 17

THE FUCKERY
OF DR. COLLINS

D r. Collins introduced the extra woman at our meeting as Nancy and said she was there to "help out." We'd worked closely with our surrogacy coordinator, Tricia, but we'd never seen Nancy before, and we had no idea what she was really doing at our meeting. She wasn't involved in our case and she didn't seem to be a Zika expert. Nancy sat behind us, making us uncomfortable for the entire discussion.

Collins began the meeting by explaining that fetal Zika infection was *very bad* and must be avoided. "Don't worry," Jeremy said. "We don't want to spend a million dollars on a brain-injured baby, either." Collins added that risk could last over six months after infection. That didn't matter to us; if Meghan had been infected, we just wouldn't use her eggs.

Then Collins shocked us. Because of the "heightened risk" (was it, though?), Collins said she could not use Meghan's eggs unless she spent six to eight weeks quarantined in the United States.

"She runs a *business*," Alan said, mystified. "She isn't wealthy. She can't just . . . not work for two months."

But that wasn't all. Collins wanted Meghan to have PCR testing at the end of the quarantine, which made no sense to me. "To be completely clear," I asked, "you're saying Meghan has to stay in the United States for six to eight weeks because it's safe from Zika, then we have to spend $500 on a test that is only positive for a week after infection? So she *is* at risk of infection here? Do you require testing of *American* egg donors?"

"That's the only way I would feel comfortable proceeding," Dr. Collins answered.

"I hear you, but that didn't answer my question. It doesn't make any sense to say she needs to be protected in the United States, but we need a PCR to see if she got infected here in the last week of her quarantine. If you can't use people who might be infected, by your logic, you can't use any Americans."

"Yeah! What you're saying doesn't make any sense," said Alan, after a narrow-eyed look at Nancy, who smiled enthusiastically. "If Meghan's a high-risk donor, per your own guidelines, you simply can't use her. You said the duration of risk is six months, which is far longer than the quarantine you proposed."

Jeremy jumped on that point, too. If the risk was six months, then by having Meghan as an egg donor after only six weeks in America, we were saying that we trusted Zika tests to exclude infection. So why couldn't we use the tests to clear her when she arrived in California? Next, Jeremy asked if we could quarantine Meghan's eggs and retest her months later. Collins didn't trust foreign labs and thought that was an option only if she flew back to the United States to be retested. But why?

"This is what I recommend," said Collins.

I found myself momentarily speechless. As a physician, I didn't understand Dr. Collins's testing strategy at all. It didn't sound like a doctor's plan to me. It didn't sound like a *medical student's* plan to me. So I took a deep breath and opened my file of Zika research. "I prepared carefully for this discussion," I said. "Here are the latest documents from your own professional society that detail how Zika risk should be managed in

South America. Nothing I found contains the recommendation you're making." I showed her all the position statements I'd brought. None of them mentioned anything like what she'd proposed. Even the most conservative guidelines said women with possible exposure—people at higher risk than Meghan—could get tested with serology two weeks after exposure—not Dr. Collins's six to eight weeks.

Another guideline said, "Routine serologic testing is not currently recommended" for patients without symptoms. Citing FDA guidance, it said that women from low-risk areas like Meghan could donate eggs, as long as everyone involved understood the risks. We had the reproductive society's recommendations, Meghan was at infinitesimally small risk, and we would happily sign waivers acknowledging the risk, I pointed out. Wouldn't the risk be all *ours* then, not Dr. Collins's? I didn't understand the problem.

Jeremy asked her to put the risk in context. "What do you think the risk of a birth defect is from Zika virus, in an area with no Zika virus activity, and what do you think it would be *after* this quarantine period?"

"Yeah," said Alan. "What's that risk compared with the risk of birth defects in *any* pregnancy?"

Collins wouldn't say.

I still wanted to understand where her recommendation had come from, if not a guideline. "Did you use any information *besides* these guidelines?" I asked. "Is there some other research I didn't find?"

"I did consult with experts in the field," she said. I asked her which experts. "I had a conference call with an infectious disease expert and epidemiologist." I asked her from where. "The University of California, San Diego," she said.

I could feel my eyes go wide. "Which doctor was it?" I asked. "A man or a woman?" A woman, she admitted. "Italian accent? Dr. Scaligeri? Does that sound familiar?" She nodded.

What were the odds? Out of the nearly forty million people in California, how many people had just had a consultation with

Dr. Scaligeri about Zika and IVF in the last forty-eight hours? And mine had been facilitated by a randomly misdirected email!

"I just spoke with Dr. Scaligeri myself, two days ago," I said. "She told me, specifically, not to worry about Zika or do any testing at all. She told you something different? She didn't reassure you?"

Apparently not. Dr. Collins just said she would not take any unnecessary risks. She had made her decision.

Things only got more tense from there. In frustration, Alan finally turned and confronted the woman who'd been inserted into our conversation and never properly introduced. "I'm sorry," he asked, sounding not that sorry, "what is your role in this meeting?"

"I, uh, help deal with complicated situations," Nancy said, "and, you know, help around the office."

"I'm sorry," Alan replied, sounding even less sorry, "but no, I *don't* know. What job is that, exactly? Are you from risk management? Are you the office attorney? Why are you sitting in this meeting, with us, right now?"

"We just all thought it would be helpful," she offered lamely. Brick walls in all directions. We wrapped things up quickly, since the discussion wasn't going anywhere, and also we didn't want to end up yelling at Collins or her mystery probably attorney partner Nancy. We ended up leaving the office without an adequate explanation of her role in the meeting, or even a title.

"Let me be perfectly clear about one more thing," Alan said as we prepared to leave. "Ian came in early to do his sperm donation and lab tests. I just wrote you a check for $500 to pay for it. And now you're throwing up a practically insurmountable roadblock to using our egg donor. I am not happy."

"Sounds like we'll need to speak to other IVF specialists," Jeremy said.

"You won't find anyone willing to make the exception I'm offering you," Collins warned. "They'll just refuse to work with you."

"We'll see," said Alan. "I don't understand why *you* won't work with us."

"I *do* want to work with you," she said. "We just have to make sure that Meghan is a safe donor."

"No, do not put this on us," I told her. "Meghan is safe. I confirmed that with the infectious disease specialist running UCSD's Zika response team. You aren't an epidemiologist specializing in Zika, correct?"

She wasn't. We left, fuming. Alan said what we were all thinking as we paid for parking and headed home: *"Fuck* that shit." We needed to get ourselves a new repro med doctor—and quick, because Meghan was scheduled to arrive soon. As it turns out, Jeremy made both our wishes come true with a single phone call.

CHAPTER 18

ESCAPE TO BLUMBERG

"I found a new guy!" Jeremy exclaimed breathlessly. "Dr. Blumberg. A lot closer to us than FISC. And he gave us an appointment—tomorrow! On a Saturday!" He had something else to tell us, and he wanted us to sit down, which felt rather ominous.

"I hate how tense this week has been," he said. "But I want you to remember two things. First, in about two weeks, this will just be an annoying memory. And second, if it doesn't work out, we'll be okay. We'll resent having wasted all that money, but we have such a nice life and an amazing family. If we end up pregnant, I'll be so excited to begin a new chapter with you. If not, I have two amazing people who I love and cherish so much. Either way I feel so lucky."

Jeremy's pep talk took the sting out of the Collins meeting so we could make a fresh start with Blumberg. We drove to downtown San Diego and took an elevator to what seemed like the hundredth floor. Alan pointed to a mezuzah on the door frame of the clinic. "See? He's Jewish, like Delilah. Our baby is part of God's plan." Blumberg's office was hopping, full of young women and a few men, coming and going, many of them speaking Mandarin and one with an Australian accent (California is an IVF destination for a number of countries). The receptionist took us back to Blumberg's office to wait for our consultation. Skyscrapers crowded the panoramic view. Piles of thick patient charts in manila folders covered every inch of Blumberg's desk. It looked like a doctor's office from a TV show.

"Check this out," said Alan, pointing to framed photos on the wall of the office. "His house was featured in *Architectural Digest*!" Blumberg's Spanish-style mansion, beautifully illuminated for a dusk photo shoot, looked like he'd bought it from Pablo Escobar and built an addition. He had exceptional taste. We wouldn't have changed an atom.

"Well, he's doing all right," said Jeremy. "Must be good at making babies."

Soon after, Dr. Blumberg joined us, wearing burgundy surgical scrubs branded with his clinic's logo. Ignoring his desk chair, he plopped onto a little doctor's swivel stool like he might do a pelvic exam, and faced the nervous throuple on his couch. "So," said Blumberg, "I understand from Jeremy that the three of you are in a committed relationship, and you're looking to have a baby via assisted reproduction." We nodded.

"You know, I've taken over for other patients of Dr. Collins," he said. "A doctor who'd trained at UCSD and his husband. They said Collins's office told them their case was too complicated, too." Another UCSD-affiliated doctor? What a small world! It turned out the parents who'd jumped ship from Collins to Blumberg were actually our super-nice friends and neighbors, Suri and Dave—what a *tiny* world, in fact! Dave worked for an organization that helps conduct clinical research, and Suri was a gastroenterologist and former colleague. We just exchanged a look of astonishment at the coincidence, and let Blumberg address the elephant in the room: Zika. Collins had said other doctors would simply refuse to work with our Argentinian egg donor. What would Blumberg say?

"I don't get it," he said. "Meghan hasn't been exposed, so there's no risk. We can do a serology so we all feel better. No problem."

It just got better from there. Blumberg explained that he'd done the IVF procedure for the first gay couple to get listed on a birth certificate in California, about twenty-five years ago. Aghast, his peers tried to have his board certification revoked but failed. Since that time, he'd done fifteen hundred fertility cycles for male-male couples. It's amazing how quickly society has changed. A few decades ago, doctors were morality police; now, discriminating against gay couples would make you an asshole and possibly a criminal. "I've never worked with three guys before," he said, "but there's a first time for everything!"

"It's not a little weird for you?" asked Jeremy.

"My attitude is that everyone who comes to me has given parenthood a great deal of thought and has the resources to care for a child. My job isn't to judge who should or should not be parents but to help people make their dreams come true."

What a stunning relief! It was like we'd been teleported to the climax of an inspirational movie. "Yes!" said Alan. "*Yes!* Exactly. *Thank you!*"

We were hooked. We sat back while Blumberg gave us his whole spiel about the process. Meghan would receive hormones to stimulate the production of multiple eggs at once, each of which would mature in an ovarian cyst.[vii] An anesthesiologist would sedate her, and Blumberg would remove the eggs by passing a needle through her vagina. Hearing him describe the egg-collection procedure made *my* vagina hurt. Under a microscope, the eggs would then be fertilized with a process called ICSI, or intracytoplasmic sperm injection. I figured it would be best to mimic nature and let some sperm fight it out, but Blumberg said no, best to pick the winner.

We felt both supported and in capable hands, and with Meghan's arrival only days away, we were all relieved to have a replacement doctor.

---

vii "Ovarian cysts" have a bad reputation because we only talk about them when they rupture painfully or grow large enough to cause discomfort.

As we drove out of a basement parking garage onto bright city streets, Jeremy said, "This is good. This is where we should have been the whole time."

Indeed.

CHAPTER 19

THE SWIMMERS

Sperm are an endangered species. In 2017, an analysis of 185 studies on almost forty-three thousand men concluded that the average sperm count has dropped 50 to 60 percent in forty years.[80] That's an astonishing figure. If you plot out the rate of decline, you can predict a civilization-wide infertility crisis by 2060. As an environmentalist, I'm all for declining fertility and birth rates, but I was shocked to learn that 8 percent of kids in Denmark are now conceived using assisted reproduction. And that the percent of men who qualified as sperm donors in China fell from 56 percent to 18 percent in only fifteen years![81]

Why? Researchers point to different causes, but modern lifestyles are likely culprits. Cigarette smoke, alcohol, obesity, stress, poor exercise habits, pesticides, medications, and pollution all harm sperm. For example, a Taiwanese study linked air pollution to worse sperm quality—the more pollution, the worse the sperm quality.[82] Even ibuprofen, the ubiquitous painkiller in Advil and Motrin, can weaken testicles.[83]

Endocrine-disrupting chemicals found in plastics, in which many of our foods are now stored and heated, may also be at fault. Many Americans avoid plastics that contain bisphenol A (BPA), a chemical that has been linked to cancer, obesity, early puberty in girls, and genital deformations in boys. Many plastic products now advertise that they're BPA-free. That sounds super, but it's not, because most are BPA-free only because they're made with another toxic bisphenol,[84] like bisphenol S, F, B, Z, and others.

For years, I'd been buying BPA-free plastic items, thinking I was keeping my family safe, but according to research recently published in the journals *Current Biology* and *Toxicological Sciences,* I'd been deluding myself. BPA substitutes are just as bad, some BPA substitutes are even worse, and bisphenols cause genetic damage not just in animals who consume them, but in several generations of descendants.[85,86] Notably, while sperm counts have plummeted in some populations, the sperm counts of African men have not declined significantly. These African men were presumably exposed to fewer man-made chemicals; they also suffered less testicular cancer.

What to do? Plastic-free grocery shopping is nearly impossible, but we replaced our plastic food containers with glass ones, which we bring to restaurants to reduce waste and chemical exposure. I've even convinced the local Thai takeout spot to fill my home containers. And we have found stainless steel bottles and cups with silicone nipples, sippy tops, and straws for growing babies.

Anyway, while we'd donated sperm in Collins's office, we'd gotten caught up in her Zika fuckery so quickly, we didn't think much about our test results until we had a new IVF doctor. Short version: we didn't have the most amazing sperm.

	Volume	Motility	Sperm (total)	Sperm (concentration)	Morphology (% normal)
Normal	≥1.5 ml	≥ 32%	≥39 million	≥15 million/ml	≥ 4%
Alan	3.8 ml	55%	410 million	108 million/ml	3%
Jeremy	3.5 ml	63%	140 million	40 million/ml	1%

Jeremy's sample came with the additional finding of severe teratospermia, or abnormal-appearing sperm. Jeremy submitted an additional sperm sample, by mail, for a sperm chromatin structure assay to estimate his odds of successful fertilization. To assist in this process, he received a nearly three-foot-high, bullet-shaped, dry ice–cooled shipping vessel. A hassle, but if there's one thing to say about sperm testing, it's a heckuva lot more fun than having eggs extracted. Jeremy's supplemental test came back describing his DNA fragmentation index as showing "excellent to good sperm DNA integrity." I still couldn't tell you if this test is good at predicting pregnancy outcomes or fetal health . . . we were just told it was necessary. It cost $750.

I had the stupidest sperm by far:

	Volume	Motility	Sperm (total)	Sperm (concentration	Morphology (% norm al)
Normal	≥1.5 ml	≥ 32%	≥39 million	≥15 million/ml	≥ 4%
Ian	2.1 ml	15%	36 million	17 million/ml	2%

To put that into perspective, Alan's sample had *forty-two times* as many motile sperm as mine. "Huh," I said, as we looked at my results. "Looks like we haven't had a kid because I have stupid sperm. I always thought it was because we're all men."

I have stupid swimmers. That's okay with me. I've been asked why I would want to admit that in a book, but it's not a big deal. I was forty-two at the time, and sperm counts decline with age. Quality goes down, too, increasing the risk of Down syndrome, schizophrenia, and autism. Besides, men everywhere have crummy sperm counts, and I am more than my sperm count, which would matter perhaps once in my whole life. I have other redeeming characteristics.

Prior costs	$41,359.00
Initial sperm testing, Alan:	$530.50
Initial sperm testing, Jeremy:	$530.50
Initial sperm testing, Ian:	$530.50
Jeremy's additional tests:	$750.00
Subtotal:	$2,341.50
Total:	$43,700.50

CHAPTER 20

THE MEGGS

When Meghan arrived from Argentina, we took her to dinner and a movie. It seemed like the right thing to do, since we wanted to have her baby. We saw 2016's *Arrival,* starring Amy Adams as a linguist asked to interpret for a pair of giant, squid-like aliens who arrived in an enormous hovering spaceship. She establishes rudimentary communications with the aliens, nicknamed Abbott and Costello, but the soldiers escorting her become frightened of the aliens' powers. They do what humans do best and bomb the alien ship, killing one of the aliens. Explains Costello, "Abbott is death process."

"I loved that," Meghan said as we left the theater. "*Abbott is death process.*"

Jeremy handled the numerous calls and emails it took to navigate our transfer of care from FISC to Dr. Blumberg and transported our precious sperm samples, sealed in a bullet-shaped container in a bath of liquid nitrogen. With our records and gametes transferred to Dr. Blumberg's office, I took Meghan in for a final premedication visit. Blumberg explained the process, called our prescriptions in to a pharmacy, and warned us that Meghan would feel bloated. "Some of this is fluid retention and ovarian swelling," he said. "Constipation is common, so take a daily laxative. Watch out for rapid swelling and weight gain." This, he warned, might signal a dangerous side effect of her medications: ovarian hyperstimulation syndrome, or OHSS. At its worst, OHSS can cause aggressive fluid build-up, blood clots, trouble breathing, and even death. Cheery!

Blumberg then gave us a semilegible medication plan.

After years of practice, I can read almost anything doctors write, even most of their crazy abbreviations. You have to know the context. When I first came across the abbreviation *NAOE,* at the beginning of a hospital progress note, I realized it meant "no acute overnight events."

For those of you who can't read Doctor Scrawl, it lists Meghan's medications: Gonal-F and Menopur. It looks like her dose of Menopur is 37,510, but it's actually 375 IU. Precisely because "IU" (for "international unit") can be misread as "10," hospital regulatory agencies have actually banned the use of this abbreviation. Underneath the drugs, which Blumberg wrote out carefully for obvious reasons, it says "prenatal vit" (vitamin). That Arabic-looking word is "aspirin," so the word before it is presumably "baby" or "Preg," a reference to a commonly used dose of 81 mg. I'd never heard of "Preg" aspirin dosing before (why not just write the dose?), so I confirmed the dose and wrote the standard doctor abbreviation for aspirin, "ASA," next to it. By the next block of instructions, the handwriting had switched to "you get the idea" mode, and "menopur" is indecipherable. Later on he refers to "Apt here with clinic"—"apt" means "appointment." Down at the bottom, it says to expect "prob egg retrieval" in early December.

We took our prescriptions down to a nearby pharmacy, where we picked up a grocery sack stuffed with supplies—medication boxes, syringes, needles, adapters, vials of diluent, reams of drug information bulletins, and a sharps box for safe needle disposal. The medications alone (just the medications, not the fertility cycle, collection, or implantation) cost $4,731.63. With an icy, sinking sensation, I realized we hadn't bothered to shop for deals, which I suspected might have saved us a small fortune. How many less well-off families get soaked on the downtown San Diego specialty pharmacy because they forget, like we did, or don't feel comfortable speaking up about wasting their money? Oh well.

"I had no idea they would cost so much," Meghan said. "The Meghan eggs. The 'Meggs,' I guess we should call them."

We did save $22 on overpriced laxatives, though. Meghan assured me she was as regular as a clock and ate plenty of fiber and therefore didn't need them. Besides, they were ordinary over-the-counter medications. We could pick them up any time. For less.

With our supplies in hand, we returned to the office for a primer on drug injection. Meghan had already made it clear that there would be no Meggs if she had to inject herself. "I don't do needles," she said. "But be gentle. You'll have to woo me." So I paid close attention—or tried. The nurse ran through the complicated process at eighty miles per hour. For drawing up the Gonal-F, you used adapters, but not for the Menopur. For this one, draw up some saline first, but not for that one. Use these needles for this and those needles for that. If we made a mistake with the medications, we could overdose her, or we could spoil a vial of drug that cost hundreds of dollars, and if that made our supplies inadequate, we might need a whole new *box* of vials. Meghan's eyes widened. Eventually we shared a nervous laugh.

"Sorry to interrupt," I said, "but that's a lot to remember. Don't you have printed instructions?"

"Oh, our patients don't need any," the nurse replied. "It's pretty simple."

"To *you* . . . but I find it confusing, and I'm a hospital doctor. I promise you some of your patients are just afraid to tell you."

The nurse cocked her head. Apparently this had never happened before. Either I was an idiot, or patients truly didn't feel comfortable speaking up. Perhaps both. "Well, we tell our patients if they have any questions, they can just come into the office, and we'll do the injections."

"That's very kind, but rather than drive forty minutes each way, every day, is it possible to get some printed instructions?"

It wasn't.

We did okay anyway. I knew that music would be the trick, ever since Iguazu Falls. For the duration of Meghan's egg-collection trip— lying on the bed, or driving to clinic appointments—she and I sang until our throats hurt. We sang Brandi Carlile, Indigo Girls, and even menstruation-themed songs from Ani DiFranco, prompting Alan to ask if we were actually driving to lesbian rallies instead of ovarian ultrasounds. For her daily injections, we needed to dial it down from protest music, so I picked a daily selection of soothing music. I played her DiFranco's "You Had Time," Loreena McKennitt's "Dante's Prayer," and Chopin's "Andante Spianato in G Major, Tranquillo," which eventually won Best in Show. Meghan reclined on the couch and took deep breaths like we were about to do an amputation in a Civil War field tent. I buttered her up with words of appreciation for her Meggs and drew up her meds, hiding the needles from sight. She grabbed my hand tightly until I reminded her I needed both hands to do her injections. Then I poked her as gently as possible.

One day I started laughing. We were making a baby just like straight people, I said: holding hands, playing mood music, laying Meghan down in the missionary position. "I even had to woo you before I could gently poke you!"

Meghan switched to her serious voice. "You do realize there are significant differences."

"Of course! Remember, I've had two girlfriends."

"But you didn't make any babies with *them*, right?" she asked, as if I might accidentally impregnate *her*.

"Not to my knowledge."

"Okay. Just checking."

Meghan claimed to be a difficult patient, but she never flinched and only grimaced intermittently. I've dealt with truly difficult patients (if you ever need to give Jeremy eye drops, I suggest you bring a SWAT team and an elephant tranquilizer). But she handled it all with aplomb, except for one thing: that constipation we'd been warned about. It hit her like a bolt from the blue, and she did *not* like it. "Guys," she said, holding her belly with a fearful look I'd seen on people who had ruptured organs, "my colon is *death process*."

We got it sorted out, and Alan later teased her to peals of laughter: "Come on, brood sow! Stop lollygagging and give me my Meggs!" Much of the bloating, I suspect, was actually her ovaries, swollen with follicles, ready for harvesting. Things seemed to be going just fine.

We didn't know it, but beginning Meghan's medications when we did would come back to bite us in the butt. Our egg-donation contracts and parenting agreement weren't quite done yet—we knew that, of course, but we figured we weren't collecting any eggs yet, and certainly not implanting. Besides, Dr. Blumberg had started Meghan on the drugs, and we figured he could handle the legal issues. But we would hear about the timing of the contracts one more time.

In San Diego Superior Court.

Prior costs:	$43,700.50
Meghan's initial Zika testing:	$750.00
Consultations, Meghan and Delilah reevaluations:	$1,629.50
Redoing Delilah tests with Blumberg:	$479.00
Another Zika test:	$305.50
IVF medications and supplies:	$4,737.00
Airfare for Meghan:	$2,122.00
Meghan's time-away-from-business expenses:	$1,500.00
Subtotal:	$11,523.00
Total	$55,223.50

CHAPTER 21

MAKING BABIES

Delilah's ultrasounds looked great. Her uterus had a healthy lining built up by daily, intramuscular hormone injections (sorry, Delilah!), ready for our future baby to implant. Now it was up to Meghan's ovaries. Alan drove her to the clinic and held her hand as they placed her IV. An anesthesiologist knocked her out with a milky infusion of a sedative called propofol, and Dr. Blumberg performed a transvaginal aspiration of her ovarian follicles. She woke in tears, not from pain but from the emotional roller coaster of anesthesia, which was hard to watch. But she had produced eleven eggs, so things had gone well.

We thought.

Blumberg explained that a teenager might have made twice as many eggs or more. With older gametes of both genders, each egg had a lower chance of success, and many fertilized eggs just died. "From this collection," said Blumberg, "I hope we can get you an embryo to implant."

"*An* embryo?!" I thought. "*One?*" Blumberg warned us not to get our hopes up. As he put it, "otherwise, sexually active people would all get pregnant the first month."

None of us said aloud just how badly this could all turn out. We'd adopted two embryos, paid for genetic testing, and implanted one in Delilah, who'd suffered through fertility treatments and plenty of doctor visits. This cycle, we'd flown Meghan to the United States, treated her with ovarian stimulation medicines, and put her through transvaginal needle egg collection (shudder), and prepped Delilah's uterus with a course of painful intramuscular injections. After all that, she might show up on implantation day and find that there were no zygotes to implant, jilted on the big day.

We'd agreed that we would each fertilize a third of the eggs. We thought we might each eventually have a biological child, all half siblings united by Meghan's gift. So Alan and Jeremy got four Meggs to fertilize, and I got three. Then the waiting started. Five days after extraction and fertilization, surviving embryos would have several cells extracted for genetic testing to ensure they had the right number of chromosomes and to determine their sex. Blumberg would update us whenever the lab had news. This felt utterly bizarre. Our children were developing in petri dishes.

"Ian, you're a champion!" Jeremy said after taking the first call. All three of my embryos were developing, compared to two of four Jeremy embryos and three of four Alan embryos. I didn't make much of it. I had stupid sperm and I viewed the whole thing as a gamble, just like the 50 percent risk of abnormalities on our donated embryos.

Jeremy got the next call a day later and sat us down for the news, which he said was mixed. "First thing. Delilah's estrogen level is way out of whack. They called it 'sky high,' so high they think she overdosed on her medications. They said that five times." That hardly made sense. Delilah was a pharmaceutical developer with lab experience; Richard was an orthopedist who regularly gave injections at work. If any mistake had been made, I would have bet an illegible (or nonexistent) medication instruction was to blame. My heart started pounding. High hormone levels increase the risk of dangerous blood clots, and they're how Plan B—the morning-after pill—prevents pregnancy. But according to Jeremy, Dr. Blumberg thought things would be okay and wanted to proceed. I never told him my concerns about Plan B and preventing implantation. The levels were what they were, and Blumberg was the IVF specialist, not me. "So what about our little zygotes?" I asked.

"We have five developing," he said. "Blumberg is confident we'll have some to implant. There's bad news." He paused. "None of your zygotes made it. They all stopped developing. I'm sorry."

I'd gone from first to last in the zygote race in five seconds. Oh well. I was okay. I knew it was a crapshoot going in, so I had no expectations. Now there would be fewer tough decisions to make. More than having a dozen potential kids, I had wanted to avoid any strife over picking whose embryo got selected. I'd made things simpler by disqualifying myself. Now we'd only have to pick between Alan's and Jeremy's embryos. That is, if everything worked out.

We were doing a fresh cycle. This meant extracting eggs, fertilizing them, doing genetic tests on the ones that grew to one hundred cells, and picking one for implantation, all within a one-week time frame. Our embryo would go from warm petri dish to warm Delilah oven without ever being frozen. But there's a big downside to fresh cycles: they're an emotional minefield of nervous waiting. Meghan's eggs were extracted and fertilized on a Friday. The five surviving embryos (two from Jeremy, three from Alan) were biopsied for genetic testing the following Wednesday, with results and implantation expected the next day. We might show up on the day of implantation only to find out we had no viable embryos. And we couldn't do a thing about it.

On the big day, we all got up early. I had to work. Alan and Jeremy picked up Delilah and drove her to the IVF clinic white-knuckled, jittery with anxiety. She was, as usual, a bundle of positivity. "I have a really good feeling about this. I just know we'll have healthy embryos." Jeremy wasn't so sure. We'd had so many setbacks already.

We figured Dr. Blumberg would share our results in person at the clinic. But just as they entered the lobby, Jeremy's phone rang. He checked the number: Dr. Blumberg. Alan saw him turn as white as a sheet. Why would he call, other than to say that none of the embryos had survived and they should just turn around? Thankfully, it was our luck that had finally turned around. "I'm happy to report that you have two healthy embryos to choose from. A girl from Jeremy and a boy from Alan. Both embryos are rated excellent." Blumberg said that a second Alan embryo of fair quality would be tested and frozen for a later cycle.

We had children! Well, potential children. Alan, Jeremy, and Delilah all wiped their eyes, hugged, and got in the elevator, headed for Dr. Blumberg's office.

Alan and Jeremy had only a few minutes to pick an embryo. And while cycle one had taught us not to get too attached to plans, we had discussed the issue of boys v. girls at length. Almost everyone told us to have a girl first. Friends with both girls and boys swore that boy babies were definitely more stupid. "I kept thinking something was wrong with him because he was so far behind his sister," one said. "Nope, he was just a boy." A girl would make an easier first baby for us, they said, and a more reliable older sibling for future babies.

Having to choose between two dads added another layer of decision making. Which dad would go first? Jeremy had always said he didn't want to be a bio-dad first, or possibly ever. He kept saying Alan and I were smart and handsome and we should have the babies. Alan and I thought *he* was smart and handsome, and we outvoted him. We'd hoped to get a girl from Alan and a boy from Jeremy (to avoid a six-foot-tall girl), and ideally, we'd have Alan's girl first. This is why you don't go into IVF with expectations. My partners found themselves in the elevator on the way to implantation, choosing between a girl from Jeremy who hadn't wanted to go first (or father a girl at all) or a boy from Alan.

"We always said we wanted a girl first," said Alan, around the third floor. "Let's implant your girl."

Jeremy silently weighed his desire to have a daughter against his desire to avoid going first. Between floors four and five, he decided Alan was right. We would implant Jeremy's giantess and freeze Alan's embryos for later. Jeremy called me to make sure I agreed. After my yes, I heard a cheer from Delilah. She'd had three boys of her own and had her heart set on carrying a girl. Everything felt right.

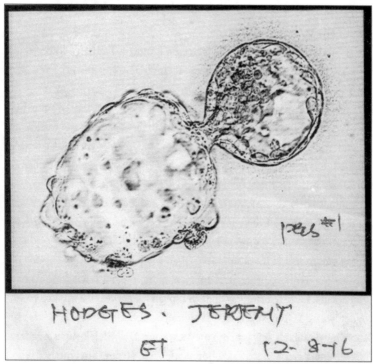

Baby's First Photo

Up in the clinic, Delilah hopped into stirrups and crossed her fingers. Blumberg drew our hundred-cell ball of hope into a syringe attached to an ultrathin catheter and injected it into the rear of Delilah's uterus. A little puff of fluid visible on ultrasound, and that was it. The impregnation was the simplest part of the entire process. While this was a medical procedure, I wish I could have been there. Usually, fathers are present when impregnation happens, and it's a special moment (in a different way). As my partners later explained, something special *did* happen.

"This is not scientifically proven," Dr. Blumberg said, "but if you agree, I would say a prayer over your daughter."

"What do you think, guys?" Delilah asked, unable to hide an excited grin.

"Yeah, go for it," said Alan.

Blumberg bowed his head, placed a hand on Delilah's lower abdomen, and prayed solemnly in Hebrew. Delilah's eyes misted up. Even Alan got a little emotional.

I love that our baby got a prayer. I attended Jewish preschool, where I played dreidel and made hamantaschen, little cookies made for Purim. Then I ended up at a famous Jewish hospital for my medical training, where I learned about Sabbath elevators (they stop at every floor so you don't have to press buttons), and where I worked overnight every Christmas with Jewish colleagues so the Christians could celebrate with their families. I even once managed to get a kosher cake *on Sabbath* for a hospitalized rabbi's ninetieth birthday. I'm all about Jewish tradition unless gefilte fish is involved. And when my partners told me about the prayer, I remembered that Jewishness is matrilineal—Jewish moms have Jewish kids. I figured the Torah didn't specify whether this applied to surrogacy, so . . . we'd have a Jewish daughter. Cool.

Nine days later, it was pregnancy test time. Delilah felt superpregnant, but we knew from experience how little that meant. She got her blood drawn, and we began the nail biting. The clinic promised results by 4:00 p.m.

The afternoon came and went without news.

Jeremy called the clinic. They didn't have any results. "They have to know this is killing us," he texted me. He called again; the clinic had closed. Night fell while I worked late. Jeremy called me, asking me to

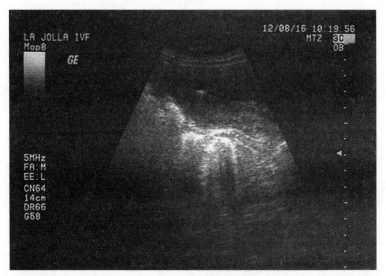

Apparently this shows a successful embryo implantation. Baby's second photo!

pick up a pregnancy test and drive it to Delilah's before I came home. I wanted to wait until the next day. I was ready to call the pending test a good excuse for a glass of red wine; I figured I'd earned one, and I honestly didn't know if I could deal with a negative result. But I knew Jeremy couldn't rest without knowing, so I picked up a kit and drove to Delilah's.

I got the call as I pulled up to her house. I ended up giving her hugs instead of pregnancy tests and bouncing around her driveway. We were pregnant.

Prior costs:	$55,223.50
Delilah's meds:	$560.30
One IVF cycle with transfer	$25,000.00
Ovulation monitoring visits	
Egg retrieval fee	
Sperm preparation and ICSI	
Embryo incubation	
Assisted hatching	
FDA coordination fees	
Genetic analysis	
Hormone levels:	$80.00
Duplicate semen analysis x 3:	$750.00
Sperm storage fees:	$750.00
Anesthesia:	$550.00
One pregnancy test:	$9.00
Subtotal:	$27,699.30
Total:	$82,922.80

CHAPTER 22

THE BLUEBERRY CONVERGENCE

Although we'd gotten a positive pregnancy test, we felt like we were barely clinging to parental life. We still faced a fetal loss rate of 30 percent, which would drop to 5 percent once we saw that heartbeat. Things would not feel real until we saw the baby on ultrasound. That seemed like the quintessential parent experience: listening to the rapid whoosh-whoosh-whoosh of the heartbeat while staring at grainy ultrasound images and squeezing your partner's hand, your other partner's hand, and your surrogate's hand while thinking about your out-of-country egg donor.

In a stroke of luck, everyone but Meghan got to come to that critical first ultrasound: all three dads' work schedules aligned—even Delilah's husband got to come. "Would you believe that they let me out of my hospital for this?" he asked with a face-splitting grin. "It's awesome. I didn't even come to my own kids' ultrasounds." The five of us crowded into an exam room, drawing stares from patients and office assistants alike. Blumberg inserted an ultrasound probe and pointed to the screen. We saw a little bump on the lining of the uterus.

"That little blueberry is your daughter. And that flashing there is the heartbeat. Congratulations!" Tears were shed, hugs shared, and excited squeals emitted.

We left the office elated and weepy.

"So cool that everyone could make it," said Delilah.

"A grand convergence," Alan agreed.

"The blueberry convergence," said Richard. "Hey, if you're this excited about a blueberry, you're going to be great parents."

"Thanks, man. Sorry we knocked up your wife," I said.

"It's all good. She loves being pregnant."

"It's true," Delilah agreed.

After goodbye hugs for Delilah and Richard, we celebrated at brunch. "My god. I'm really going to be a dad," said Jeremy, to the clink of champagne glasses. "If this were a Lifetime movie, this would be the part where I died. Think about it. It'd be so dramatic."

"Don't say that," said Alan. "You're the zookeeper. We need you to raise her!"

We hadn't really planned on a girl from Jeremy, but now that we had one cooking, everything felt right. Well, mostly right. "She's going to be enormous," said Jeremy. He put his face in his hands, but I could see he was smiling.

"Do you want her to play basketball or volleyball?" Alan asked.

"She could be a model," Jeremy said hopefully.

"STEM career or senator," I said. "Unless she wants to be an impoverished performance artist, I guess. Her life, her choice. Although she *is* still just an embryo. We probably shouldn't read her books about Malala until she's formed more organs."

"You know," said Alan, "since Meghan's 100 percent white, and you're 99.6 percent white, we're going to have the whitest baby ever."

"Not white," said Jeremy. "Remember those crystal shrimp I used to have in my fish tank? She'll be beyond white. She's going to be *clear*."

We live in sunny San Diego, and I've seen skin cancer kill my patients.

So I decided our baby would get all the sun she wanted. But not before she reached adulthood and left the house. Until then she was going to spend her life dipped in sunblock and wearing such a dorky hat it'd double as birth control.

When the giddiness and champagne wore off, we realized we had to secure her legal status with a birth certificate before we worried about her complexion or career. Poly families face different hurdles getting the birth certificates they want. A woman in a poly relationship with two or more men can generally list whomever she wants as the father. But if she's married, some states will put the legal spouse's name down automatically, and if the family wants to change it, they'll have to shell out hundreds of dollars for court-admissible genetic testing.[87]

The next day, we emailed our attorney about the pregnancy. "Dear JEREMY ALLEN HODGES and ALAN RICHARD MAYFIELD," his reply began (apparently I was still the spare-wheel parent). "Congratulations!" He said that he was so happy for us, and now that the pregnancy had been confirmed, we could proceed with the judgment phase of the surrogacy process. He attached information sheets for the three of us and Delilah to fill out, so they could craft the judgment pleadings, the documents that argued we should be the parents of our child, for filing with Superior Court. They also listed the costs for acquiring our baby:

Intended parents' court filing fee:	$435
Surrogate couple's court filing fee:	$435
Intended parents' attorneys' fees:	$3,500
Surrogate couple's attorneys' fees:	$500
Court hearing fee:	$60
Court reporter fee:	$30
Certified copies of judgment (three certified copies):	$90
Overnight shipping fees/incidentals:	$150
TOTAL BALANCE DUE	$5,200.00

We also paid fifty dollars a person for criminal background reports on each of the three intended parents. You know who doesn't have to pay for their own criminal background check before they can be a parent to their own child? EVERYONE! That includes career criminals, as far as I know (sixteen, beer, pickup truck). Some of these costs were bogus. There was one case, not two; why did we *and* Delilah have to file? Did she really need to pay $435 to escape the parental duties on a kid who had fifty different surrogacy contracts and a parenting agreement?

I decided not to be pissed about the court fees. My hospital used to staff the in-jail clinics at several local detention facilities. I'd spent many days fending off requests for Percocet, lancing skin abscesses, treating lice, soothing heroin withdrawal, recoiling from skull-exposing lacerations, and marveling at front-and-back boot prints acquired "falling out of bed." From what I'd seen, San Diego court could use the money. It was basically a tax, and Californians *love* contributing to the government.

While Delilah gestated our little girl, we helped our lawyer with the court filing. Basically, he needed to document the story of our relationship to convince the judge that we should be parents. He had to do this for all intended parents, but our case was more complex than previous cases by exactly one extra dad.

"It's never been done," he explained. "Unprecedented. There's never been a three-parent birth certificate. Third parents have been added, way down the line, but that's different." We sat down with the attorney and hashed out how we met, how we lived, and how we'd become parents-to-be of our little blueberry. He worked to make everything sound as healthy and normal as he could for the judge. Throughout the pleading, for example, he called us a throuple instead of a triad, because the former sounded folksy and family-like, and the latter sounded like a legal arrangement.

"Never been done," he said as we wrapped up, "but that doesn't mean it can't be done." He'd worked with the judge a thousand times before, and he said she was fair and understanding. "Uh ... 95 percent chance."

Super?

Ian Jenkins MD

Prior costs:	$82,922.80
Postimplantation IVF clinic visits:	$1,860.00
A birth certificate:	$5,200.00
Three background checks:	$150.00
Extra meds for Delilah:	$156.00
Subtotal:	$7,366.00
Total:	$90,288.80

CHAPTER 23

OUR SCANDALOUS
POLY LIFESTYLE

I
t's weird having lawyers write up a story about your relationship and parenting plans to make the case that you should get the baby that your legal contracts already say is yours. But that's what happened. We had to provide heartwarming, reassuring anecdotes to our lawyer so he could write up a court filing that promised we'd make the most wholesome family since the Cleavers of *Leave It to Beaver*.

We decided to leave out the fact that our neighborhood was calm and peaceful before we moved in, and afterward, it's been the scene of crazy parties and public sex. Coincidence? You decide.

We live in an older neighborhood in the process of turning over. There are young families to either side of us, but three original owners live nearby. One woman is seventy-seven, the spring chicken of the bunch. Next come the Englemans. We only really know Sam, unfortunately, because his wife, Sue, suffers from severe dementia. She's homebound now, but when we first moved in, she wandered. Once I found her blocks from home, dressed for temple but sweating in the heat, heading to an imaginary meeting. We learned to lock our front door because otherwise she'd charge right in, driven by a tumult of delusions. Sam was stealing her money, she'd say. She'd ask us to take her to a bank, but she didn't know which, and she only had scraps of paper with confused scribblings on them, notes that terrified her when she flipped through them and realized that none of them made any sense. Sam always followed, pleading with her to return home in a Brooklyn rasp: "You can't bother these nice boys!" At that point, she'd ask if she could move in with us.

Our neighbor to the west used to argue with Sue, tell her Sam was a nice man, and even offer to sort things out at a bank. Alan, the psychiatrist, knew better than to argue with delusions. "Sue, wow, I love your dress!" he'd say. "Where did you get it?" After some small talk, Sue would agree to go home, as long as Sam waited outside. After a particularly bad spell, Sam had to wait an hour in ninety-degree heat while Sue calmed down. He refused our invitation to wait with us, preferring to keep an eye on the house from his car, fifty feet closer, so I brought him some ice water.

"I'm really sorry you've got to go through this," I said.

"We've been married fifty-six years," he replied. "Fifty-four good. Well, this is what you do for people you love. She'd do it for me."

We give Sam assortments of eggs from our pet chickens; he brings us blood oranges and grapefruits. Lots of grapefruits. "Here. None of my friends can eat these. They interact with our medications." Sam's a great guy, ninety years old. While he had some gay acquaintances in Brooklyn back in the fifties, he'd never met a polyamorous family before us. And our relationship doesn't matter to him. "I don't care about someone's religion, or if they have no religion, or whether they're straight or gay, or what color they are. It only matters if they're good people," he told me. The only tricky part is what to call us. "Share these with your . . . friends," he says when he gives me citrus, because he doesn't know whether to say "boyfriend" or "partner" or "husband." The poly gays are new, and the lingo is complicated, but we are not.

Our favorite senior citizen, however, is our other neighbor, Betty Mae Brown (sorry, Sam). She weighs about five pounds soaking wet, she has all her teeth, she lives alone at ninety-seven, and she's an absolute gem. Betty grew up on farms in Georgia before moving to San Diego and giving up her college plans to help America win World War II. She's tough, and she's seen some shit—friends from her high school were killed at Pearl Harbor, and her husband died from a vicious pancreatic cancer a few years ago. She's done the math and knows she'll join him soon. She's relentlessly positive anyway, even when she's trying to give us one of her original oil paintings because she wants her place tidy when she dies. We check on her and help with gardening tasks. Our reward is that she'll snail-mail us thank-you cards that she could probably have folded into paper airplanes and sailed our way, except for that arthritis in her shoulder. And the awesome stuff she says:

"They tell ya not to feed the coyotes, but I do anyway. They were here first. Besides, old Betty does what old Betty wants."

"There sure are a lot of young people staring at phones instead of books these days. You can bet your sweet bippy they're not learning anything on 'em."

"Lemme tell ya, the Republicans have turned into a real bunch of blankety-blanks these days."

"You look thirsty. Can I get you an Ensure?"

Betty doesn't give a damn that three unmarried men live together in her neighborhood, either. We've got more important things to worry about, like swapping succulent cuttings to propagate. Sometimes she gets me mixed up with Jeremy, but she knows our character, and I don't mind getting the credit when Jeremy brings her a slice of cake.

Three Dads and a Baby

Maybe it seems like the neighborhood would be low on scandal. Perhaps, especially after Betty offered me an Ensure, you feel mislead by the chapter title. I admit *we* are pretty boring people, but our neighborhood really did have scandal aplenty after new renters down the street turned out to be party promoters. Their ads showed up all over Facebook and college campuses, and until they got evicted, their events drew astonishing crowds—literally thousands, crowding the streets for miles, drinking and tossing their beer cans in broad daylight without a care. I stood outside, thinking that might deter people from littering. One of the revelers stopped to check me out. "Hey," I said, with a wave.

"Hey," he said, and he pulled out his dick and pissed on my yard.

We spent the afternoon watching the crowd, our windows shaking with the bass lines of music from vehicles with shiny rims and tinted windows. The police, safe in their cruisers, told everyone to leave, but the partiers just raised their drinks in salute as they passed, and leaned back into the garage doors of the driveways they'd colonized. Safety in numbers. The spectacle mesmerized me, like a trashy version of one of those enormous synchronized schools of fishes, which I now realize are just fish block parties. With mako shark police.

I visited Sam and Betty after all the revelers had been chased away. They know I keep a running tally of the pieces of trash I've picked up in the neighborhood (over seventeen thousand now). I told them the party had added 383 pieces to my tally.

"You won't believe this," said Betty, "but I saw two of them kids making love, right there on my lawn! I thought they were just kissing till I saw them showing their bare bottoms to heaven."

"Damn kids," I said.

"Damn kids is right," said Sam.

CHAPTER 24

COMING OUT POLY

I n truth, our poly family has brought zero drama to the neighborhood; the minor bumps in the road came with family. When one settles down with two boyfriends, friends and relatives must eventually be told. Friends didn't care. With family, the three of us had been through the coming-out process, and for the second round of disclosures, we followed a key principle: wait until you're sure. After Jeremy redecorated his room, we knew it was time.

Alan's parents took it pretty well. I figured his mom would be more bothered than his father, since she grew up Catholic and continues to attend Mass and volunteer at church. But in truth, her value system is more "nice and accepting" than "Catholic dogma." She made her peace with polyamory immediately. "I guess," she said, "if you're all in a relationship, then no one is cheating on anyone, and it's okay!" Good summary, Maddy! Alan's father, Michael, didn't handle the news as well. He said our arrangement was immoral and Alan needed to honor his commitment to me (not guessing, apparently, that I was the one who brought

Jeremy home). But after seeing our relationship in action, Michael quickly came around. He's said poly families work just fine for the right people, and he tells us he loves us when he says goodbye.

Jeremy had the hardest time. When we met him, he'd just come out to his parents as gay. His parents raised him in the conservative Nazarene community, whose members neither drink nor use playing cards, which is considered gambling. His father is actually a Nazarene pastor. Not surprisingly, Jeremy had taken a while to come out to them, but surprisingly, his dad did something really sweet: he called his son and said, "You'll always be my baby boy, and I'll always love you more than life itself."

His mom hadn't taken it as well. She'd sent him a five-page, single-spaced typed letter. She'd written from her experience in a community that considers homosexuality "unnatural" and "immoral," and from a time when she knew Jeremy as an innocent boy who performed carols in a bell-ringing choir with dozens of white-gloved elderly women. She'd suffered a serious jolt and a real loss. Still, as she compared stable gay relationships to brother-sister and father-child incest and bestiality ("If you said, 'I'm in love with this monkey,' I'd feel about the same"), the hurt had mounted. It hadn't helped Jeremy to read that she'd wanted his identity kept secret from friends and family. Some of those people, she'd realized, sometimes said they wished all the "queers" could be shipped off to a deserted island to die, but she didn't want Jeremy to lose them.

Jeremy loves his mother. They've always been close. Her elaborate and emphatic rejection had hurt him deeply. He'd lived for family and church his whole life. His identity automatically severed his relationship with his church, and his mother had shut him out. He grieved for their relationship like a person had died. He broke into tears out of the blue; he had to take days off work. Jeremy genuinely loves both his parents—they both raised him well, and they're lucky to have him.

We started dating Jeremy not long after these events, and needless to say, he didn't update them immediately. That took a year, once he'd moved in with us and felt like a true part of our family. He sent an email, so everyone could have their emotions in private and think about our "unconventional and odd relationship" before responding. He said he knew they'd need some time to adjust, and he expected questions, but since we loved each other and hoped to spend our lives together, he was not open to criticism and judgment. "Big adjustment for me mentally," his father admitted, "but no matter what, you are loved."

His mother said she never wanted to see or hear from him again. She didn't mince words. She didn't spare words, either; she sent thirteen hundred of them. The choicest: *My son Jeremy is gone. Only the physical shell is there. My heart is exploding with grief. Wires came loose in your hard drive. You should seek counseling. Doctors are often the biggest abusers of scrip drugs. I hope your fascination with wealth does not destroy you. You are the one who brings me the most hurt. I cannot be a part even on the superficial level with what is now your world. I am now completely dead in my heart. I wish you would Facebook defriend everyone I know. I hope this bizarre arrangement comes to an end. I have no questions. I have no answers. I will not be a part of your life and world anymore.*

This time, Jeremy had prepared himself for the worst, but the words still stung. They stung me, just copying them into this chapter, and she's not my mother. Jeremy knew he would get along with his father, and she could eventually come around. So he sent a measured reply saying he would talk with her whenever she was ready. Several months later, Renee contacted Jeremy for advice about a trip to Rome, where he'd traveled twice before. "I don't want to talk about the other stuff," she began, and he didn't. She didn't offer an apology, he didn't ask for one, and they rebuilt their relationship by email and then by phone. Two more months passed.

Knowing how important Jeremy's family was to him, I offered to fly his folks out to visit. Shortly after, Bob and Renee came for a daringly week-long, alcohol-free, playing card–free, even "scrip drug" abuse–free visit. It went . . . remarkably well. Alan and I obeyed a previsit request to limit public displays of affection. We drank iced tea at restaurants instead of margaritas. As our guests departed, Bob took me aside and gave me his heartfelt thanks. He said he loved Jeremy very much, adding, "You're very important to Jeremy, so you're very important to me, too." Since then, we've seen his family regularly, and they love and accept the pair of sons-in-law they never expected.

Jeremy holds no ill will toward his mother. She'd always hoped he'd get married and have children, and her community taught her to oppose same-sex relationships and to believe that being gay was a choice. His coming out gay, then poly gay, surely felt like a repudiation of her values and how she raised him. She had no preparation for having an unusual son, and she felt like she couldn't turn to her friends and church for support. From her perspective, Jeremy's announcements were personal tragedies, and her resistance had been an act of love.

Jeremy responded with empathy, and he focuses on their relationship since then. We know that parents don't always have perfect responses when their children come out. The growth that follows is what matters. Although her first letter said she'd never be able to visit him knowing he would be sleeping next to a man, she visits regularly and happily, and we enjoy her company. She gave us a chance and accepted us, and she didn't have to.

These days, she sends us thoughtful gifts wrapped with her trademark care (precise folds, double-sided tape hidden in seamed edges, elaborate ribbon and bows), which convey her affection.[viii] She's a private woman, so perhaps the most courageous and awe-inspiring thing she's done is to allow me to share this story. Now, other parents with conservative backgrounds who are struggling with their kids' sexuality can imagine a bright future, enjoying their children and grandchildren—maybe even a bonus in-law. So for her initial reaction, we gave her a mulligan. She gave Jeremy life and raised him to be kind; it's the least we could do.

I had the easiest time coming out poly to my parents. My mom had such a blasé response I can't even remember the conversation. I told my

---

viii She has since become our best babysitter, the most entertaining grandparent on toddler FaceTime calls, and the only grandparent to turn to for leading children's songs.

father and stepmother over Mexican food on a trip to the east coast. "Alan and I are dating a wonderful guy named Jeremy, who's moved in with us."

"Oh," they said, and went back to eating guacamole. Years later, they told me they hadn't known what to say. No one prepared my parents to have a gay son (in 1994) or a poly son (in 2013), but in truth, there isn't a whole lot to say. Having an extra kid doesn't make a family wildly interesting, and it turns out, neither does having an extra partner. I'm sure people are bothered by us in principle, but I can't really imagine rational people being bothered by us in practice. We work, we do chores, we ask each other what we should have for dinner. It's not exactly reality TV material.

Our drama usually comes from outside the home, like when we heard our surrogate had suffered heavy bleeding eleven weeks into the pregnancy.

CHAPTER 25

BLOOD

"I'm bleeding," Delilah's text said. "A lot." Delilah had an ob-gyn she loved, Dr. Gordon, who'd delivered all of her children. But because of her age, a high-risk obstetrician named Dr. Lee had been following her for our surrogacy. Delilah called Dr. Lee's clinic. They told her to take it easy and come in the next day. For now, there was nothing to do.

We knew, immediately, we either faced a good chance of losing our baby or that we'd already lost her. What the hell else could heavy vaginal bleeding mean at eleven weeks? We felt completely helpless. I thought, *Hope for the best; prepare for the worst.*

That's what I tell patients when all signs point to advanced cancer and they have to go through the awful experience of waiting for biopsy results. Lots of people think that breaking bad news is a singular event, maybe even one sentence. It's actually a process. Patients don't need to hear all the bad news at once. In fact, they usually *can't,* because people go into shock when they hear horrible news. Besides, I have to start by telling them *why* they need a biopsy.

"Tell me straight," many of these sick patients ask. "Do I have cancer?"

I say, "Hopefully it's an unusual infection. But it's best to hope for the best; prepare for the worst. If it's good news, it'll be a pleasant surprise. If it's cancer, you'll be ready, and we can start planning the treatment."

Here's a secret: *It's always fucking cancer.* When that teenager had that seventeen-centimeter monster displacing his heart; when that young mother had nodules in her liver; when that nonagenarian told me the thing he dreaded most would be losing his speech if that thing in his brain ate his language center—it was always cancer. *Once,* I went through this process with a good friend who had cancerous-looking masses throughout his abdomen. That one time, the biopsy was negative and the illness melted away on antibiotics: the exception that proves the rule.

When I told myself, *hope for the best; prepare for the worst,* I was already preparing myself for the loss of our baby. Every miscarriage is a tragedy, I know. I already felt a deep sympathy for everyone who'd suffered one. But let's be honest . . . we had worked so hard to get where we were. We'd spent $90,000 on IVF and hired most of the lawyers in California, and we'd accepted a great gift from Delilah, putting her health at small but measurable risk. We only had two embryos left, and each try would cost another $25,000. Our surrogate would probably be tired of trying (and was not getting any younger), and that would mean locating a new surrogate and another flurry of legal fees and time.

A miscarriage could mean the end of our parenting plans.

There was more. Since enrolling in medical school twenty years ago, and developing a role in error management at my hospital, I'd witnessed, or heard about, several obstetric disasters. In fact, if I met a pregnant woman, it was usually bad news. Obstetricians don't call me when things go well.

Once, after a terrible day dealing with a dying young person, I made the mistake of telling Jeremy and Alan. They told me in no uncertain terms to keep future tragedies to myself, and I have. That goes double for obstetric disasters. But I'd been thinking about the long list of problems

I'd seen women suffer, and now my brain went into overdrive worrying about them. A partial list:

Placental abruption: The placenta peels off the uterine wall, causing rapid, painful bleeding. It can kill both baby and mother.

Placenta increta and percreta: invasive placenta. In one case, a mother suffered massive bleeding from placenta in her bladder and rectum. She got over fifty units of blood and died anyway.

Pulmonary embolism: pregnancy hormones increase the risk of blood clots, which can float to the lungs and kill a healthy woman without warning.

Preeclampsia is a poorly understood syndrome of high blood pressure and leaking protein in the urine. Swelling and seizures may develop.

Sepsis: Pregnant women downregulate their immune systems so they don't reject their fetuses. This increases the risk of deadly infection, or sepsis. One common cause is chorioamnionitis—intrauterine infection. I've seen it put a woman on life support. She woke up two weeks later, only to find out she'd had emergency surgery and lost both her baby and her uterus.

I thought about the risks facing Delilah and baby, and I thought about them often. My greatest fear was *not* losing our baby. It was losing Delilah. If her generosity killed her and the baby, we would have ruined Richard and her kids' futures for nothing. If we lost Delilah from postpartum complications, we'd think about Delilah's death every time we looked at our baby. So with great trepidation, we went to Delilah's appointment with Dr. Lee and awaited her ultrasound.

It wasn't great. The images showed a dark space under her placenta that shouldn't be there—a big collection of blood. "Subchorionic hematoma, about six centimeters," said Dr. Lee, moving the ultrasound probe around for the best view.

"That sounds big," Jeremy said. "Is that big?"

Dr. Lee paused. Ah, the doctor pause. Sometimes they're truly figuring something out. Usually they're planning how best to present bad news. "It's not small," she said.

Subchorionic hematoma, bleeding under the placenta, is the most common cause of first-trimester bleeding. The main risk is that blood will peel the placenta off the uterus, which suffocates the baby, causing spontaneous abortion.

Dr. Lee told Delilah to return for weekly ultrasounds and take it easy. No exercise, no kids jumping on her lap, and stop taking the aspirin she was using to facilitate early pregnancy. She didn't need bed rest, which was great news. Most importantly, it meant the doctor wasn't that worried. Also, if Delilah *had* needed bed rest, we would have had to pay her lost wages. We'd have hired a pharmaceutical developer to lie in bed. That could cost tens of thousands of dollars. So we crossed our fingers, and Delilah relaxed at home ("Having a doctor's order not to exercise is the best excuse I've ever had!"), and we told her to order off Jeremy's Uber Eats account as much as she wanted.

Then we made sure her care was appropriate. When it comes to other physicians, my motto is "trust but verify." I've intervened to save family members from incompetent doctors on several occasions, doctors who missed stuff I could figure out over the phone. Jeremy had read *What to Expect When You're Expecting,* and he'd had to remind one doctor to give Delilah a whooping cough booster vaccine already. We loved Dr. Lee, but I researched subchorionic hematoma myself anyway, and learned it causes abortion in about 10 percent of cases. We were facing higher odds, since Delilah'd had a big one, and because of everyone's age. But there was nothing we could do except cross our fingers.

Delilah bled three more times before she finally stopped. Each time scared the bejeezus out of us, but less and less bejeezus each time. Serial ultrasounds showed the hematoma was shrinking, and the blood that she lost was dark, old blood, not fresh red blood. This convinced us the hematoma was just gradually making its way out, and she was not having new bleeding. Nevertheless, it reminded us how little control we had over the pregnancy. Nature will do what she will.

I worried (privately) that Delilah would get an infection. Bacteria love blood so much it's used to feed them in petri dishes. Delilah still had a clot of old blood in her uterus, and since she'd bled, we knew it was open to the vagina, a notoriously nonsterile body part. Only later did Dr. Lee tell us just how worried she really was about that hematoma, too. But Delilah never got an infection. We actually enjoyed seeing Delilah and our developing baby at the frequent ultrasounds that she now needed, and nothing went wrong for the rest of the pregnancy. After the bleeding stopped, the only pregnancy drama occurred outside the uterus.

Prior costs:	$90,288.80
Numerous clinic visits and ultrasounds:	$0.00
Total:	$90,288.80

CHAPTER 26

WHAT'S IN
A NAME?

I told the boys we really needed to name the baby. Also, we needed to name some *chickens*. We'd gotten four new ones, and we'd already burned through great choices with the previous generation, which we named after the Golden Girls (Blanche, Dorothy, Rose, and Sophia) and Whoopi Goldberg's character in *Sister Act* (Deloris Van Cartier).

Two names came easily: one adventurous chick took to riding her mother around the coop, and I named her Dora the Explorer. Another laid olive-colored eggs, so we named her Olive. The last two proved tricky. Jeremy and Alan would not commit. Eventually I forced the issue. "A family that can't name a chicken in two weeks can't take care of a baby," I said, and I named them Elvira and Jackie Brown, because something had to be done. Now it was time for baby.

We tackled her last name first. I've come across some unfortunate last names, shouldered by children because of the sexist tradition that they couldn't take their mother's, presumably better, name: Seaman, Fuchsman, Shart, Rautenbush, (Richard) Handler, or just something difficult, like Skrlj or Khsithesh. But we all had fine last names. I decided to take Jenkins out of the running right at the beginning.

Why? My stepmother is a librarian, so my folks stop in libraries in every town they visit. In a small town in North Carolina, to their shock, they found a fifteen-pound book about the history of our unimportant clan during Civil War times, titled *Abigail's Story: Tides at the Doorstep—the Mackays, LaRoches, Jenkinses, and Chisolms of Low Country South Carolina, 1671–1897.* From this tome, I learned a number of important things. First, people will apparently write a book about anything. Second, collections of letters from eighteenth-century commoners are soul-crushingly dull. Third, the Jenkins family crest displays three chickens and a . . . mutant griffon (?) with mange (?) and may have been drawn by a child. Fourth, and most importantly, I learned that my father's great-great-great-great-grandfather was a devout Christian who heavily endowed the local church. And who owned about a hundred slaves.

Yuck.

I know that I'm not to blame for what my ancestors did. I know they didn't give the family motto (*"Vigilis et virtute"*) any serious thought, because owning slaves means maximum negative virtue. And I can gladly report that the monetary spoils of this evil didn't pass on to me—the Jenkinses of South Carolina justifiably lost everything in the Civil War. If I ever see this "devout Christian" relative in an afterlife, I'm going to tell him that I donated to the ACLU and NAACP and lived in a gay poly family and *loved* every minute of it, and find out if he repented. Depending on the answer, I may kick his ass. But every time I meet another Jenkins and that Jenkins is black—and most of the Jenkinses I meet are black—I can't stop thinking about our ancestors. My father tells me there were abolitionists among them as well as slavers, but that doesn't help me feel any better about using the name. And my brother has two girls, which meant I likely got to decide the future of the Jenkins name. I decided it would belong to black Jenkinses. And to drive home the point, here's that family crest, which indicates we're just a family of drunkards:

At least it proves that chicken farming is in my blood.

Jeremy bowed out next. We loved Alan's parents, the Mayfields. His whole family is made up of sweet, funny people. So *without passing any judgment on any of my or Jeremy's relatives,* except the slavers, we decided that kiddo would be a Mayfield. She could take a middle name from the Hodges clan.

When we started thinking about names, we mistakenly told our families. Suggestions started pouring in. Jeremy's mom had an endearing strategy of changing the name she used in each call or text. Baby went from Allison to Julie to Buttercup. None of this was pushy. My mom, on the other hand, wanted definitive action: "Name her Bella." I rejected Bella because it reminded me of the *Twilight* books. She hadn't heard of them. I told her everyone else had. A slew of alternatives spewed forth:

Victoria, Nina, Sunny. I told her we were considering Harper and Parker, and she said that Parker wasn't an option because of Parker pen company: "Other kids will call her a pen." I was pretty sure the other kids wouldn't.

She plowed ahead with the silly names: Athena. Artemis. Luna. Skylar. Xena—"your own baby warrior." After that, she suggested Gertrude, because she had a mischievous cat named Gertrude (and one named Barack). Who could argue with that logic? "She's not eighty," I said, and she came back with Pearl and Rose, to which I replied, "She's not ninety, either." Then she suggested the name Elliot. For a girl. She made two points: first, both Sting and George Stephanopoulos had daughters named Eliott and Elliott, respectively. Second, historically, Elliott had been a girl's name. I replied that historically, aristocratic men strutted around in high heels and pink, but no longer.

"No, seriously," she texted. "I think it could be bisexual." Did she mean "unisex"? Then she really hit me with the good stuff: "Ok, Bella is beautiful, so you could name her Hermosa from Spanish, Schon from German, Bonita in Portuguese, or"—I am not making this up—SMUK. Just like that, in all caps. SMUK means *beautiful* in Danish, apparently.

I told her without hesitation we were going with SMUK. She texted back, "Yes I love smut."

I knew she'd been tricked by the auto-correct on her phone, but I still told her, "I've known you were into smut since I found your stash in ninth grade! Fifteen years of *Playgirl*. Lucky me."

She insisted she was really fond of SMUK. I told her I was planning her involuntary psych hospitalization. When she said it a third time, I swore that we would give the baby a terrible name just to spite her.

I told the story to Alan and Jeremy that night in the hot tub. They laughed, and we discussed a number of terrible name options to terrorize our parents with. Jeremy had heard about one at work: ABCD, pronounced "ab-ci-dee." I'd met a kid named Sixth, because his parents had already had three kids and two dogs. These were great parental torture names, but suitable more to email than to phone conversation.

"What's the most horrible thing to name a baby right now?" Alan wondered. "I know: Zika."

Jeremy laughed. "That *is* the worst."

"No," I said. "Zika Palin."

"Zika Palin," Jeremy repeated approvingly, and once we'd brought in the Alaskan queen of word salad who nearly became our vice president, I knew we had our placeholder name.

"So we've decided," said Alan. "If your mom mentions Smuk again, we tell her we settled on Zika Palin-Mayfield."

Prior costs:	$90,288.80
Maternity clothes:	$700.00
Total:	$90,988.80

CHAPTER 27

LEAVE

As of 2016, of the 193 countries in the United Nations, only a handful lacked national paid parental leave laws: six tiny Pacific islands and Suriname, a small South American nation sandwiched between Guyana and French Guiana—and *no,* I did *not* have to look that up.[ix]

Oh—and the *United States of America,* the only high-income nation without mandatory paid maternity leave. Fifty nations offer new moms six months of paid leave, and some offer more.[88] Sweden offers sixteen months, to be divided between two parents. Parental leave not only helps women recover from childbirth, it stabilizes family incomes at a key point, and it encourages bonding and breastfeeding, which have a number of health benefits for babies, including improved IQ scores and reading and writing performance.[89] As if that weren't enough, paid leave reduces infant mortality.[90] These are gifts you'd think a nation would want its infants to get.

---

ix I lied. I totally looked that up.

But not America. About half of American workers qualify for up to twelve weeks of FMLA (Family Medical Leave Act) time, but it's unpaid time off, so families and babies either miss out on these benefits or they pay dearly for them. Only 12 percent of workers have paid parental leave through their employers.[91] Oh, America. If you didn't have so many missiles I would seriously wonder about your priorities.

There's a lot less support for paternal leave than maternal leave, however. Ninety-nine countries offer fathers nothing, and forty-six offer less than three weeks. Saudi Arabia, for example, offers mothers ten weeks, while dads get three days. *Three days?* What, are you supposed to make your newborn infant independent in three days? The article I read about this didn't say if Saudi Arabia provides more parental leave if the father is in a gay polyamorous relationship, but I won't be traveling to the kingdom to ask.

Anyway, when we realized the baby thing was definitely happening, it was too late to move to Sweden and claim our sixteen months, so we explored the parental leave benefits offered by our employers. The short version: check the policy, speak up for yourself, and join the Teamsters.

I had the trickiest negotiations. I'd been with my hospital for thirteen years, had advanced to full professor, and ran a medical school class and hospital committees. My division had provided me with an excellent mentor, free advanced training, and numerous research opportunities. It had also made major improvements in the compensation and experience of the physicians—all while becoming one of the highest-ranked academic medical centers in the nation by dramatically improving the care it provided to patients. But because of one manager who handled my benefits (no longer with my institution), I wouldn't get my full allotment of leave time without advocating for myself.

Actually, I'd had issues with the leave policy for a decade. Soon after I joined the faculty at my hospital, previous division administrators asked for comments on their policy. It said that mothers got six weeks off and fathers got two. I reminded them that not all of their employees' families *had* mothers, and that it seemed discriminatory to give men a third of the leave time women got.

As Delilah got more and more pregnant, I started asking the mothers who worked or had worked in my department how things worked out for them. I got surprisingly different answers. Apparently my group's definitions of "off" and "leave" had evolved over the years. As schedulers and administrators changed, different mothers got different benefits. Some got a solid three months off, while others got two months, but only by moving shifts around—they got *flexibility,* but no time *off.* I'm no manager, but this seemed like a great way to piss off employees. Imagine finding out that you got zero minutes of maternal leave and Suzie got three months!

So I went back to my benefits manager to ask what I was entitled to. Nothing had improved in the last decade—in fact, things had gotten worse. The manager, someone I'd worked along side for a decade, offered me *one week* of leave, admitting the discrepancy seemed hard to defend. "Sounds illegal," I said. "How can you justify that policy?"

"Well, Ian, that's how it's always been."

"Not true, and it still sounds illegal."

"Let me get back to you."

A week later they called with a clarification. "I figured it out. My wording was vague. I meant a woman would get six weeks off to recover from *childbirth.* But *parental* leave would always be *two weeks*—I don't know why I said one week."

"You're joking," I said. "Did you just reword the policy to screw me out of my parental leave?"

"Of course not!"

"Oh really? You're telling me that if a woman adopts a newborn infant, you'll expect her back at work in fourteen days?"

"I guess that's what the policy would imply."

"Don't guess—*you* just rewrote it yourself! Well, I'll be speaking to the benefits office for clarification."

That turned out to be an empty threat. The people I spoke to handled benefits for an entire university, and didn't know the specifics for my group. They referred me back to my division or an online maze of benefits information that did not clarify anything. I started asking other departments what they did. One said they had *no* policy—I have no idea how they manage their physicians' absences, even to this day. But another sent me a university-wide policy document, which specified the minimum benefits all departments were required to offer their faculty. These benefits included twelve weeks of parental bonding leave, of which six would be paid. I could request my leave up to twelve months after the birth, which was great for my poly family, since we planned to space out our parental leave over months.

Fantastic! The explanation had apparently been distilled from my university's academic leave policy, which is publicly available online.[92] But we *still* weren't done. My benefits manager, like all the colleagues and benefits specialists I'd spoken to, hadn't known about this policy. I later learned there were a lot of competing documents and policies that had caused the confusion. But even after reviewing the university's policy, they still said she didn't think it applied. I spoke to my division admin staff, who knew me and would be responsible for managing my schedule changes, and they agreed with me that the policy was unambiguous. I told them I'd be taking my six weeks paid leave, they nodded, and *then* we were done. One great thing to come of my parental leave journey: it ended up clarifying leave benefits for my division and beyond. Our current administrator called it a "leap forward."

Alan, who's employed by the federal government, had to fight for leave as well. I've heard about the bureaucracies of all four branches of our armed forces from a number of friends, family members, and coworkers, from Boston to Japan. They've convinced me that our government is an institution of profligate waste hiding behind ostentatious belt-tightening. On the surface, government physician salaries and wage freezes make federal positions less attractive than private ones. Below that, things get outright weird.

One example: according to a number of family and friends with firsthand experience, the military sometimes has to deal with recruits who lied about their physical or mental health when they enlisted. Instead of firing them, the armed services will sometimes give them "medical separations" (about $1 million of lifetime disability benefits) for conditions ranging from fibromyalgia to bipolar disorder, after as little as a few months of service. You didn't misunderstand me; they basically say, "Oh, your enlistment was fraudulent? Here's a million bucks."

Or consider a story I heard about an army officer. He completed a twenty-year career, at which point three things magically happened at once: first, he started collecting retirement; second, he started getting disability checks for a non-service-related condition; third, he was *immediately rehired as a civilian doing the same work*. What kind of disability prevents you from neither finishing a career nor starting a new one? In this case, sleep apnea, which is treated by the application of a pressurized mask for sleep. It's not disabling.

Where I work, you can be working, retired, or disabled—but not more than one, and certainly not all three at once.

So imagine our surprise when Alan learned that the federal government behind these generous programs provided *no* paid parental leave for many civilian employees. None. Zero. Nada. Zilch. You're having a newborn baby? Fine—but every hour you spend with it is expected to come from unpaid Family Medical Leave Act time. It drove Alan crazy. "This place is nuts. They give their active-duty women twelve weeks of parental leave, but they only give active-duty men ten days, and they won't give a single *minute* to civilians?"[x,93]

Alan researched federal policies and learned that, with the approval of his hospital's director, he could use accrued leave days to cover parental leave.[94] This approval, however, was usually given to women who were recovering from childbirth. Alan met with the director and politely, yet

---

x In a major advance for families, the 2020 National Defense Authorization Act provides for up to 12 weeks of paid parental leave for most federal employees, effective October 1, 2020.

directly, pleaded his case—and voilà, he got permission to use leave days to cover paternity time. He'd have to use up his vacation and sick days, but he arranged eight weeks of paid time off.

Jeremy had the most generous benefits. For this, without question, we owe the Teamsters, who negotiate the benefits for their union members, including their talented and handsome zookeepers. Jeremy had to spend his vacation time toward parental leave, but he got three months paid and eligibility for another three months unpaid leave. So he planned to stay home with baby from August through January. Alan would take his leave at the beginning while we were sorting things out. I'd take over at the end, to give baby the maximum duration of dedicated parental care at home. After I moved some shifts around and leveraged a visit from my parents, we realized baby would get stay-at-home parenting, *paid,* for seven months.

We had to fight for it, but we know we're lucky. If any of this seems unfair, I highly recommend getting yourself a second partner with membership in the Teamsters union. No one's stopping you.

CHAPTER 28

DREAD
& PRECEDENT

U p until the day of the court hearing for our three-dad birth certificate, our lawyer—our eighth lawyer, I mean, the one tasked with
writing a court filing about our relationship—told us not to worry. He'd
done many surrogacy cases, many with gay men, and he knew the judge.
She was a kind and open person, and he had no doubt she'd want to help
us. The hearings were so routine, he didn't ask his clients to attend them.
With us, being a throuple added a wrinkle, so he asked us to come, to
convince the judge we were upstanding people. But we wouldn't have to
fight. "Show up and have fun," he said.

So we planned a celebratory legal hearing. We invited Alan's mother
and mine, plus Meghan—lots of family were coming in for our baby
shower the next day—donned our suits, and headed off to meet the attorney an hour early to prep. We left our family outside and met in his conference room.

"I'm really worried," he said without warning. "Now she's ambiva-
lent. She reviewed the law, she's quite concerned, and she had me come to

an emergency briefing yesterday." The warm fuzzy in our chests vanished, replaced by anxious ice water. "She said she lacks the authority to designate all three of you as parents. It's because of her reading of SB 274."

I reached for Alan's hand as we listened. Jeremy sat across the table, and we shared a frown.

SB 274 is the California law that lets courts add a parent to a birth certificate if it's detrimental to the child to be deprived of that parent (e.g., two lesbian moms and an involved sperm-donor dad). The court can find that not having the dad as a third parent could deprive the child of the bio-dad's assets, or just his role as a parent.

"The problem," he said, "is that there's no child. The baby can't experience a detriment because she doesn't legally exist until birth. The judge suggested I bring you back to the court in a couple of years to show detriment to a living child."

"How can she say there's no detriment," asked Alan, "when our daughter would get deprived of someone's assets or health insurance? And a parent?" Our lawyer shrugged.

It got worse.

"I also pleaded your case under the California Supreme Court case *Johnson v. Calvert,* which says that a 'parent' is a person designated on the surrogacy contract or parenting agreement. Our judge isn't buying that, either. She says the legislature wasn't talking about throuples.

"I've got to convince her she has the authority," our lawyer said. "She's got nothing against you, but she doesn't think she has the authority because there's no precedent. She says that's the job of the appellate court. She kept saying, actually, 'Why don't you just appeal me?' In other words, let the appellate court sort it out." There was no precedent in California for having a polyamorous family on a birth certificate. No precedent anywhere, in fact.

"You're saying we'd have to file an appeal?" asked Jeremy. "That sounds horrible. We want a daughter, not a legal battle."

"I probably should explain how this works," our lawyer said. "We're going to Superior Court. That's step one. If she won't help you, you can go to appellate court. You know in the movies, when lawyers are opening books and referring to case law? That stuff happens at the appellate level. If she decides in your favor today, it won't set any precedent. There's only precedent if someone appeals a case. If we win, and someone goes looking for throuple cases, they won't find it. But if it's an appeals court decision, they would. If the appellate court doesn't help you, you can appeal *that*, and it would go to the California state Supreme Court, and then on up."

Fighting our way "on up" sounded like we could end up spending half a million bucks only to get to the United States Supreme Court and lose the case when I threw tomatoes at Justices Thomas, Alito, and Roberts for their hateful decisions, and at Neil Gorsuch for sitting in a stolen seat *and* his hateful "opinions."[xi,95]

Alan pointed out that there was legal precedent. He mentioned an article he'd read online that described court victories for nontraditional families. The main story in the article was about how Madison Bonner-Bianchi, who'd been raised by lesbian moms and a sperm donor, won a spot on her California birth certificate for her second mom in 2017. The article also noted some setbacks, like a family that lost a decision in Wyoming.[96] I didn't think the nice judge our lawyer had described would want to side with the Wyomingites against a well-dressed triad of smiling California gays, but we'd see.

Our lawyer had Alan send him the article, and he made us all copies and one for the judge.

With two moms and Meghan in tow, we walked to court. I'd never been to court, other than to weasel out of jury duty, and it's basically a low-rent airport with wood paneling. As my mother went through the security process, she asked if she needed to remove her shoes for the metal

---

xi Thomas, Alito, and Roberts sided against marriage equality in the 2015 case Obergefell v. Hodges. Justice Kennedy, who authored the majority opinions in *Obergefell* and *Lawrence v. Texas* (invalidating sodomy laws), has also now been replaced by Justice Kavanaugh, who refused to say if he agreed with them during his confirmation hearing. Gorsuch, to his credit, wrote the 2020 decision extending federal protection against employment discrimination to LGBT citizens.

detector, and the security guard looked at her like she had two heads and shook his head reaaaally sloooowly. The guard locked us in the courtroom with our lawyer and the judge. Our lawyer sat at a table before the judge, and we sat in the witness seats.

Before we got to our case, our lawyer had a simpler case to dispense with. Imagine a case just like ours, except with two straight parents (who didn't come in) instead of three dads. This took less than five minutes, almost all of it boilerplate. Our lawyer read a brief statement saying his clients needed a birth certificate for a child by surrogacy. The judge responded with a long statement about how she had jurisdiction, because the parents lived in San Diego and the child was going to be born here. Then she said she was granting the two parents their birth certificate and ordering it to be written, while the court recorder tapped away at her stenotype in that familiar way from the movies that makes them look like they're faking it.

After watching a routine surrogacy hearing, I became convinced that $5,300 for a birth certificate was a pretty good deal and I could lead a very comfortable life as a reproductive law attorney. But, on to our case.

The judge didn't ask any questions. She just talked at our attorney about surrogacy law for a full ten minutes. Code section 7612, she said, didn't apply because "Seventy-six twelve would require this court to find that it would be detrimental to the child not to name a third party. Since the child is not born yet, I can't find detriment." Section 7601, on the other hand, which dealt with naming parents from a surrogacy contract, did not mention triple parentage. "My read of it is that if the legislature wanted to allow more than two parents under the surrogacy section of the law, they would have done so."

She explained how lower courts apply existing law, not make new law. Our three-daddy birth certificate would be unprecedented in California, and it wasn't within her authority to set precedent. Granting our request could open a "Pandora's box." She recognized a bind our request put the court in—that picking two of us as parents and leaving one out seemed like an unpleasant prospect—but she had an out for that. "The parties anticipated, via their contract, that this was a possibility and already made that decision." Otherwise, she said, "how would I even pick two, if I was to decide that I can only enter a judgment for two?"

"Goddamn it," Alan muttered, as I continued with my best court posture and court silence. "I bet she couldn't have ruled against us if she would have had to pick herself. We're about to lose because we were conscientious."

The judge suggested two avenues forward for us: we could appeal her decision and fight the ruling, possibly up to the California Supreme Court. Or we could come back in a few years and argue that Baby had suffered because one of us had been left off the birth certificate, and she'd add the name then. *Dammit,* I thought. *We lost. We'll have to wait unless we want to spend a bunch of money to be those weirdo polygamists on TV who appealed the case of their left-coast family situation.* She gave us a steely look like she'd just dropped the mic, or possibly her gavel. And she turned things over to our attorney. "What do you want to point me to and argue to change my mind?"

CHAPTER 29

A FEW
GOOD MEN

Our lawyer stood up straight and began to fight for us. He established our right to bring an action and jumped into the California Supreme Court case that had found, "It's the intentions of the parties at the time of [surrogacy] contracting that's going to determine who the parents are." He argued that detriment would surely befall our baby if the law didn't recognize the reality of her situation. He pointed out that she was going to have three parents—that much had been set in stone—and denying this reality on her birth certificate wouldn't benefit anyone. Why risk harming an infant when tri-parentage would avert that risk? He asked her to consider changing social norms, like the increasing recognition of different gender identities. Next, he explained that neither the law nor court precedent specifically restricted their scope to two-parent families. Maybe they didn't say "three dads," but they also didn't exclude single moms or single dads; wouldn't the judge grant single parents sole parentage without hesitation? What was the difference?

As the judge pushed back, I started thinking about whether we'd have the fortitude to fight our loss at the appeals court, or whether we'd just return in a few years to apply for my parent status. And that's when Alan went full mama bear.

First he whispered to our attorney, interrupting the judge, and told him to make the case for detriment more strongly. Alan also asked him to remind her she wouldn't be making precedent—since we all wanted the ruling, no one would appeal it, and no one would hear about it. The judge noticed the conversation and interrupted, at which point Alan asked to testify, and the judge agreed! The security guard motioned us through the little swinging door, and we swore to tell "the truth, the whole truth, and nothing but the truth" about our throuple. Our unrehearsed comments would determine whether I ended up a mere coparent by contract, or full legal parent on the birth certificate.

"Thank you for letting us speak," Alan began. "I know it's a complicated and unconventional case. I can only say we really did enter it with the utmost planning and care and concern." He explained how much we thought about raising a child, and laid out all the benefits of our child having three parents—our assets, my pension, Jeremy's health insurance. "If something were to happen to Ian, if he were to die or be killed and the child were still a minor, she would be legally entitled to those pension payments if Ian is a parent." It was true. My partners wouldn't get my pension if I died, but our child *could*.

Using just the right amount of passion and frustration, he explained how no trusts or marriage arrangement could benefit our daughter the same way tri-parentage could. "I really don't want the child to be penalized for our unconventional relationship. It would be in the best interest of the child for all the intended parents to be legally named parents." Alan wiped away a tear as he spoke about protecting his daughter, and the look on the judge's face was one of . . . discomfort? Unease?

Jeremy spoke second, explaining how we loved our daughter as a full person already. "God forbid, if someone were to attack our surrogate, he would be attacking two people." He echoed Alan's concerns about inheritance: "If something happened to Ian right now, or shortly after birth, it would be nice if the child was able to receive the rights she would be due as his heir." He went on to remind us all that the proceedings weren't about anyone but our baby: "We never tried to push our relationship onto society. We understand it's very unconventional. That changed . . . suddenly we were very worried about this little person that we've created. And it *must* be to her detriment not having her three dads as legal parents."

Then it was my turn. "I'm so proud of both my partners and their comments. I second everything that they've said." Then I told her about a video Delilah had sent us. "Her whole abdomen is moving—she's dancing, really, and we were like, 'she wants out!' There are legal definitions. But from our perspective, she's our daughter now, and we just want to protect her."

The judge took a long breath, followed by a long pause. "Let's just be clear for the record. The contract originally started with two of you," she noted, "and the second amendment . . . added the third party. Was it your intent in entering the contract that all three of you be named the parent?"

"Yes," said Alan.

"Yes," said Jeremy.

"Yes, it was," I said.

"We were legally naive," said Alan, explaining that it took lots of legal advice before we understood we could apply for triple parentage.

"We just didn't know," I said, "that it was possible to arrange a three-party parentage."

The judge dived into the details of the family code with our lawyers once again. Back and forth they went, discussing the details of 7630 (b), parts (d) or (f) of 7611, 7620 (a) and (c), and the 7900 series, whatever that is. We didn't understand the legal details, obviously, but we knew that Alan had revived our case. The judge took a deep breath. Our lawyer cut in during her long pause to remind her that her decision wasn't going to appeals court, so it wouldn't set formal precedent: "*Nobody* is going to appeal this case."

"I know," the judge said. "All right. I have heard from you. I have read the pleading, I've read the case law . . . I'm going to find that 7601 and 7612 do not apply in this case. I'm not finding detriment. However . . ." She paused. Her face seemed to say: "Crud. I can't rule against these nice gay people, so how the hell am I going to justify *that?*" The three of us sat forward in our seats. Our relatives held their breath.

"I am persuaded," she said reluctantly, and we knew that somehow we'd won, turned things around from "dead on arrival" to "three-dad birth certificate," and our hearts leaped up. "Where [section 7620] says a person who causes conception with the intent to become a legal parent by assisted reproduction, it talks about *one or more* parties."

She recapped all the applicable codes, but then told us that Delilah had begun her medications before all the contract amendments were finished. We had violated California law, section 7962,[97] which says that parents may not "undergo an embryo transfer procedure, or commence injectable medication [. . .] until the assisted reproduction agreement for gestational carriers has been fully executed . . ." You would think that a billion dollars in legal fees and the experience of a well-paid reproductive medicine doctor would have protected us from making this mistake. You would be wrong.

Luckily, the judge forgave us, finding "substantial compliance" in the fact that the amendments were underway, and we finally heard the words we were waiting for: "I'm going to grant the judgment to establish a parent/child relationship. Stay the enforcement of the judgment until the birth of the baby. Good luck to you all."

If there was a movie of our life together, this would be the part where we'd jump up and down and yell like maniacs. Instead we just smiled and behaved like responsible future parents, waiting for the judge to finish the court proceedings. There was one minor catch: we'd have to get a two-parent certificate and pay to have it amended, but it'd be the real deal. I checked the clock: forty-five minutes had passed. While I held Jeremy's hand and waited for her to finish, something clicked inside me. I thought about how well we fought together and complemented each other, and I fell even more in love with our crazy little family. We'd done it.

Prior costs:	$90,988.80
Amending birth certificates to recognize all three dads:	$193.00
Total:	$91,181.80

CHAPTER 30

THE COLANDER

Outside the courtroom, our attorney congratulated us, and we celebrated with our families. My mom cried until she looked like a lightly pummeled, red-eyed jellyfish—in a *good* way, Mom, I promise!—and Alan's mother dabbed away tears. Jeremy thanked all our relatives for their support: "It means so much to have our families behind us." And I finally understood that expression viscerally. Our families had literally been behind us.

Meghan had a solid case of the feels, too, and summed up how I think we all felt about the roller-coaster court hour: "I think I need an adult beverage!" Later she told me, "Alan and Jeremy seem really worried you're going to get killed soon!" I think they were just looking out for our baby. At least, they haven't asked me to get life insurance yet.

From court, we headed straight to preparations for our baby shower. But before I tell you about that, I need to rewind all the way back to eighth grade. That year, I went from being an asexual kid to having an all-consuming crush on a friend. Instead of that friend being a girl, the way it was supposed to happen—the way it worked for everyone in my universe—I had a crush on a charming boy I'll call Jeff.

I spent years amazed by the antigay rhetoric that people choose to be gay. How the hell would straight people know, apart from the fact that so many antigay pundits and politicians seem to be tortured closet cases themselves? Do they think straight people choose their orientation? Or are their minds so small, so closed, that they think everyone must be straight by default, so that every gay person or lesbian represents a deliberate, presumably evil, choice?

I certainly didn't choose to fall for Jeff. Why would I? I literally did not know a single gay person. I saw older ones, on television, marching in San Francisco. My impression was that all of them would die of AIDS. I didn't conceive that any of them knew love, or happiness, or the acceptance of their families, or that they had relationships. My friends played a tackle game called "Smear the Queer" and deployed the slur "faggot" as an insult of the highest order, and although I doubt anyone ever suspected me, their attacks landed on me just the same. Worse, I thought I was the only target of their hatred in the world, the sole homo in my community. I realized only years later that I *did* know many gay people; they were just closeted, like me.

LGBTQ+ kids hide who they are because they are fearful (or certain) of the negative reactions of friends and family. I worried that my friends and family might reject me, which made me feel that I didn't have friends or family. I was alone. And if I wanted to hang on to the illusion of friendship that I did have, I needed to hide, so instead of telling Jeff about my feelings, I stopped spending time with him. But the best way to hide was to participate in the name-calling. So to my loneliness, I added regret in hurting any anonymous gay people stuck in the closet with me and complicity in building my own prison.

Years later, I even gave up my first chance at escape. One day, I visited my friend Mike, who lived down the street from me. In the privacy of an afternoon with no friends, siblings, or parents around, he offered me a massage. It was just a friendly thing, he said; his dad was a chiropractor and had showed him some techniques. How beautiful that touch could have felt! I felt years of longing rise up—longing that I had never been able to discuss, let alone share, with another person. There could have been touch, a smile, a moment of vulnerability and companionship. Perhaps even a kiss? The possibility beckoned at me like a sweet, clean drug, and of course I rejected Mike's offer, promptly and firmly. A massage sounded gay, and gay was poison.

When I reconnected with Mike a quarter century later, I found out something amazing: at the time, he hadn't even known he was making a pass at me. He realized what he had been doing only years later. Mike's fine now, and happily married to his partner. But in high school, he'd gone so deep in the closet he'd even hidden from himself.

College was better than high school, but not great. The welcome schedule at the University of Virginia included a meeting for the LGBU, the lesbian, gay, and bisexual student union—we didn't add the *T* and *Q* until later—in a garden designed by Thomas Jefferson himself. Some students, gathered in the common area of our dorm, grimaced at the event schedule when they realized the LGBU was meeting in half an hour. "We ought to go spy on the fags. At least we'd know who they are," said one. "Hey, Ian, where're you going?"

Oh, just out, I told them. *You know. Exploring.* In a way, I *was* exploring. That day I told thirty people my truth just by showing up; until that moment, I'd only told two friends. The LGBU kept me sane, but larger UVA did not welcome me. The LGBU had to meet off campus because too many students feared discovery. They had good reason, considering what happened at the football games. I went to the first game of the season, in the stadium across the street from my dorm. Following tradition, students dressed in blue and orange, and every time our team scored, they put their hands on each others' shoulders and swayed, singing the university's "Good Ole Song," which includes the line, "We come from old Virginia, where all is bright and gay." Also following tradition, they yelled, "NOT GAY!" after that line, in a shocking, stadium-filling roar.[xii] I walked out and never went back.

My first year at college, I met a sweet and handsome guy named Alex at the LGBU and began eating dinner at the cafeteria near his dorm in the hopes of seeing him again. It worked. He came to my dorm room after dinner and suggested we eat at the cafeteria again. I told him I would, if he agreed to go on a real date. He nodded, blushed, and kissed me. I felt an inferno of passion mixed with the fear of discovery, like we were spies for the resistance in occupied France. He stumbled out, weak-kneed, and I fell onto my squeaky twin bed and listened to my heart race.

Months later, I was holding Alex's hand when an SUV screeched to a stop. Five students jumped out and chased us through the center of campus. Long-legged, we outran them and took shelter in a computer lab, wondering what they'd have done had they caught us outside in the lonely dark. Then, I found death threats in my email—from college kids in *other states,* who apparently had time to worry about the company I kept. Had low-level involvement in the LGBU been enough to make me a target to strangers? I never found out. Neither Alex nor I thought to notify the police or campus security. Hate was just an ocean we swam in. Instead, I redoubled my martial arts training and started carrying a concealed folding knife whenever I left home.

I didn't learn my lesson, though. I came out university-wide with an article in the student newspaper that detailed the assault and the death threats. I warned nine friends, one by one, before it ran. My roommate didn't care a whit (thank you, Michael). Two others left the room, stunned, and came back five minutes later to say, "You're still just the guy who edits my English papers, right?" The rest of them—six people!—avoided me like the plague from then on.

I still hadn't told my family. Curled up together one night, Alex and I came up with a life goal: we hoped that one day we would be welcomed,

---

xii Some fans have continued the homophobic chant up to the present day, despite pleas from student council and notable alumni, including Tina Fey.

together, to celebrate Christmas with our families. And that was it. We knew with great certainty that we would never be able to serve in the military or get married. We just wanted to be accepted by our loved ones. It didn't happen overnight.

"I fell in love," I told my mom after my first year of school. "With a boy."

"He'll try to give you AIDS," she said.

"We're virgins."

"Hepatitis, then," she replied.

Within a week, I'd moved to my father and stepmother's place. Things went better there. "We don't understand it," my stepmother said, "but we love you and we support you," and the three of us shared a long hug. It wasn't their fault—they couldn't have supported me until they knew I was gay—but that was the first time since my crush on Jeff that I felt loved by parents, without second-guessing, caveats, asterisks, or conditions. It had been six hard years.

My mother came around, of course. She joined the Human Rights Campaign, and she donates to them and forwards me their news bulletins (and yes, Mother, if you're reading this, I am *also* on their mailing list; you can stop). All three of my parents befriended Alex. And his family got used to me, too. For a long year, his parents seemed to tolerate me. Then I started receiving little gifts, like bottles of dried spices from his mother's garden, and invites to dinner . . . to spend the weekend . . . to Thanksgiving with Alex's ninety-year-old grandmother . . . and *Christmas*. The tree, the tray of hot chocolates, the long-needle pine garland on the hearth above the crackling fire—it felt like living a Hallmark card. Today I would call it a Pinterest moment. Alex's parents got me a colander from Williams Sonoma, a true extravagance at a time when I was buying dried beans instead of canned to save pennies.

We never suffered much from discrimination in Virginia. Yes, after I described our assault in the school newspaper, several students told me they couldn't be suitemates with me, because I might lick their dishes to give them AIDS. Yes, a potential landlord refused to rent to us because we were gay, which was perfectly legal, but we just rented a different apartment. During our college days, the state not only banned gay marriage, it banned civil unions and even partnership contracts—any attempt to bestow the benefits of marriage to a same-sex couple. This pointless cruelty arguably denied same-sex couples even the ability to leave property to each other in their wills or to write parenting agreements. But Alex and I each had our own health insurance and didn't need any other marriage benefits. And our families accepted us. Some gay students weren't as lucky and ended up without college funding or homes after their families disowned them.

I didn't write out these experiences to complain. Life dealt me just enough adversity to make me tougher: an activist, an advocate, a public speaker, a martial artist. The six great years I spent with Alex are now part of my distant past. I have a wonderful life, with two wonderful partners, and my throuple has seven parents who love us and dozens and dozens of friends and coworkers who treat us like just another family. But you never leave your childhood behind. Every time I strain something, my fancy colander reminds me that my greatest teen aspiration was to be accepted with my life partner at a family Christmas. That loneliness, and the joy and relief at how that dream was met and exceeded, are still part of me, just like that colander, which is tucked away in the back of a drawer in the kitchen.

Growing up, I thought of marriage as an institution of a society that didn't want me. I protected myself by having relationships in secret, and then discreetly. I never envisioned having a marriage ceremony or a reception. I expected my unions to be sacred to the participants, not to a god. I never wanted my government to bless my relationships. And I didn't appreciate the value of affirmation from friends and family that comes with a wedding and reception. Not, that is, until the baby shower.

CHAPTER 31

THE SHOWER

Jeremy grew up in a deeply religious community where the expectation of a fancy, heterosexual wedding celebration was absolute. He didn't really come out to *himself* until twenty-four, go on a date until twenty-six, or drink until twenty-seven. The confines of his Nazarene upbringing had some costs, but he treasures his memories of the Nazarene community in small-town Montana, from youth group to summer camp to devotional music to the way they teach children empathy. He loves the lavish ceremony of Christmas, and he's always liked the idea of an extravagant marriage celebration. Joining Alan and me, he had to grieve for that celebration he knew would never come. Some people throw throuple commitment ceremonies . . . but not us.

But our idea of a baby shower grew to fill the void. We thought of it as the reception for the wedding we'd never have. Friends and family wanted to come from all over. We realized it was a great chance to get our seven parents and extended families together in celebration. And then there was Neha, the friend who had encouraged our parental aspirations and who wanted us to live up to our potential as hosts. We'd finally have an occasion to throw a party that would make her proud. Best way to make Neha-approved party choices? Sign her up as your party planner.

She researched caterers and bartenders and presented ideas to Jeremy, who made decisions, designed the invitations, and planned the decorations. He knew our guests would want to see a finished nursery. We'd been working on it, but the shower gave us a firm deadline. Alan, chief of purchasing, redoubled his efforts.

Our house became a hotel. We housed Alan's and Jeremy's parents, my mother, and Meghan, which meant crowding the three of us into one bed. Our throuple almost never sleeps all together, largely because the middle position is hotter than the sun. That, and our four dogs sleep with us. Braiding twenty-eight limbs together and sleeping is possible, but not ideal. We told ourselves we were practicing for baby.

When we host parties, we usually cook. If the guest list tops a dozen, we provide trays of Indian food or a taco truck. For the shower, we had professional catering, servers, and a bartender—so once the decorations and tents went up, we had little prep to do. I had just one crucial shopping trip to make. For marijuana.

Before my mom flew out, she asked me for medical evidence that marijuana fixes various types of ailments, particularly arthritis. I told her the data wasn't great. "Isn't CBD oil fantastic for epilepsy?" she asked, and I replied that there are a bunch of different kinds of epilepsy, and, crucially, *epilepsy is not arthritis.* Then her physician's certificate of need for marijuana showed up in our mail. A doctor in Los Angeles, a city she's never visited in her life, had provided documentation she had been "evaluated in [his] office for a medical condition." He promised to monitor her use and to provide medical advice, at least annually, clearing her to possess and use marijuana, pursuant to California Health and Safety Code Section 11362.5.[xiii]

---

xiii The doctor, I learned, claimed that he'd switched from surgery to pot prescribing because he was so impressed with the results, but I had a sneaking suspicion it had more to do with being sued at an astonishing pace in several states and surrendering one license after accumulating over three dozen malpractice lawsuits in one state alone.

"I'm trying it," she explained by phone. "It's going to fix my hands. And I never get to have any fun. I'm in my seventies and I never got to enjoy the seventies." And you know what? I'm proud of her. All her life, she'd taken nothing stronger than Chablis, then, at seventy-three, she decided she needed to get high for the first time.

Off to the dispensary we went. Without a medical marijuana letter of my own, I couldn't help her shop, so I joined a dozen potheads in the waiting room. My favorite was a guy who looked like he'd come from an audition for the part of 1970s pimp, complete with a cane and a white velvet, wide-brim hat with a leopard band. "Tell yo mama not to stack her edibles," he advised sagely. "I bought a fifty-serving brownie once and kept eating, and *bam*, I'm puking up things I ate in the nineties!" Mom emerged with a bottle of CBD oil, a tin of blueberry edibles, and a first-timer gift of a large brownie. I told her if she ate the brownie, she'd turn into a pimp. She nodded trustingly.

Back home, the guests piled in, bringing gifts for . . . *our infant!* Parenthood felt more real than ever. And that was before Delilah stopped me on my way to set up the dessert tables. "Ian!" she said, beaming. "Come here!" And she grabbed both my wrists and guided my hands onto her belly.

Until then, Delilah's pregnancy felt remote, even abstract, because while we saw Delilah for her OB appointments, the pregnancy still happened thirty minutes away, not in our home. We marked the progress of the pregnancy each Friday, when apps on Jeremy's phone announced organ formation and growth milestones. We'd cuddle up on our bed and watch videos that compared fetuses to a fruit of the week, as if plums and papayas were international units of measure. But even as Delilah's belly swelled until she looked like a skinny model trying to steal a basketball from a sporting goods store, she was still pregnant *out there*. No longer. Our daughter was having hiccups, and they were adorable.

"Oh, Delilah," I said stupidly. "Wow."

"I know, right? There's a little person in there!"

There really was. We were going to be parents. "Wow," I said again. Things like this make me cry.

On the other hand, nothing makes Jeremy cry. He didn't cry when the old man's wife died in Pixar's *Up*. He even likes watching *Love, Actually* with Alan's dad, while Alan and I roll our eyes and drink in the hot tub, and he doesn't cry at *that*. If you're not touched by the wedding proposal in broken Portuguese or the kid evading airport security to say goodbye to his would-be girlfriend, what's the point?

But *Jeremy cried at the shower*, because he loves our family and our baby more than anything else in the world! Once our seventy-five guests had filled the balconies and deck, the black-clad servers had passed a few rounds of appetizers, and everyone had quaffed a drink or two, Jeremy whistled for everyone's attention. The five parents gathered on the deck with our arms around each other, and he gave an impromptu, unscripted, and totally endearing speech.

"We just wanted to say thank you. We are so grateful we have so many friends and family here and that you're all here to support us." Jeremy thanked Neha for her party organizing, and she curtseyed to much applause. Then he got adorable.

"I might get emotional. I blame the mai tais. We are so excited that in less than seven weeks, we're going to be parents. I want to thank Julie and Stephanie, because they started us on this journey. They were the first ones to convince us we could be parents and saw that in us, and I"—this is where his voice started breaking—"really appreciate that. We would not be here without you. I want to thank Meghan. This beautiful creature is going to be the mother of all our future children, and I could not imagine doing this with anyone else. We're so glad you're a part of our life, forever." We took a break to share some hugs.

"For those of you who don't know, we're so excited to say that as of yesterday, we had our court case and we're going to be the first three dads on a birth certificate!" People cheered. Lots of people. I never thought I'd care that dozens of friends and family would turn out to support our weird little family and our victory in court. But that support moved me deeply, and I will never forget it.

"It was a long and expensive legal battle," Jeremy continued, "and the only reason we won was because Alan stood up in court and went full mama bear. He got us our baby. He was incredible. It was so validating to have California say we are in a legitimate relationship and we are the parents of our child." More cheering, much wiping away of tears.

"Now our biggest thanks, where is she . . ." Everyone laughed, because our conspicuously pregnant surrogate was standing right next to him. ". . . ah! Our biggest thanks go to our dear friend Delilah. It has been the easiest relationship anyone has ever had with a surrogate. She's been our trouper, our cheerleader, our supporter, and we are so grateful. We're so excited that our child was created in this love, in the love of her, her husband, and her kids. And we're so grateful we have all of you to help us, because we don't know what we're doing, so expect a lot of phone calls. Thank you very much, and it's an open bar, so have a great night!"

We adore a photo of this moment, the five of us crowded together for an embrace. Jeremy would later frame three copies—one for us, one for each mom. That image will always anchor our unique family, even though Delilah has her own family across town and Meghan may stay in Argentina.

We did our best to chat with all our wonderful guests. To those I missed, let me relay my genuine gratitude. I'd been dead wrong about the value of a wedding, or at least some kind of celebration. It meant so much to feel the love and support of friends and family and to share our joy with them. They didn't have to accept the poly weirdos, but they did, and that filled a hole in me I didn't know I had.

Later, after the desserts were served and the bartender started to pack up, Neha congratulated us on a job well done. "The service was delightful. Your speech? Exquisite."

"You always wanted us to throw catered parties on the deck and get on the baby train," I said. "Have we finally made you proud?"

"Well, you've come a long way," she said. "I'm a tiger mom; I can't go around dispensing excessive praise." Then she leaned in and whispered, "It was perfect."

Previous costs:	$91,181.80
Shower reception catering:	[$8,250.00]
Total:	$91,181.80[xiv]

---

xiv I decided I couldn't include the shower costs in our total, since we didn't *have* to throw a party. But it sure was worth it!

CHAPTER 32

THE NURSERY

Our guests had left. I was passing the pool on my way to clean up the bar, using my phone as a flashlight, when my phone leaped into the water, like a ghost had smacked it out of my hand. I heard a melodic little "plunk!" and watched the light spiral into the pitch-black of the deep end. I dived in, scraped it off the bottom of the pool, and lifted it above water like it might take a deep breath. Then I did what I always do when facing a technical problem: I ran directly to Alan. He was talking to a dozen relatives in the living room, and I was soaking wet.

"Alan, help!" I pleaded. "Resuscitate my phone!" He set up a dehydration system: a vacuum-sealed pouch containing the phone and a bunch of desiccant packets he'd saved from shoes and other deliveries. He'd read a bunch of articles, he told me, and this was the best approach. Seriously, how many people can count on a spouse to preemptively save desiccant packets and read about wet phones? The whole thing was emblematic of Alan's technical support. You can count on him having previously studied the issue and stockpiled the supplies—and to deliver one snarky comment you're better off ignoring. This time it was "I don't understand why you threw your phone in the pool."

The next morning, I opened up the vacuum pack and plugged in my phone. Sadly, it was officially dead. "We should have sacrificed a chicken," I said.

"The good news," said Jeremy's dad, "is that you probably won't hesitate to rescue the baby, either."

"Great," said my mom. "Maybe he should let Jeremy carry her, though?"

I think she would have really chuckled the night before, watching a puddle grow at my feet, asking for help with my drowned phone like a little kid. She missed the whole thing, passed out on the downstairs sofa from marijuana edibles.

My point is that Alan handled my whole phone crisis. One of the magical aspects of making babies with Jeremy and Alan is that they took care of all the details. They handled the IVF appointments. They acquired our embryo donors, surrogate, and bio-mom. And they bought *everything*, from carefully researched diapers and butt paste to blankets and organic cotton onesies and beyond. One of my favorite moments was when Alan looked up from his online shopping to say, in all seriousness, "I'm having trouble finding any baby kimonos that I like." Our stroller just showed up at the door after my boys test-drove some and picked the best—and the steering is *so* smooth. Like butter! While Jeremy single-handedly managed our registry, I just got to sit back and watch.

They both took on the crucial role of nursery design. It began with the unicorn head. "Is that a . . . black unicorn head with a gold horn?" I asked when Alan opened an Amazon delivery box to reveal said unicorn head.

"It sure is," he said. "Baby's nursery is off to a great start!"

That had been many months ago. But as I said, nursery remodeling had really taken off in the weeks leading up to the shower. The boys found a stylish end table with gold legs and a black-and-gold lamp and clock.

Jeremy tested a half dozen paint samples, and I repainted. Alan picked out a new carpet, and the two of them jointly selected a dresser, crib, and rocker in tasteful French gray. Admiring our handiwork, we felt the slightest sense that we'd gone astray.

"You know how we want a fancy but tasteful midcentury modern vacation house in Palm Springs?" asked Jeremy. "We've been designing *that* instead of a nursery." But baby hadn't arrived, and when she did, she wouldn't be able to see farther than two feet, so we had time. Jeremy finished an art project he'd been working on, a mosaic of colorful wood triangles; Alan found triangle-print curtains and a felt-ball mobile in the same cheerful colors. After applying forest and cuddly animal wall stick-ons, we finally felt our nursery was ready for baby—and guests.

We had plenty. Jeremy's parents are innkeepers, and the morning after the shower, they cooked brunch for the masses. Jeremy thought we might just collect presents and go through them later, but one of his cousins, hands on her hips, sternly corrected him: "Yesterday was the gay baby shower. Now you're going to see what a *real* one looks like." We rearranged every sofa and chair in the house for the shower and unwrapped a veritable mountain of baby gifts. People gave so much. They gave too much. We realized we'd have to donate a lot of gifts, because otherwise our baby would only get a chance to wear each outfit once.

After the unwrapping, we took groups of guests down to the nursery for tours. The same nursery where my mother had been sleeping on an air mattress . . . and aggressively treating her arthritis with CBD oil. She might as well have put it in an aerosolizer. It smelled so much like weed that I wanted to start singing Bob Marley songs. I could see our guests' heads turn and noses wrinkle as they admired the black-and-gold unicorn head mounted on the wall.

"My mom's really into patchouli right now," I said, and everyone either believed me or made a really good show of pretending.

Three Dads and a Baby

Prior costs:	$91,181.80
Crib & dresser/changing table:	$1,190.00
Adorable fox clock:	$75.00
Bookshelf:	$199.00
Paint:	$28.00
Black unicorn head with gold horn:	$110.00
Mom's marijuana:	$60.00
Subtotal:	<u>$1,662.00</u>
Total:	$92,843.80

CHAPTER 33

BREECH

Jeremy and I attended Delilah's next ultrasound, which went south in about five seconds. "Hey baby, what's your head doing up here?" asked Dr. Lee. "And what are your feet doing down here? Sorry, folks, but baby is breech."

This was Not Good. Breech babies come out feetfirst. This doesn't sound like a big deal, but think about how a normal delivery works: the biggest part, the head, stretches the cervix before the baby enters the vagina. You know the narrower bits can pass once the head has gone through. In a breech, the head can get stuck at the cervix. If mom needs a C-section *then,* baby's half in, half out. Plus, the umbilical cord usually enters the vagina *after* the largest thing, the head. In a breech birth, the cord has to squeeze through the cervix with the head, and it can be squished. That's like applying a jujitsu choke to a baby already stressed by the birth process.

Thus, 90 percent of breech babies are delivered by C-section. Surgical delivery is generally safe, but a C-section would increase Delilah's hospital time and her risk of infections, blood clots, bleeding, hysterectomy, and cardiac arrest.[98] Plus, vaginal birth would benefit our baby. The squeeze of delivery improves Apgar scores and reduces the risk of breathing problems by removing fluid from the lungs,[99] and the birth canal transmits healthy bacteria to the baby, reducing the risk of immune disorders later in life.[100] Breech position was Not Good.

"Wasn't she head down the last time?" asked Jeremy.

"I think so," Dr. Lee joked, "or maybe that was another baby. Do you have two in there?"

We were not amused. We, and Delilah, just had questions: Could she flip on her own? Did a breech always require a C-section? What could we do?

"Well, we could do an ECV," said Dr. Lee. "External cephalic version. Maneuvers to reorient the baby. We don't do it till thirty-seven weeks, because she could just flip back."

If the baby is so mobile she could flip back, I thought, what's the big deal about her being breech now? And what if Delilah goes into labor next week?

"This happened with my last one," said Delilah. "I did all the stuff from the old wives' tales. I ate pineapple. I ate spicy food. We had sex. Didn't work, but he eventually flipped on his own."

"Wasn't a total loss," I said. "Sounds like you had pineapple curry and got laid."

Delilah laughed. "We'll figure this out. Me and baby. It'll be fine. We'll run the program!"

"She's big. She's off the charts for size, like ninety-fifth to ninety-ninth percentile. Now she's breech," said Dr. Lee. "Let's just go ahead and schedule a C-section. It's hard to reserve *or* time, and I've followed you this far. I might as well see you through."

Dr. Lee was referring to her practice patterns. She only did deliveries by C-section. Apparently she felt weird about being Delilah's doctor and not handling the birth, but she was the only one of us who thought a C-section would be a good outcome.

Delilah saw me grimace at Dr. Lee's comments. "Nature's got a plan," she said. "Let her run the program. We'll get this baby flipped." She winked at us dads.

"Would an ECV work?" asked Jeremy.

"Maybe," said Dr. Lee. "She's got a lot of amniotic fluid, so it's easier to flip, or to flip back." Apparently the ideal thing at thirty-six weeks is a baby head-down, without too much amniotic fluid, restrained by antibreeching straps. "You've got a huge baby. It's best to prepare for a C-section." True, Delilah'd made us a big baby, but she'd also vaginally delivered an eleven-pound child of her own (and while most people assumed six-five Jeremy was responsible for our large baby, he was born at seven and a half pounds).

Out in the parking lot, Delilah told us Dr. Blumberg wanted her to visit. "I think it's a good idea," she said. "I always remember that blessing he did over me. I think going back to him would be really good juju."

I thought of the mezuzah hanging outside Blumberg's office and Delilah's heritage, and for a moment I thought she'd said "good Jew-Jew." It's a sign of my increasing social skills that I kept this thought entirely to myself, up until the point I published it in a book.

"I'm glad that he doesn't just impregnate people and disappear to his sea-cliff mansion," said Jeremy. "It's really cool that he checks on his patients when he doesn't have to."

"Right?" said Delilah. "He checks up on them, he cares about things, and *then* he retires to his sea-cliff mansion!"

"We'll read up on debreeching babies, and let you know what we come up with," said Jeremy. "My baby book has a section."

"Great!" said Delilah. "I know we can do it!"

"I'd feel terrible if Delilah had to have a C-section," Alan said that night. And then, as an afterthought: "Doesn't our contract specify some additional payment if she has to have one?"

"It's maybe a couple thousand bucks," I said. "Don't worry, I'm sure that when the Republicans finish passing their health-care legislation, all surrogacy expenses will be reimbursed at 200 percent if you're gay." This was mid-2017, and Republican congressmen were arguing against mandatory coverage for women's health and pregnancy care.

But I digress. Jeremy sent Delilah a bunch of information about methods to debreech a baby, from our pregnancy guide and an online article, "5 Ways to Flip a Breech Baby." "Some of this sounds a bit hippy-dippy," he admitted, "but so am I!" Most of it looked like yoga: variations of child's pose and downward dog. You needed to do it twenty minutes, three times daily for best results ("I'd love to see the study *that's* based on," Alan said skeptically).

Other remedies included placing a bag of frozen vegetables on your upper belly and a warm compress on your lower belly, and playing soothing music. The genius idea behind the frozen peas/warm compress is that baby would flee the cold in favor of the warmth, which raised two important questions: (1) how much can you cool a baby's head through the abdominal wall, and (2) following the same logic, shouldn't Mom squat on the speaker playing the soothing music? The webpage recommended peppermint oil and my personal favorite: the chiropractor. "If your hips are out of line, it may be preventing your baby from getting into the head-down position." Yeah, right. Your hips are a millimeter off, so baby flipped 180 degrees. I didn't want to rain on Jeremy's enthusiasm, but we had entered the realm of total bullshit.

Delilah got a bonus text from lead pregnancy researcher Jeremy—about home labor induction. Options included walking, sex (because semen contains uterus-stimulating hormones), and maternal orgasm, which releases oxytocin and promotes uterine activity. The book warned that sex late in pregnancy could trigger labor, fail to work, or extend pregnancy. You know what else might induce labor, prolong pregnancy, *or have no effect?* At last check that list includes pecans, *Gilligan's Island* reruns, internet cat memes, and *anything*. No one has any idea what works, but that doesn't stop them from writing books filled with gibberish. Other ideas included uncomfortable nipple twisting "for several hours a day," or castor oil, risking a delivery in the midst of "diarrhea, severe cramping, and vomiting."

Some unsolicited advice for pregnant ladies out there: unless you really like pineapple, I'd stick to the sex.

For debreeching, I was much more optimistic about external cephalic version. We quickly found a few videos on YouTube and watched physicians cover a woman's belly with ultrasound jelly and reposition a fetus in two minutes. It looked easy, but the American College of Gynecology website does warn that ECV can rupture the membranes, start labor, or even cause placental abruption. It did *not*, however, provide any guidance on what we should do.

Plus, a pediatrician friend tried to talk us out of it: "So painful for the mother." But while ECV didn't look like something I'd do for fun, it looked a *hell* of a lot more fun, faster, and safer than a C-section. Avoid ninety seconds of discomfort so you could heal an abdominal incision for six weeks? I guess you could get a Percocet prescription out of the latter, but *damn*, I'd go for the belly massage if it were me.

We left it up to Delilah, who wanted to trust baby, trust nature, and "run the program." We really did not want baby born by C-section, and, it turns out, neither did baby. Delilah felt an achy stretch as our baby turned herself head-down; the following morning, hiccups she felt at the diaphragm had shifted to her lower belly. At the next appointment, ultrasound confirmed that baby had flipped herself head-down, loooooow in the pelvis, ready to pop. Good work, baby!

CHAPTER 34

THE FUCKERY OF DR. COLLINS, PART DEUX

One of my friends asked me about assisted reproduction doctors when she heard about our pregnancy. I couldn't really tell our story without including our unpleasant departure from Dr. Collins's clinic, and after hearing about it, my friend had two important questions: "Wasn't she required to refer you to another clinic?" And "What are you going to do about it?"

To which I sighed and said, "Well, shit." Assisted reproduction is stressful enough *without* having to scramble to change clinics, and I wanted to spare anyone else from having an encounter like ours. And who knows? Maybe if I reached out to them, I could find a way to get some gay porn into the collection, as a little treat for the next gay guy who needed to produce a sample there.

I was going to have to complain about our experience.

I started by writing FISC's lead physician and listing our concerns, which included expensive and unnecessary Zika tests, involving a risk management person in our meeting without notifying us, the lack of support for Dr. Collins's recommendations in professional guidelines, and how we never heard her acknowledge Dr. Scaligeri's recommendation, which was not to do any Zika tests on Meghan. I didn't mince words, concluding:

> We got very different recommendations from Dr. Scaligeri and Dr. Collins, who did not disclose the duties of the risk management person she had sit in on our meeting. Life goes on. We are not fragile people, and we don't wish Dr. Collins ill. But we think your clinic should be aware of a doctor who does not thoughtfully order tests or disclose and follow the advice of experts she's consulted with.

Twenty-seven emails and three phone conversations later, we have a much clearer picture of what transpired that day. I even spoke and exchanged emails with a FISC doctor who had joined the Zika conference call with Collins and Dr. Scaligeri. He explained, "We based the recommendation on multiple factors: CDC recommendations, the advice of two UCSD infectious disease experts, and the opinions of our risk management staff—with the goal of minimizing the risk of a client or baby being affected by Zika."

That was weird. We'd never heard Dr. Collins mention speaking to colleagues. As a doctor who sees tons of cancer patients, I know that difficult cases are discussed with colleagues all the time to improve care. There's even a formal meeting for it: tumor board. A team of specialists reviews cases and makes joint recommendations, which are documented in the medical record and shared with the patient. Such discussions are risk reducing (the doctor is following consensus, not a whim), and reassuring for patients (who get automatic second, third, and fourth opinions). If I were Dr. Collins, I would have just said a committee met and made a joint decision. She knew Alan and I were doctors. We would have considered a FISC committee process entirely reasonable, and it would have made us feel better about the decision, even though we disagreed with it.

Things got even weirder. I pressed Dr. Collins's colleague about Dr. Scaligeri's advice to me, which was to neither test for nor worry about Zika. By phone, this doctor agreed that the infectious disease consultants were *not worried* about the Zika risk. He even said that despite the quarantine period the clinic suggested for Meghan, they would have let us use a surrogate from tropical Brazil, the highest-risk area in the world, if we simply signed a waiver! I didn't understand—why accept a patient at maximum risk and refuse a patient with negligible risk? As the clinic committee saw it, the point was that Meghan's risk was modifiable, because she could just stay in the United States for two months. If I could insert an eye-roll emoji here, I would. Any high-risk surrogate in Brazil, in theory, also *could* take a long vacation out of the country to reduce her risk, and if at all possible, *should*.

Replies to my emails turned into a bit of a mess. I'd remind the doctors that FISC had complicated our life plans beyond what guidelines required, disregarded Dr. Scaligeri's recommendations, caused us stress and additional expense by disrupting our care, and failed to refer us to another clinic. They'd reply FISC only had our best interests at heart. Maybe they thought that would mollify us?

It didn't.

Alan joined in, writing a deliciously blistering, fourteen-hundred-word response. He pointed out that the Zika cases in Argentina were as far from Meghan as the Zika cases in Miami were from our current location in San Diego. He called the unexpected inclusion of a risk management person "very unprofessional and unethical," and described how stressed he felt trying to figure out who she was. He said it was "appalling" that we, the patients, knew more about Zika testing than our doctor.

But the clinic simply wouldn't address the discrepancy between their recommendations and the guidelines and expert advice, no matter how many times I asked for an explanation. At that point, the universe provided another chance encounter: I got assigned to a physician leader training session, only the second in thirteen years, and bumped into Dr. Scaligeri yet again. I'm not religious, but it seemed increasingly likely that a bearded, toga-wearing deity was helping us out with this whole five-parent-kid thing.[xv]

I told Dr. Scaligeri everything. Hearing how FISC had advised the testing and quarantine after consulting with her, in short, confused her. "We certainly did *not* tell them your case was too risky," she said. "And a quarantine in the States makes no sense. We told them there was no concern in the Buenos Aires region, and we told them there was no reason to test. That didn't satisfy them. They wanted to send all patients with any Zika risk to our infectious disease clinic. But why? They have the same tests we do. They just wanted us to take on all the malpractice risk by promising nothing bad could happen. That wouldn't help patients, so we said, 'No, thanks.'"

Now everything made a lot more sense. I certainly don't feel like we heard the whole story from FISC, but this is how I assume things really went down: Zika felt new and scary to this corporate-owned reproductive medicine group. Their very risk-averse risk manager heard about our case—maybe she reviews them all, maybe Collins brought it up, maybe there was already a Zika meeting planned. When the infectious disease clinic declined to shoulder all the Zika risk, perhaps the risk manager asked Collins to change her plans. She did, but she collected our fees for the day before telling us. Maybe that was thoughtless, maybe she thought she was the only show in town and we would follow her recommendations. And she likely cited guidelines and mentioned consulting with experts because that sounded better than attributing the changes to risk management. It was just very bad luck that she tried that approach with us, probably the only IVF clients in the region who'd thoroughly educated themselves about Zika—or consulted with the *same doctor.*

---

xv I'm kidding. Our deity looks like Oprah.

Armed with Dr. Scaligeri's testimony, I wrote the IVF clinic once more. With customer service issues, it helps to be direct. Don't just tell them you're dissatisfied; tell them what you want. Dream big. I asked for two things:

▸ We'd like an apology from Dr. Collins.

▸ We'd like a refund for the inappropriate Zika PCR plus whatever expenses had to be repeated with Blumberg due to the disruption in IVF services.

I got a prompt reply offering a partial refund, as well as an "apology" from Dr. Collins, who said she felt sorry for any distress, inconvenience, or expense we "feel" were due to her decisions. It's always nice to be told someone is sorry you *feel* distressed. It's just short of being told you imagined the whole thing. She also added, oddly, that it made sense for us to end up with Dr. Blumberg. He had, she believed, established himself as a "regional referral center for male-male couples," although she would "really appreciate" working with any gay couples we could refer to her.

When I showed Alan that last email, he sat back, cocked his head, and said, "Huh." This last bit made no sense to us. We did *not* know that Blumberg was the go-to doctor for male-male couples. Neither did Suri and Dave, our male-male coupled friends who had been turned away by FISC. We had a lengthy conversation about the whole matter with them, and they had never understood what about their case (they'd just said they were gay men who had a healthy egg donor, a healthy surrogate, and wanted to do IVF at an IVF clinic) made them too complicated for FISC.

And fishing for referrals in a nonapology? Ha.

Dr. Collins concluded her message by saying that everyone at FISC just wanted to maximize the safety of our intended offspring. She reminded us that Zika can be devastating. She said it was unfortunate that not all regulatory agencies or experts were in agreement about the best way forward. However, FISC now appreciated how "sensitive" all their staff must be in every communication with their patients, and she thanked me for bringing my concerns to her attention.

After reading this, I felt one-third each tired, disappointed, and pissed off. I'm a doctor. I fully understand that an IVF specialist would want to control risk. Doctors are obsessed with risk. I'm even sympathetic to the idea that fears of malpractice risk can scramble your reasoning. But think about it: our egg donor lived in an area without Zika transmission, which Collins never disputed. And we would have happily signed a release for Collins absolving her of any Zika risk.

For a doctor to have malpractice risk, something has to go wrong, and the doctor has to be at fault. Since there was no appreciable risk of Zika, and we would have consented to any risk going in, *there wasn't any malpractice risk!* I think their risk manager was worried about the *appearance* of risk (since there had been Zika elsewhere in Argentina).

We were glad Collins had consulted with experts and colleagues. But we only knew the differences between her recommendations and actual guidelines because of my research. And we felt wounded that we found out about those experts' recommendations only because one of them happened by tremendous coincidence to be a friend of mine who mistakenly emailed me about Zika two days before our clinic appointment. Whatever.

Prior costs:	$92,843.80
Refund:	- $1,061.00
Total:	$91,782.80

HUNDRED AND FIFTY DOLLARS FOR VITAMINS?! The fuck is this?" I got so mad I had to apologize to Jeremy later. I stormed off and searched pubmed.gov, an online repository for medical literature, for information on supplements to raise sperm counts, and also found an excellent nutrition guide from, of all places, Dr. Collins's website. Her site said to avoid junk; eat fruits, vegetables, and olive oil; enjoy some dark chocolate and green tea; and consider an array of antioxidants similar to those we'd bought. They sure as heck didn't need to be branded, though.

I emailed the pharmacy and got permission to return the fancy vitamins. Then, armed with my research and the list of supplements from Blumberg's office, I went shopping. I picked high-end fish oil and coenzyme-Q supplements (only the best for my babies, right?), but it only cost me seventy-nine dollars to replace the $750 vitamins (I'd also gone to Costco, so I had a year's supply). The only things missing were a zinc supplement (it's found in nuts and chocolate, so I probably have zinc toxicity) and the nitric oxide booster, which I decided was nonsense anyway. Nitric oxide was supposed to improve sperm counts by improving blood flow, but supplements to increase production of it in the body worked by supplying vitamins, amino acids, and antioxidants I already had. Notably, I did get B vitamins, vitamin E, and selenium supplements that *did* seem to raise sperm counts or quality but that Blumberg *had not* recommended.

So what did all this work get me? Well, for starters, I got pee that looked like highlighter fluid. I also got some peace of mind. Maybe I could increase the odds of success by taking vitamins, but then again, maybe not. A lot of Americans live on soda and fast food. America's top vegetables are iceberg lettuce, which offers little besides fiber and water, and potatoes, usually served as French fries. I, on the other hand, often eat a huge plate of organic greens, piled with other vegetables and sprinkled with nothing more than walnuts and extra virgin olive oil, and call that dinner. I don't think I corrected a vitamin deficiency by taking my supplements, so I was probably just making expensive pee. It was worth seventy-nine dollars to know that I'd done my best. It just wasn't worth $750.

Waiting at the pharmacy to return the vitamins, I noticed they had branded pens to give away. I grabbed one. Doctors misplace their pens all the time. When the staff members found out why I'd come, I got a bunch of concerned looks. "Uh, who approved this return?" one asked. "We never allow returns on vitamins." I told them that I'd driven thirty minutes after receiving approval to do just that. They huddled to discuss the matter; I grabbed another pen. "Sorry, we can't accept the return on the vitamins," they concluded. "We couldn't resell them. They could be compromised." I pointed out that all of the vitamins were still protected by their safety packing. "But what if they'd been damaged by being left out all day in your car?"

"You're saying they're heat sensitive? Well, they've been safely stored in our kitchen. More importantly, we were never told to protect them from heat, nor do the instructions say that. Many of your customers could have accidentally heat-damaged their vitamins, and they could have wasted $750 and possibly have a failed IVF cycle. I just want to be sure that's what you're saying." The pharmacist blinked nervously. "Sort it out, I'm in no rush," I said. The staff huddled again. I took another pen.

As I waited for the final verdict, I thought about what was really going on here. This place had assembled some possibly helpful vitamins and jacked up the price over ten times. Make a sale, and even a profit, but why gouge your customers?

Especially vulnerable customers. People go to IVF doctors, often, because they're desperate to have a child. It's very difficult for anyone to question their doctor or pharmacist, and it's even harder when the condition is infertility. I'm sure many normally levelheaded people who would negotiate the price of a water heater just swallow their tears and shell out hard-earned cash for brutally expensive vitamins, because *otherwise they're those assholes who care more about their money than their future children!* But you can do some really nice things for a kid with the $750 some executive would otherwise have put toward a third Lamborghini. And people don't even know if the services suggested by doctors and pharmacists are legitimate. For example, if your doctor says you need your hormone levels checked to predict fertility, almost everyone would simply agree and spend the $325.[101] It sounds reasonable. But a recent student found that ovarian reserve testing was useless. Thousands of couples, including us, wasted money on the tests. I took another pen.

The specialty pharmacy wasn't even upcharging for a service. Nothing had been individualized, no one had asked about my diet—they just handed me their standard vitamin bag. And the pill bottles, which the pharmacists had filled and labeled themselves, recommended different dosing from the instruction sheet. Even that sheet struck me as incomplete. For example, it said to take the folic acid every other day, rather than daily, as per the bottle's labeling, but not why. The why is important: research suggested that folic acid might increase the risk of *colon cancer.* Good to know, right? Dr. Collins's website, and several others, provided this information free with their recommendations, but it didn't make it into the $750 goodie bag.[xvi]

While I waited for the staff to decide on accepting their vitamin return, I remembered that I was wearing boxers. After ten years wearing briefs, I'd switched to boxers because they improve sperm counts (things shouldn't get too warm down there—that's why testicles are outside in the first place). I'd also skipped the hot tub, knowing the high temperatures harmed my swimmers—we really wanted our second fertility cycle to succeed.[xvii] But we never heard about briefs or hot tubs from *any* of our doctors. A cynic would say that was because that advice couldn't be sold. Much of the infertility industry feels like a racket, facilitated by parental desperation.

---

xvi Subsequent studies found no convincing effect of folic acid on colon cancer risk, one way or the other (Qin Ti, *Sci Rep* 2015).

xvii Sadly, this second round of egg collection yielded zero embryos, a result Dr. Blumberg attributed to the elderly parents involved. We did save money by getting medicines for Meghan from Israel, so they cost $2,400 instead of $4,737. But with the clinic costs added in, we spent another $23,050 trying to make siblings for a baby still in utero, with nothing to show for it.

Behind the counter, the huddle ended. "We'll be able to refund these vitamins to your card on file. Will that be okay?"

"Super," I said. "Mind if I take a pen?"

CHAPTER 36

EMERGENCY

T wo weeks before our due date, Jeremy went to an ultrasound/pelvic exam appointment with Delilah, while I went to a riveting meeting about diabetes algorithm implementation (I'd tell you all about it, but they're going to make it into a movie, and you can just watch that). When my meeting ended, I looked at my phone for the group text between the three dads and the surrogate, only to find that during the pelvic exam, Dr. Lee had tried to "strip the membranes" through the cervix, which can induce labor, just to get things rolling.

Whoa! What happened to running the program and trusting nature? If baby were ready, she'd tell us—kick, break the water, send a text message, start contractions, something like that. I knew that hospitals are graded on how often they end up inducing women preterm, or before certain milestones. And we weren't at thirty-nine weeks. Why were we trying to induce labor? I asked a few innocent questions to express my unease with this attempted labor induction.

"Oh, I didn't know they tried to start things this early, in a normal pregnancy," I said.

"No, you're not listening," said Jeremy "Dr. Lee *tried,* but she couldn't do it—the cervix was still closed."

That's what I said: *she tried.* "Able or not—I didn't know they tried to induce this soon," I responded.

"It's not an induction—this would have just been trying to get labor started."

"Induction" of labor v. "getting labor started"—it sounded like an attorney was parsing our birth plan, and I knew to drop it right there. Baby was full-term, a doctor had recommended this, so . . . fine.

But, holy shit! What if we'd ended up in labor *that night?* We hadn't picked out baby's formula yet. We hadn't packed a bag of clothes and toiletries so we could rush to the hospital on a moment's notice. We hadn't finished adding appliqué leaves to the nursery's stick-on forest, populated with stick-on birds, raccoons, squirrels, and other adorable animals. We hadn't yet guaranteed the outcome of the birth with a burnt offering to the Mesopotamian deity Nanshe, goddess of prophecy, fertility, and fish (lots of people say the homos are in league with Satan, but most of us actually worship Mesopotamian deities). My responsible boyfriends had read *What to Expect for the First Year,* but neither of them had yet prepared me a one-page cheat sheet on how often/how much formula Baby Mayfield would need to consume, and I sure couldn't keep her alive without that.

But the real emergency was that we still didn't have a name for this kid, cause we sure weren't going with Zika Palin-Mayfield. I convened a family meeting, and Jeremy got out the list of names on his cell phone (mine having been drowned in the pool with my phone), and Alan pulled out a baby name book.

Baby naming is a process driven by vetoes more than passion. We revisited the old debate about whether a kid's name should be easy, or whether she'd like something interesting, or whether she might hate her interesting name for fifteen years *then* like it. One of Alan's friends insisted on giving his kids truly interesting names. They settled on Zuly for their daughter, and their son didn't fare any better. Combine an old family name with something that apparently sounds normal in Poland, and voilà, you get Romulus Telek.

"Well, that's great," said Jeremy, "but I refuse to name my daughter Romulina Telek."

"What about Ren?" asked Alan.

"That's a bird," Jeremy replied.

"You're thinking of w-r-e-n," said Alan, but then I said I knew a guy named Ren, and it didn't work for me. "How about Chloe?"

"As in Kardashian?" I replied, gagging.

"Ellen?" asked Jeremy.

"Too lesbionic," said Alan. "Ellen Page, Ellen DeGeneres."

"Those are awesome lesbians," I said. "Ellen is fine for me. A little generic."

"Willa?" Jeremy suggested.

"That's a cow's name," said Alan, thumbing through the baby name book. "What about M names? We could be bold." He chuckled. "What about Morag?"

"That's a devil name," said Jeremy, "but I can't promise my daughter won't be a devil."

"I found it!" said Alan, but he hadn't—he had to spell his next suggestion: "Mairghread!"

"Is that Welsh for 'I tried to name my daughter Margaret after smoking ten rocks of crack'?" I asked.

"Esme?" asked Jeremy.

"What the fuck is an Esme?" I asked. "That's a human name?" Jeremy promptly told me there was an Esme in the *Twilight* series, and Alan informed me the wife in *Babe, Pig in the City* was an Esme. "Ok, very impressive memory, Alan, and Jeremy, to make sure I understand, you suggested naming our daughter after a character in the *Twilight* 'books'? Veto."

I took that moment to shoot down any C name on Earth. I have brothers named Chris and Craig. Chris married Cheryl and fathered

Claire and Caroline, and Craig was engaged to Carrie and, I thought, would likely produce Caleb, Clementine, Cyrenia, and Cleantha. "No C names," I said.

Over the next fifteen minutes, I learned that Kevin can be a girl's name, that Cody was English for cushion (didn't we just agree, no C names?), there are people running around named Gaelin, and that Ceridwen is the goddess of Bardism (for the last time—no C names!?). Also, Murphy was out, because that was Jeremy's coworker's dog's name.

"Riley?" asked Alan. I thought it was nice, but Jeremy thought it sounded like she'd been born with a piercing. "Rowan?" he asked.

I shot that one down: "Rowan, like Rowan Atkinson? Mr. Bean? Veto."

So we came back to the favorites we'd had for months: Harper and Parker. I was leaning toward Harper when we made a dreadful discovery. Alan checked all our name ideas on the Social Security website, where you can graph name popularity by year of birth (expecting parents: *you have to do this*). I would have guessed that the only Harper anyone would know would be Harper Lee, author of *To Kill a Mockingbird,* and I figured the name would be uncommon without being difficult. Boy, was I wrong. House researcher Alan announced that Harper had shot up from 847th to ninth in just a decade. "Must have been the Beckhams," said Alan, and I gave him a look as if he'd just worked quantum computing into the conversation. Apparently, the Beckhams had named a kid Harper, and people everywhere were following suit. Harper was out. We realized we liked Avery, too, but Avery had risen to sixteenth in popularity.

But Parker still held promise. And when I mentioned how I felt drawn to the -er names, Jeremy put Piper on the list, too. I immediately thought of *Orange Is the New Black* and author/reformed money launderer Piper Kerman, but apparently Piper *hadn't* become a thing: Piper was eighty-eighth and falling in 2017. Plus, what better way to signal to a daughter our confidence that she should be a flutist? Somehow, in ten minutes, we settled on Piper. Add in Jeremy's mom's first name, Joy, and Alan's surname, and we had it: Piper Joy Mayfield.

My mom called me the next day with more name suggestions. Before I could tell her we'd decided, to my great astonishment, she said she'd always liked the name Gay, and how about that?

Holy freaking Jesus Christ. Can you imagine burdening a child, already a potential target for teasing because of her three dads, with the name Gay Joy Mayfield? Her life until college would go like this: "Hey Gay Joy, which of your three gay dads enjoys gay joys the most?"

The nice thing about my mom is that pleasantries and phone decorum have been stripped away to about nothing over the years, which allows me to say such things as, "Gee, that sounds great. Let's call the kid with three dads Gay Joy, and she can be bullied to death by the age of one month."

"*I* think it's a lovely name," said Mom.

"Oh, it *is*," I replied. "But let's go all in. Why not call her Sodomy Delights Mayfield? Or Prostate Pleasures Mayfield? Or, if we want to go with the whole subtlety thing, we could call her Pearl and quietly change her middle name to Necklace. Great idea." I tried to audibly roll my eyes over the phone. My mom made a great recovery. My mom is such a master at the non sequitur that I call her zigzags *mom* sequiturs.

"I mixed in some cocoa with my coffee this morning. Delicious. I think we should all eat less meat. Do think you Trump is really going to get us into a nuclear war with North Korea? I heard they can hit California with their missiles."

All true, I thought. Just the day before, Trump had threatened North Korea—a country thought to have dozens of nuclear weapons and missiles that could hit most of the United States—with "Fire, fury, and, frankly, power, the likes of which this world has never seen before."

All bad news, whether about our politicians or environmental disasters, made me worry about our baby's future. She's going to face some incredible challenges over her life. She sure didn't need a name like Sixth or Gay Joy as one of them.

CHAPTER 37

GLAMPING

As Delilah's due date approached, and we got worried about our super-size baby getting stuck, Delilah's OB made plans for an induction. Meghan flew into town so she could share the experience and help for the first two weeks. Dr. Gordon, the semiretired OB who'd delivered Delilah's children, even offered to come in to deliver our baby. We only faced one wrinkle: Delilah's OB group had moved its inpatient OB ward from an old hospital to a sparkling new one midway through our pregnancy. The new one had the feel of Google headquarters and tons of amenities but fell short on one key feature: beds. The new facility had fewer beds than the old, even though the plan had acquired thousands of new members. The OB unit overflowed as soon as it opened.

Delilah wanted to induce labor on time anyway. She called the morning of the appointment, and the hospital told her not to go in. She called for Jeremy to pick her up. "I'll wait it out. Let them leave a massively pregnant woman in the lobby wearing a patient gown for six hours. They'll find a way. Besides, if we don't do this, Piper's going to get stuck!"

I arrived hours later for my shift (we knew this was going to be a long affair) with birthing food: steaming Taco Bell bean burritos, which are doctor-recommended to fuel contractions. "She's gonna like this so much she'll fight her way out looking for more," I said.

Delilah brandished her patient ID bracelet. The labor and delivery department was full. But true to her word, she'd changed into a gown and was camped out in the lobby. "I'll give birth in the waiting room if I have to."

Eventually the hospital found Delilah a bed in the triage area. To get started, she first had to ripen her cervix—otherwise it would be like trying to push Piper through a locked door. The doctor gave her misoprostol, a chemical messenger that relaxes the cervix and stimulates the uterus. Delilah's contractions started, and while she could feel them, they didn't bother her at all.

Hours later, all three dads had joined the party. We finally got a room, but not in L&D, which was still full. They put us in postpartum, where we immediately started exploring the room's features, starting with the seventy-five-inch LCD screen and bedside keyboard, which allowed you to text your nurse directly or access a catalog of movies. We unfolded a couch into a bed and set up a fancy picnic. We passed around chocolates, dried mango, and a selection of cheeses and salamis, and watched the *Ghostbusters* remake. When Kristen Wiig got showered with an eruption of green ectoplasm, Delilah announced, "Guys, that's basically a preview of my vagina any minute now." After a moment's reflection she added, "This is basically the most civilized labor ever. How many women labor with a cheeseboard? You know what we're doing? We're *glamping*. Epic."

At that point, a unit coordinator named Destiny showed up to discuss how we'd handle the whole poly-surrogacy thing. We handed over the legal judgment so the hospital could use it to create her unique birth certificate. "Great . . . now, I know the social worker had a plan," said Destiny, "but she went home, and no one can find it. We'll have to wing this. Okay, first thing: we don't provide rooms for surrogate parents. Baby can stay in the nursery, or with Mom, but you might want to think about visitation shifts and resting at home." No problem—we didn't expect special treatment, and we didn't want a woman laboring in the waiting area because we'd turned a patient room into our hotel.

But then Destiny lost her mind. At least, she lost *us*. "Second thing: normally we open a birth packet, and there's a bracelet for Mom and a bracelet for Dad, to allow you to visit baby. So there won't be enough for all of you." We all looked at each other like we weren't really hearing this.

"Destiny," said Alan, "we discussed this with the social worker, and she explained that we'd each get a bracelet."

"I was thinking that you could just attach the bracelets very loosely," she said, "and slip them off to give to each other."

"What have you done for other surrogate families?" Jeremy asked, rather sensibly. "Don't you just open up another packet?"

"Exactly," said Destiny, "but we give one of the bracelets to the extra parent, and we throw the fourth one away."

"So here's what we do," I said. "We don't throw that away. Four parents, four bracelets. Problem solved."

"But that's not our process," insisted Destiny.

On Alan's face, I saw an expression I've grown to know and love: one-third disbelief, one-third pity, and one-third "I'm going to eviscerate you," concealed behind a diplomatic smile. "I'm sorry," he said, "I can't tell if you're being serious. I just handed you the legal judgment declaring the three of us parents. Since I'm sure you don't want to bar us from seeing our baby, we'll just use the four bracelets." Alan had handled a Superior Court judge—he could dispense with a unit clerk with his left pinkie. His Jedi mind trick worked. Destiny retreated and returned with four bracelets.

Delilah's labor went peacefully over the night, but by 10:00 a.m., her contractions had picked up. She moved to a real L&D room and got an epidural. Her husband, Richard, sat holding her hand, a placid "no big deal" expression on his face, and I remembered he'd seen her give birth three times already. But Alan, Jeremy, and I could not relax, and we paced the room, which must have been thirty feet square. We watched Delilah, and we watched her steady contractions on her toco monitor. Eventually, at two thirty, her midwife came in and broke her water to speed things up. At three, a nurse commented that she still didn't know "where the dads were going" after the birth. "Where the baby is," muttered Alan.

We reviewed our birth plan—Jeremy would hold the baby first, getting himself that vaunted first skin-to-skin warming and bonding time. He replaced his shirt with a patient gown, open to the front, so he could plop baby right on his chest. Jeremy also planned to cut the cord—he promised not to pass out—but only after it stopped pulsating. Allowing that extra circulation would give Piper a higher blood count than immediately clamping the cord.

Another hour passed with nervous jokes. Alan whispered that he had a nervous stomach. Jeremy asked if he'd miss the birth to run to the bathroom; Alan said he'd just let it go and blame the smell on Delilah. Jeremy posed in his patient gown, and I told him to give us a runway walk to show it off. I got a random text from my mom, who hadn't given up on influencing name selections: "How about Skylar?" it read.

"My mom thinks baby's going to be a porn star," I said. Delilah, who's a bit of a mystic, said she hoped baby still knew the way out. There was an eclipse coming, she said, and energy-sensitive animals are known to freak out during an eclipse. "Don't think that's going to be a problem," whispered Alan. "I doubt Piper's seen any Facebook posts about the eclipse."

At four, Dr. Gordon showed up to say hi to Delilah in what seemed mostly like a social visit, since we all thought she still had a long way to go. She said she was honored that he came in for her; he thanked her for graciously delivering in the daylight. "So you were three and a half centimeters dilated at the last check?" he asked. "You've probably got a little ways to go. Shall we check?" As Dr. Gordon did his exam, a curious expression crossed his face. "I can't feel your cervix," he said.

"I found it far posterior," the midwife said.

"No, I can't feel it, like it's gone," he said. "She's fully effaced and dilated. So Delilah—you ready to push?"

CHAPTER 38

THE PUSH

Suddenly we found ourselves only minutes from parenthood. This was that weird moment where the primacy of expelling a fetus takes precedence over the usual privacy concerns, and of course Alan, Jeremy, and I all had a compelling interest in the goings on at Delilah's vulva, but we huddled at her side—close enough, *but* not too close. There's a lot of pressure during labor, and during medical school, I saw moms push something out of every orifice (in front of friends, family, and wide-eyed children, actually). Conveniently, Delilah's gastrointestinal tract had great timing, and she'd had a bladder catheter right up until she began to push. Piper's birth was immaculate.

Delilah immediately proved that she was a baby-making expert. Or baby-making machine? No, scratch that—Delilah is a baby-making *Olympian*. She wiggled into a comfortable position, told us how she wanted her legs positioned, and pushed like a boss. "Feeling any pain?" Dr. Gordon asked, and she said she felt *better,* because Piper had shifted lower in the pelvis, and our little one was no longer kicking her liver. We watched her toco monitor, and as each contraction began, the doctor gave her the go-ahead for another push. Delilah took a breath and bore down, a look of focused concentration on her face, her eyes closed; Alan and Richard held her knees back toward her ears. "She's on her way," Dr. Gordon announced after a quick look.

Delilah nodded. She never made a sound. Except for a tiny dot of perspiration on her upper lip, she looked like maybe she was a day late with a bowel movement. *This is some Scientology birth,* I thought. *Little Piper's not going to have any Thetans stuck to her. Delilah's a champ!*

Delilah pushed for less than thirty minutes (I didn't get the exact time—sorry, distracted). Halfway through, I noticed fetal heart rate decelerations (aka "decels") on the monitor. This is a classic sign of fetal distress. Fetal hearts beat as fast as a rabbit's. Under stress, that rate drops. That commonly happens when the head is compressed as a normal course of labor—these decels are timed to contractions and are called "early decels." But when something is wrong, and baby doesn't get enough oxygen, it compensates by restricting blood flow to nonessential parts of the body. This shunts oxygen to the heart and brain, so, you know . . . the brain doesn't die. This raises the blood pressure, causing a reflexive "late decel," which lasts *after* the contraction.

Piper had late decels. For most of labor, her heart rate ran about 150, and the nurses told us over and over how that showed she was handling the contractions well. Now she had decels to the hundreds . . . and to the eighties. The nurses stopped talking about her heart rate. Dr. Gordon remained perfectly calm, but he saw the decels, and I saw that he saw them. You know that smile people make for photos when they're not actually happy? A performance smile? That's what Dr. Gordon was doing. Did Alan notice? Did Jeremy? I sure as hell did.

Every horrible thing I'd ever seen or heard about happening to an infant (or mother) started to run through my mind. Amniotic fluid embolism. Placental abruption. Umbilical cord compression. Maternal hypotension. Pulmonary embolism. *Fuuuuck.* The good news was that because of Piper's fetal macrosomy—or large size—the delivery team knew there was an increased risk of complications, like shoulder injury, and had already requested the presence of the neonatal ICU team. The best doctors to help were already in the room.

Delilah bore down and pushed three times in succession. "She's got your hair!" a nurse exclaimed, and Jeremy leaned in for his first, probably only, view of a vulva. And yeah, little Piper had lots of golden hair! Her parents' genetic tests had predicted she'd be bald. More importantly, our child would be born in seconds.

"She's coming! Push, push, push!" said Dr. Gordon, and Delilah obliged. I could see Piper's hair . . . her forehead . . . her nose . . . Holy shit, we were having a baby! "Again!" he said, watching those worrisome decels on the monitor, and most of Piper's head emerged. "She's caught up right at the end. I'm gonna make a small epeese," he said, meaning episiotomy, a cut to widen the vaginal opening. He wanted baby *out*. Delilah gave him the okay, and I heard a spine-chilling scissor snip.

We were close, just the shoulders now, except . . ."Ooops, I get to cut the cord," Dr. Gordon said calmly. Piper was a dusky, vernix-coated blue. Her umbilical cord had wrapped around her neck. It was supposed to be supplying oxygen to Piper through her abdomen, where she was *not* getting crushed. But it was squashed between her neck and Delilah's birth canal, choking her instead of sustaining her. Dr. Gordon clamped the cord in two places and cut between them in five seconds flat. So much for leaving the cord alone until it stopped pulsing, and so much for Jeremy cutting it—at least the cord could no longer strangle her.

But neither could Piper breathe. She had no oxygen coming from her placenta now, and she had not taken a breath. Piper had to rely on whatever oxygen remained in her (blue) blood to keep her brain alive until she could breathe. She hadn't made a sound. I hadn't even seen her mouth open or her nostrils flare.

"I'm going to use vacuum," said Dr. Gordon, and he briskly applied a cap-like suction cup to Piper's scalp, squeezed a hand pump several times to make a seal, and with Delilah's next push, he pulled Piper free at 5:49 p.m. As he handed her over to the NICU staff, my anxiety went into overdrive.

Parents will tell you that they can hear a baby cry a mile away—that the sound distresses them like no other. I promise you, a silent newborn is worse. Piper hadn't made a sound, and she looked lethargic and limp. I couldn't breathe, either.

The NICU team placed Piper in a heated bassinet and got to work. "Intercostal retractions, weak ventilation," the doctor said. I heard "struggling to breathe."

"Seventy-eight percent," said a nurse. I heard, "Critically low oxygen." (Yours is probably 99 percent.)

"Diffuse rales," a doctor said, examining Piper's chest with the world's tiniest stethoscope, and I heard "crackle sounds from wet lungs."

And all I could think about was: *respiratory failure. Hypoxic brain injury.* Or even *cyanotic congenital heart disease*—somewhere along the line, the complex work of making her heart might have gone wrong, and her blood vessels could have connected in the wrong ways, depriving her of oxygenated blood.

Nurses clamped Piper's umbilical cord close to her abdomen and let Jeremy shorten it. "Keep cutting," one said. "It's chewy." They wrapped her and briefly handed her to Jeremy for a quick cuddle and a photo, but I knew I could not share in the moment until Piper had turned around. *Finally,* Piper cried, and I cried with her, half in fear and half in joy.

"We're going to take her to NICU for ventilator support," the neonatologist said. "Her lungs are wet. She can't breathe on her own just yet. She should be fine."

She should be fine. But I knew all the ways that things could go wrong with someone's breathing, and I saw the way they whisked her back from Jeremy to put her on high-flow oxygen—goodbye, vaunted skin-to-skin contact! I saw their hands move at emergency speed, and I heard the tension in the doctor's voice when he said, "Have chest X-ray meet us in the unit."

She should be fine. I saw how happy Jeremy looked, and I wondered if he knew the doctors were worried, and if he knew that *I* was worried. Maybe he thought this was all reasonably normal because he'd never seen a birth before. I just knew I was holding back as many tears as I could because I didn't want to upset him. I'd completely lost track of Alan and Richard, and I felt terrible about basically ignoring Delilah, who'd just gone through labor for us. Worse, I heard Dr. Gordon tell her she'd had a tear and needed stitches. But I reminded myself she had a husband and a doctor, while I had a kid. A sick kid. I felt like I was falling in love with her and losing her at the same time. I can't imagine what it's like to have a child born seriously injured, or not breathing at all. Especially somewhere in the third world. Or a hospital in Syria without electricity, or any number of things a hundred times worse. Just this felt like trying to hold on to water that wanted to slip through my hands.

She should be fine, the doctor had said.

She'll be fine, I told myself.

"Move!" said a nurse. "Let's get her to the NICU."

CHAPTER 39

NICU

From the moment I entered medical school, I lived in fear of a code blue—when someone stops breathing or their heart stops. What if it were up to me to save them? What if I failed? The doctors I followed around insulated me from disaster management, but I knew my time was coming, especially as I neared graduation. To prepare for code blues, I took a resuscitation class called Advanced Cardiac Life Support. I practiced so hard in the mock-code sessions that when I took ACLS a second time during residency orientation, an instructor asked me to help teach.

During my residency, I ran to every code blue so I could improve my skills. I always deferred to a more experienced doctor, but often, there was no one in charge, just a melee of confused people. "Who is running this code?!" I would shout, and then, if no one answered, "I am running this code!" Three times, I got to the patient *before* the code blue alarm sounded, by following any nurse who looked worried. That habit got me to the bedside of a patient bleeding to death from a procedure on his femoral artery (he lived), one suffering a cardiac arrest from a massive heart attack (he died the next day), and a woman choking on her secretions (she survived a trip to the ICU). I still manage the emergencies of my hospitalized patients: septic shock, respiratory failure, massive blood clot to the lung, severe alcohol withdrawal. I'm no ICU doctor, but I can handle a crisis.

But there was not a single goddamned thing I could do for my daughter except stay out of the way. I felt completely and utterly helpless, and it killed me.

The doctors told us Piper's lungs hadn't inflated well enough, or absorbed enough amniotic fluid, for her to survive on her own. Nurses crowded around her heated bassinet, suctioning her tiny nostrils and applying a device called a CPAP (continuous positive airway pressure, basically an external ventilator). This pushed pressurized air with extra oxygen into her lungs, and helped move the fluid into her circulation. Jeremy, Alan, and I waited just outside the room, sneaking glances when we could, rubbing each other's shoulders when we couldn't. Slowly, Piper's oxygen level climbed into the normal range. Everyone's anxiety eased, and the nurses finally let us into Piper's room.

The nurses turned to their next task—placing an IV in Piper's arm. I'm amazed that anyone can get an IV on an infant at all. Many adults have thready veins that are hard to draw blood from and even harder to catheterize; Piper appeared not to have any veins at all. The nurses turned off the lights and lit her little wrists from behind. The job looked impossible. Piper's arms were made out of uniform pink goo. Not only did she not have any veins, she appeared not to have any bones. It looked like trying to put an IV in a jellyfish.

I see a lot of suffering at work. Misery ranges from mild to catastrophic, like a young man burned head to toe when his motocross bike exploded, or a woman with an unfixable broken hip because cancer had eaten away the bone. But now I know that watching needles pierce my daughter is next to unbearable for me. I couldn't stand her little jerks as the needle slid in and out of her arm, I couldn't stand her helpless cry, and I couldn't stand how *weak* she sounded, in proportion to the torture she was going through. As the only usable vein in one arm popped and a purple bruise spread across her wrist, the nurses moved on to her other arm, and tears welled up in my eyes. But it had to be done. Piper couldn't feed with a CPAP on, and without a first meal, she risked dropping blood glucose levels, so she needed an IV for a glucose infusion. "She'll probably be fine," the NICU doctor said one more time.

Of course, the doctor was right. Piper almost certainly would be fine. But I couldn't stop worrying about the ways something could go wrong. First, she'd been deprived of oxygen for minutes. Her umbilical cord had been squished, and it had been strangling her. Had oxygen deprivation damaged her brain? And had something else gone wrong? Making a heart is a complicated process. A simple tube has to twist and grow into a four-chambered heart with multiple valves, shunts, and ducts. That process can easily go wrong. Jimmy Kimmel, the talk show host, has spoken passionately about his son Billy's life-threatening heart defect. Billy required several surgeries for a complex heart condition called tetralogy of Fallot, where four heart defects occur at once. The main symptom of this condition is . . . a blue baby with trouble breathing. I couldn't stop worrying about congenital heart disease. I knew that mild cases are missed for days or longer. Piper's first hours were about the only ones in which I wished I had *less* medical training.

Luckily, things started to look up for Piper. Her oxygen levels normalized on CPAP. She wiggled, grunted, and slept; it's normal for babies to look sedated after birth. So we just stared at her . . . and fell in love.

Once we'd spent some bonding time with Piper, and we knew she was safe, we headed back to the delivery room to check in with Delilah. She'd undergone several adventures without us. First, she said, her placenta came out in fragments. Pieces of it had been retained, and since they could get infected, they had to be removed. Dr. Gordon scraped out the remaining fragments from her uterus with his hand. *Shudder.* I didn't even know that could happen. Hearing about it made my pelvis ache.

But Delilah was happy enough about the birth that she still had a sense of humor. First she joked about getting extra payments because the OB had to punch her diaphragm from the inside, then about getting a few extra stitches "to tighten things up" for her husband. But she admitted the uterus scraping felt worse than the delivery.

Then there was the matter of that tear. Tears are pretty common, but most are minor, either first degree (through skin), or second degree (into muscle). One in twenty-five women suffer a third- or fourth-degree laceration, which means the tear extends into the anal sphincter, or through it (shudder, again). These injuries aren't just painful. They can cause fecal incontinence, or allow feces into the vagina, and in a resource-limited setting where repair is not available, that can ruin your life. No one wants poop in their vagina, and few men want a wife with poop in her vagina, either. And that doesn't take into account some other pelvic floor problems that can plague women after childbirth, like urinary incontinence and hemorrhoids. Seriously, if you're lucky enough to still have your mother around, call her right now and apologize.

Delilah had suffered a third-degree tear, and we felt awful about it. Later, she admitted to us that the first few poops she'd had were so painful they made her eyes water. We winced again. Have I mentioned that Delilah has given us an incomprehensible gift and we're forever in debt to her?

Back in the NICU, Piper continued to improve on CPAP, sucking and looking around more. As the hour grew late, we asked if one of us could spend the night. But Piper's nurse said that because we couldn't feed Piper until she came off CPAP anyway, this was a fantastic opportunity for all of us to rest. "She's got a full-time babysitter, and there's nothing you can do for her tonight. We'd call you if she looks worse. Go sleep." We didn't like the sound of that. We knew we couldn't help, but we felt like we were abandoning our little girl. So Jeremy called a friend who'd gone through a similar experience with her daughter, and her reply was immediate. "Get home and rest! Have one more peaceful night." So we did.

* * *

The next morning, Piper looked great. She'd been weaned off her CPAP and oxygen hours after we left. Now, she looked like a regular baby with an IV and remarkably chubby cheeks. I assumed the hospital would want Piper transferred out of intensive care. Adult patients pretty much have to be on death's door to get into the ICU. Piper was so vigorous, and so big. She not only looked like she didn't belong in the NICU, she looked like she might crawl out of her bassinet and go *eat* the other babies. But our nurse said no, she'd stay in the NICU until discharge.

Up and down the hall, we could see the strain of having a genuinely sick baby. We could see it in the faces of the exhausted parents who exchanged greetings with us, and we could see it in the elaborately decorated rooms of babies who'd obviously been sick for a while. The doors concealed all their individual fears and tragedies, but I had a sense of what lay behind them. I've worked with premature babies as small as seven hundred grams, which is about a seventh of Piper's birth weight. I've seen kids with the classic complications of premature birth, too, from ravaged lungs to bleeding brains to intestinal necrosis and sepsis. Reminding you how delicate all the babies were, all NICU guests had to scrub from their hands to their elbows for three minutes in a special sink by the entrance, like they were headed to do a liver transplant and not just hold their baby. We started to feel like impostors.

Liberated from the CPAP, Piper's biggest issue was getting weaned off her IV. Here's where I started to do some gentle doctoring for my baby. Jeremy, in particular, worries that I try to practice medicine out of my specialty. When he had excruciating post-tonsillectomy pain, he cringed when I asked the surgeon about using ibuprofen to control his pain, because the surgeon said ibuprofen was dangerous (she was wrong! I looked it up!). In this case, they were weaning my daughter off fluids much too slowly. And I wanted that IV out of her before it thrombosed her vein or got infected—and so we could hold her!

The nurse had orders to wean Piper's fluids from twelve milliliters per hour by one milliliter per hour, as long as she drank ten milliliters of formula in thirty minutes. Piper wolfed down thirty-four milliliters in *ten minutes*. Clearly, we wouldn't have trouble getting formula into her. "Wow, that will take at least a whole day. Do you think there's any way to speed that up?" I asked. Jeremy eyed me skeptically. The nurse looked perplexed. "She's only getting fluids as a precaution because she couldn't eat, right?" I added. "Well, she's eating like a champ."

Ten minutes later the nurse returned with a doctor's order to remove the IV if Piper did well on formula alone for another hour. Success! Now we could hold and feed Piper and take pictures of her with her adoring fathers. Pictures went out to family and Facebook, likes poured in, and we focused on feeding and enjoying Piper.

Looking back, we lucked out in some respects. Of course we'd rather Piper had emerged pink and vigorous, but the NICU came with real advantages. Our awesome nurse, Maricel, coached us on baby care. She also watched Piper while we viewed the 2017 eclipse from the hospital courtyard, enjoying the crazy crescent shadows it made through trees and sharing various viewing glasses and projection gadgets with a crowd of patients and hospital staff.

Piper also had her own room, where we could relax on a foldout bed, and Jeremy spent the second night with her. Had she not been in the NICU, there wouldn't have been any place for us overnight, because the hospital didn't provide rooms for surrogate parents. Had Piper not had trouble breathing, we might never have met our milk angel, Ashley (more on that later). And how many parents get a full night's sleep on baby's first night?

We still have our little mementos from Piper's first days, including a knit cap donated to the unit as part of a Girl Scout project, and my visitor badge, which reads "Dad #28" (for her room number) even though I've always considered myself Dad #3. The NICU eased us into parenthood, and the worst part of it—the terror of losing Piper—remains a precious memory of how much I cherish her, seared into my heart.

Previous costs: $91,782.80

Cheese board, chocolate, fruits, and snacks: $30.00
Hospital copays and fees: $0.00!

Subtotal: $30.00

Total: $91,812.80

CHAPTER 40

HOME

The doctor cleared Piper to go home on her third day. She'd been off oxygen and fluids and eating well, and she looked like a two-month-old. As we bundled her up to go, we heard the nurses talking about a baby that had been literally abandoned in the NICU. The dad had left the picture long ago, and mom had a new love interest. According to the nurses, the mom said, quote, "This baby isn't going to work with my new relationship." So she left her newborn baby to deal with whatever medical problems it had on its own, and took off.

Once we were out of earshot, we groaned.

"We love you *so* much, baby Piper," said Jeremy.

"Sixteen, beer, pickup truck," said Alan.

We'd paid a lawyer to design trusts and wills for three dads, which laid out the inheritance and succession of responsibility if one to three of us, and our families, and our friends, were all killed in some kind of successive apocalypse. America could suffer a North Korean missile attack plus the Black Death plus an alien invasion, and Piper would still have assigned parents and funding. And this mom had ditched her sick infant like a mismatched accessory.

Wow. Sorry, kiddo. Life ain't fair.

From the NICU, we headed to give thanks to both of Piper's amazing mothers. We surprised Delilah by smuggling a chilled bottle of champagne into her room, and after a toast with plastic glasses, we thanked her for her gift. What to say at such a time? Our words seemed wholly inadequate. She'd given us a beautiful daughter, and she'd paid a real physical toll to do it. I'm a sarcastic pain in the butt most of the time, but thanking Delilah brought out the sniffles that prove I'm a real softie.

Jeremy presented Delilah's birthstone push gift, a peridot pendant he bought at Tiffany's from a wildly enthusiastic, wildly gay salesperson who loved hearing Piper's story. Then it was Meghan's turn. We gave her a ring we picked out in Mykonos on a prebaby vacation, with irregular hunks of peridot and mother of pearl. She loved it and tried to convince us that something transcendent had happened.

"Guys, I know you're not that mystical, but I can feel that you're spiritual. So hear me out. We just had that eclipse—have any of you seen an eclipse before? I haven't! And right before I came here, I saw this ayurvedic astrologist, and she told me, based on my sign and where Venus is, that I should wear a pearl ring. I wanted a thumb ring, but she said it had to go on my ring finger, and this fits my ring finger perfectly! And guys, she told me it had to do with fertility. Now I have one that pairs pearl and Piper's birthstone! My name even *means* Pearl in Gaelic. Take that for what you will. It means a lot to me."

"I feel you," Delilah said with a wink.

After tons of hugs and a few final pictures of the three dads with baby secured in her car seat, we headed out the door. That's when I bumped into James, a coworker in my hospital's IT department. He'd come to an appointment with his pregnant wife, Ann. I introduced Alan and Jeremy, and we showed off our terrifyingly large infant. I could tell the dimensions frightened the mom-to-be. "Jeremy's the bio-dad, and he's six foot five," I explained.

"And you're, what, six three?" said James. "No wonder she's big—you're *both* tall!"

"Well," I said, "I'm tall . . . but I don't think that had anything to do with Piper."

James grimaced and laughed. "Ah, you're probably right. Hey, I'm a programmer, not a biologist."

Piper survived her first car trip just fine; Jeremy drove like a grandma. We plopped her on our bed. Meghan and her three dads gazed at her. She wiggled and winked and stuck her tongue out. "Have you seen *Inside Out?*" Alan asked Meghan. "The Pixar movie where everyone's emotions are little people operating them from inside a control room? It's like Piper's little people just arrived, and they're running around pressing all the buttons to see what they do."

"This is going to be a great week," said Meghan. "Just bonding and being happy. Let's make it special!"

"Yassss!" I agreed, jumping on the bed like Tom Cruise on Oprah's couch. "Let's stay in, cook organic ethnic foods, listen to the Indigo Girls, cuddle our baby, and synchronize our periods!"

Meghan laughed. Alan asked her when she first realized that I was a lesbian. "Well," she said, after much contemplation, "it's been several years." I love that she always answers these questions with complete seriousness.

Newborns don't do much besides nurse and sleep, so after we'd stared adoringly at her for hours, we hit the on-demand movie list. To start, Alan queued up the documentary *Babies,* a dialogue-free look at the development of four photogenic infants, growing up in Tokyo, Namibia, San Francisco, and Mongolia. The take-home message is that babies aren't that fragile.

"Jesus, I hate white people," Alan said, as the San Franciscan parents intoned, "The earth is our mother," at some vaguely Native American ritual, waving their infants in circles. "What a bunch of hippie zombies."

The Mongolian parents left their kid alone, tied to the yurt with a rope around his waist. As their livestock stomped around him, we wondered what the filmmakers would tolerate recording before they intervened. Naked as the day he was born, he later rubbed up against a rusty barrel sunken in the earth.

"I can't watch," I said, pretending to cover my eyes. "He's going to get penis tetanus."

The Namibian boy played in the dust, gnawing on a stray chicken bone. When he pooped, mom wiped him off on her knee, and then scraped her knee off with a corncob.

"I think we'll manage to keep Piper alive," said Meghan, a little stunned by the conditions in which infants can thrive.

"We may have bought too much stuff," said Jeremy.

"Actually, we didn't get a single chicken bone at our crappy baby shower," said Alan. To get us ready for the night, Alan bought a parenting video called *The Happiest Baby on the Block,* narrated by pediatrician Harvey Karp, about baby-soothing techniques. It was worth the five bucks in the first night alone, and we highly recommend it, but the key point is this: Dr. Karp calls the first three months of life "the fourth trimester" and recommends thinking of a baby as a fetus with a soothing reflex. To activate this reflex, you firmly swaddle a baby to simulate the tight uterine environment, among other techniques.

Armed with his infant-soothing strategies, Jeremy took Piper until around 3:00 a.m. Then, wiped out and with Piper inconsolable, he tapped out, and Alan took over (I promise I worked very hard on emotional support and home-cooked meals that night!). But Jeremy had already worked his magic—Alan found Piper zonked out in her bassinet, and in the morning when Jeremy checked on them, they were snoozing soundly with the white noise machine lulling them both to sleep. An hour later, someone we'd only met for ten minutes, once, would deliver the greatest gift Piper had yet received.

Previous costs:	$91,812.80
Champagne, thanks to Costco:	$15.00
Dr. Karp's baby-soothing tutorial:	$5.00
Subtitle	$20.00
Total:	$91,832.80

CHAPTER 41

THE MILK ANGEL

When we were planning our baby care, friends and family showered us with "breast is best" messages. They knew it wasn't up to us—they knew our breasts didn't work—but it's an appropriate message to send. Breast milk is the product of millions of years of evolution. It's perfectly designed for newborn babies, except for two significant limitations. The first is that milk production doesn't take off right away. Babies initially just get a small quantity of yellow colostrum, a "first milk" rich in protein and antibodies. It's liquid gold, just like its color . . . but it's not enough. Babies often cry for more milk than Mom can make, and they usually lose 10 percent of their weight in the first week. As Neha told us, "Just because nature hasn't yet found a solution to this problem doesn't mean you shouldn't do something yourself"—namely, supplement with formula.

The other limitation of breast milk is vitamin delivery. Pediatricians recommend supplementing breast milk with a multivitamin with iron, which is built into formula already. Apart from that, breast milk is pretty awesome stuff, highly digestible and loaded with infection-preventing antibodies. Remarkably, breast milk even adapts to baby's needs, by delivering more infection-fighting white cells and antibodies when a baby is fighting an infection. Apparently, immune tissue in the nipple can detect signs of infection during nursing. You still have to take a sick baby to the doctor, but that's pretty damned cool.

Delilah planned to pump for us, at least for a few months, or until work made it impractical. After that, where could we get breast milk? A pediatrician friend at work recommended a milk bank, mothersmilk.org. I checked out their site . . . and the take-home message is that breast milk is for rich people and high-risk babies. The site charges fifteen dollars for every four-ounce bag. It would cost more than $100 a day to feed Piper. We were looking at spending at least $20,000 to feed Piper to six months with donor milk—with the additional honor of depriving some premature babies of part of the supply. Who would have thought that milk costs more than Ivy League tuition?

We planned to use formula. Not our first choice, but not the end of the world. After all, Alan got formula and survived infancy (note: the breast-fed dads are six three and six five; Alan is five ten—coincidence?). There were still choices to be made, of course, but luckily Alan handled all the research, despite his formula-addled brain. He concluded that our best option was Enfamil Enspire, which contains lactoferrin, an infection-fighting compound, and MFGM, which . . . honestly, I have no idea what that is, even after reviewing the company's webpage.[102] I can tell you it is supposedly "clinically proven to nourish brain development," which I'm guessing means that all infants fed the stuff grew brains by the end of the study period. It's significantly more expensive than some other formulas, but not significantly expensive in the scheme of a surrogacy baby, so . . . our baby was going to get the best.

We even got a gadget that is basically like a Keurig for formula. You load it with powder and water, press a button, and voilà, you've got a nicely mixed bottle ready to go, and that sounded pretty neat to us, especially thinking about those 3:00 a.m. feedings. We were all set. But we never opened the Enfamil or the baby Keurig, because on Piper's first day in the NICU, we were visited by a milk angel.

Jeremy had just stepped out to check on Delilah when Ashley, a nurse on the unit, nervously approached him. She had three children, she said, and she pumped more milk than she needed, even though she had a six-month-old. She'd heard our story from Piper's nurse. "I hope I'm not overstepping my bounds," she said, "but I have all this milk, and I have seriously been wondering what to do with it. I was wondering if I could help your baby out."

OH MY GOD, yes, you can bet your sweet bippy we want your breast milk, Alan and I said when we heard about her from Jeremy. *For sure* we'd love to supplement formula with as much breast milk as possible.

So only a day after Piper came home, Ashley showed up with her six-month-old daughter and four-year-old son and more milk than we could have dreamed of. Three large tote bags overflowing with six-ounce bags—even some golden bags of colostrum, the liquid supermedicine moms make for newborns. Suddenly we had a storage emergency. We performed a rushed cleanout of our freezer. Somehow we managed to get it all stored, and we fell in love with Ashley and her family in the process. Ashley overflowed with energy and radiant niceness. Seriously, how many women keep pumping milk, enough to overload a deep freezer, just because they want to help out yet-to-be-identified babies?

And the milk obviously worked. Her baby, platinum blonde with deep blue, inquisitive eyes, looked like the kind of baby you find in an advertisement for organic baby food. Her son giggled and played fearlessly with our goldendoodles, who outweighed him about two times.

Not everyone was thrilled with the arrangement. One of Jeremy's coworkers (unaware that Piper had already started taking Ashley's milk) worried that our donor might have a disease, like HIV. Maternal HIV infection is one of the few reasons not to breastfeed a baby. This coworker worried, "What if she's crazy and trying to give your baby HIV!" So to summarize the possible motivations for Ashley's donation that either we or our friends dreamed up, we have:

❑ Angel
❑ Serial killer

I guess anything is possible, but an OB nurse has a lot better means for maliciously infecting babies with HIV than deep-freezing her breast milk for four months and hoping some polyamorous gays will show up so she can torture an innocent child for their sins. She could just walk room to room jabbing babies with needles and no one would know about it for years. We worried about several things while Piper boarded in the NICU, but we never worried about *that*. Considering Ashley's generosity, her medical training and obvious concern for children, her three healthy kids, and the panel of maternal blood work she'd had for her own pregnancy, which had only ended six months ago, we all came down firmly on the side of angel, and not serial killer.

So Piper got breast milk, and she loved it. On day two, she was pounding down two-ounce bottles every two or three hours (by day twelve, she'd be taking up to six ounces at a time). She didn't poop for a whole day, though, and that and a desire to track how much milk we gave her prompted Jeremy to craft an input/output chart in Excel. Remember, Jeremy's an internationally notable bird conservationist who's hatched and raised endangered Hawaiian honeycreeper chicks smaller than a quarter.

The next day, Piper announced the end of the poop drought with a series of grunts and farts. Within hours, I began thinking she overproduced poop like Ashley overproduced milk. We never did find a place to donate it. But we need to thank Ashley not just for helping out Piper, but for helping out *us*. As Neha explained, in a tone that conveyed years of olfactory trauma, "Breast-milk poop is amazing. It's yellow and seedy and doesn't stink. When you give them regular food, then it's just shit. Regular human shit. Twelve inches from your face."

It's true. Piper's poop didn't stink. It didn't smell like much at all; when it did smell, if I'm being honest, it smelled vaguely like food. I'm not saying you should spread it on toast, but it's a freaking miracle compared to ordinary poop. I decided to feed breast milk to Piper as long as possible, or until she's toilet trained, whichever comes first.

So far, Ashley has met every one of Piper's needs. She and her family even came over for dinner and game night, and they brought breast milk and ingredients for Moscow Mules—these are top-notch guests! Her boys delighted in playing with Piper, who seemed about as smiley with them as she gets. Ashley joked she's mostly pumping for "selfish" reasons: "Now I just tell myself I can have a slice of cake, because I'll pump it out in an hour." Ashley, we are delighted to help you with your cake habit! As far as I'm concerned, Piper is pooping out that cake right now, and it's vastly superior to regular feces. Keep up the good work.

Prior costs	$91,832.80
Keurig-like "Baby Brezza" we never used:	$179.95
Package of Enfamil:	$39.95
Bottles, nipples:	$60.00
Breast milk:	$0.00!!
Subtotal:	$279.90
Total:	$92,112.70

CHAPTER 42

PIPER'S DIAPERS: MEDITATIONS ON POOP AND DISNEY

One of my family goals is for Piper to look back on her childhood as a time of love and joy. I want her to remember her parents laughing, having a good time, and not taking anything too seriously, but instead making time for the things that matter. And that brings me to the intersection of family, poop, hilarity, and Disney films.

On Piper's seventh day home, we spent the day talking about poop. Some friends visited and told us they'd been scolded by the pediatrician, who found some poop in their daughter's vagina. They recommended a suction bulb to rinse her, front to back (this turns out not to be necessary). After they left, Jeremy put his hand on Meghan's knee and asked, in his most serious tone, "Meghan, how do you clean yourself when your vulva is packed with poop?" She laughed her head off and said that doesn't happen to adult women, as if we didn't know that, so we laughed *our* heads off.

Jeremy told Meghan how a coworker tried to scare him about the intersection of several things he most feared: poop and vaginas. Over breakfast (odd choice, I know), Jeremy had asked him what it's like cleaning that region during diaper changes. His coworker said, as ominously as possible, "Imagine buttering this English muffin, with all its nooks and crannies. Now imagine trying to get the butter back out." Every time Jeremy tells this story, he screams like a nonessential character getting stabbed halfway through a slasher flick.

It's not nearly that complicated. But I have often wondered just how Piper's gastrointestinal system manages to create certain problems. I was cuddling her with Meghan when she suddenly got fussy. "Look out, she's going through the great reddening!" said Meghan, and Piper grunted, turned bright red, and thunderously defecated.

Meghan handed me supplies as I changed her, and I wondered aloud how she managed to have a nearly spotless bottom and poop spread all the way up to her waist. "She's such a front-pooper. How do you women do that?" And Meghan laughed again.

That was the night we decided to catch up on our movie watching. We'd sworn not to let parenting keep us from recreational activities, and Jeremy wanted to introduce Meghan to *Moana*. Disney has mastered the art of animating films. There's astonishing animation, there's an adorable potbelly pig and a hilariously brainless chicken, and a decent depiction of the Long Pause, in which Polynesians ceased colonizing islands in the Pacific for two thousand years, before resuming for reasons unknown. True, Maui's companion goddess Hina is totally omitted, and Maui himself is animated like a giant slab of Spam. But we want our daughter to see good role models, and Disney has gotten quite good at creating independent, heroic female characters. Moana depends on her courage and wits, not a man, for her success. And Disney has a knack for churning out maddeningly catchy songs.

Piper had had an exceptionally poopy day. While Meghan and the other dads cheered Moana on her quest, I felt compelled to write some alternate lyrics about poopy babies. Apologies in advance. If you get these alternate poop lyrics stuck in your head, turn on *Frozen* and replay "Let it Go" until you're cured.

To Moana's "How Far I'll Go:"

The three of us put off having daughters
None of us getting pregnant, never really knowing why
Little Piper is my perfect daughter
But I know there is gonna be a diaper
every time I hear my daughter cry

Every toot she makes, all events lead back
From the time she ate to the sodden splat
However bad the scene, we will get her clean
How she longs to be . . .

(Chorus)
There is poop trapped inside of the folds of her vulva
No one knows, how far it goes
If I wipe carefully front to back toward the anus
Perhaps we'll know . . . If I look there's just no telling how far it'll go

When I finished the lyrics, I found the other parents in the middle of clay facials. I read them my song—and before long, irrepressible Jeremy could no longer contain himself and queued up some Disney karaoke tunes on Spotify. Piper and I settled in to watch, and Jeremy belted out "How Far I'll Go" (original lyrics) on an invisible microphone. Faces covered in gray goo, Alan and Meghan flanked him and cranked out an interpretive dance that careened from hip-hop to hula to ballet.

As Jeremy turned to "One Jump Ahead" and "A Whole New World" from *Aladdin,* I wiggled Piper in time to the music and thought about how much I loved all these crazy people. Alan cranked out his dance with one of Piper's blue feather fascinators clipped to his brow. Meghan alternated from uncontrollable laughter to dead seriousness as she moved between pirouette and plié. And Jeremy gave me murderous dagger eyes when I made the mistake of asking if he knew all the lyrics to *The Little Mermaid*'s "Under the Sea" (He does. Don't question him again.)

Piper's going to have an awesome childhood.

CHAPTER 43

#BLESSED

Going into fatherhood, I worried about being tired all the time at forty-two, but I knew I had plenty of experience working sleep-deprived, and you do learn some important skills with practice. During my medical internship, I took overnight call every third or fourth night for a year, which dragged the usual twelve-hour days into thirty-six-hour marathons: twelve–twelve–thirty-six repeat, or twelve–thirty-six repeat. Then, and with Piper, I knew I was inexperienced but qualified, and both times I never truly rested. As a new doctor, whenever I tried to sleep at work, either my pager would go off or I'd worry I'd made a mistake or forgotten something.

Caring for Piper proved to be significantly easier. I got to sleep easier, I only had one patient, she wasn't sick, and—this is crucial—instead of working all night and then having to practice medicine, I could hand her off in the morning. You know what's easier than taking care of a dozen medical patients, some complicated, some angry, and some dying? *Sleeping in,* that's what. Having extra parents around is amazing! Single mothers, you have my deepest respect. Stay-at-home parents whose partners got no parental leave? My condolences. Even the couples out there? I am *very* sorry about your sleep schedule, especially you breastfeeding moms! All we ever needed to do was stretch a late evening into another six hours of half sleep, then rest, knowing that someone else would take over. For those first weeks, we had *four* well-rested caregivers sharing responsibilities—and frequently a grandparent or two, fighting for a chance to feed or diaper our little girl.

Only with this much help could infancy go so easily. Before Piper turned two weeks old, she'd been to three restaurants and gone on several shopping trips. She'd received dozens of visitors and met three grandparents (who arranged for us dads to have a date night out on our own). We hosted a pool-and-pizza party for two other families, as well as our book club, for which we home-cooked both vegetarian and sausage baked ziti, garlic bread, vegetables, and a pistachio cake. Jeremy and I caught the *Game of Thrones* season finale at a friend's house, and we watched eight movies at home. I wrote an overview of health-care quality improvement techniques for my professional society. In my spare time I built a retaining wall in my yard and kept up with my exercise regimen, *without even taking any parental leave!* No way can an average married couple enjoy as much support and time at home to celebrate their little one.

And I'll be perfectly honest here: we get graded on a curve. An exhausted mom juggling children is too often seen as a spectacle, an annoyance, possibly just a complication for a clerk or waiter, and at the very best, a routine sight. We men, merely by tending to an infant, apparently become heroes. Gushing compliments come regularly. Once, Jeremy had bright-eyed, curious Piper strapped to his chest while we considered a shirt at a clothing store. A woman came up and clasped his hands. "You're doing a great job," she said, before leaving, and Jeremy cocked his head and wondered, "For standing here?"

Looking back, I'm sometimes overwhelmed thinking about how much love our community extended us, and how everything really came together.

Piper had a horde of caregivers and admirers from the beginning—all of them people who truly loved her. Our embryo donors never got to see us raise their biological child, but they came to us with a wonderful, generous offer, trusting us with their offspring. Delilah offered to be our surrogate out of an abundance of love, as well. We'll never forget her words: "I know that being parents will make you even better people, and that your life and hers will be full of love. That's something the world needs more of, so this is just a gift I want to give you." We made our planned donations to the charities she picked—in amounts totaling a typical surrogacy payment—knowing we would be in debt to her and her family forever.

Meghan gave us a gift, too, but with her, it feels more like we've begun a wonderful if unusual partnership, because she'll be as much a part of Piper's life as she wants. She's no longer just our friend; she's part of our family, and a delight to share Piper's first days with. Meghan, we love you! Add to that all the love and gifts we've received from friends and families. Piper has beautiful handmade quilts made by close relatives, distant relatives, and even by one of Delilah's colleagues! Then consider the mammary miracle of Ashley's breast milk donation, which eventually covered all of Piper's feedings up to and beyond solid food. Our daughter is incredibly lucky. Our family has received an embarrassment of riches, and we feel deeply, truly, *#Blessed*. As much as any polyamorous atheist pack of homosexuals in history.

Prior costs:	$92,112.70
Monthly expenses to Delilah, total:	$1,800.00
Donations to Delilah's favorite charities:	$27,000.00
Subtotal:	$28,800.00
Grand total for one perfect baby:	**$120,912.70**

CHAPTER 44

LOVE

W ay back in Chapter 3, I promised to share what I thought was the best reason to have children. It's simple: they make your heart swell with love until you think it will explode. Just the laughter of an infant can redeem all the wrongs in the world. I revisit so many memories of falling in love with Piper: the positive pregnancy test, her first ultrasound, winning the right to be her parent in court, and feeling her hiccups through Delilah's abdomen. Then I felt that horrible fear-love worrying I'd lose her in the NICU. Then came the enthusiastic smiles that narrowed her deep blue eyes, giggle storms at tickles or flurries of kisses, and our first conversations in baby talk. Then the endlessly curious wiggles so she could look in all directions whenever I carried her, puffing precious, excited baby breaths on my neck. Now she's doing everything from potty training to voraciously consuming Spanish lessons to dancing her version of *The Nutcracker* in cowboy boots.

But my thoughts return again and again to my first night on duty with her. Jeremy had taken her for her first night at home, calling on Alan for help around 3:00 a.m. I took her for her second night at home, her fourth night of life. I prepared several bottles of breast milk in the fridge, ready to go, and carried her to the nursery, on the other side of the home from Meghan, Alan, and Jeremy. Piper had a carefully prepared nursery, stocked with everything I could need, and a baby monitor I could listen and watch on. It would have been quieter to leave her in the crib, but I was terrified of some kind of SIDS or aspiration crisis and afraid I wouldn't hear her in the next room even with the monitor. I wanted her nearby. I swaddled her and laid her in the bassinet next to me on the bed. I heard every little coo and aww and gwah that she made and checked her after every one. I studied her noises and expressions and fumblings and managed every discomfort.

Sometimes she just needed a bassinet wiggle. When she really stirred, I figured out the problem pretty quickly. Once she just wanted to be cuddled. She really didn't seem to mind poop, although I changed her four times. Instead, milk fixed her nearly every time, even if she'd recently eaten. Just pop the nipple in the mouth, she'd eat, and distress vanished. As fast as you can say "Waaaaaaaaah-slurp slurp slurp."

Dead tired at 3:00 a.m., I either studied the smallest noise for signs of distress, or if no noises came, I checked her breathing. Nothing could have kept me from it. Keeping her happy and safe, my task until the morning, had become the most important task I'd ever had. Sometime in that first night, I realized that sturdy Piper could survive sleeping fifteen feet away from me. That night side by side wasn't for her; it was for me. I was falling deeper and deeper in love. And a few quick bottles and catnaps later, I woke to Jeremy coming to check on me at 6:30 a.m.

"You didn't need us?" he asked, having expected Alan to relieve me.

"I needed her," I said.

Jeremy kissed me and took Piper away so I could sleep. She gave a final "ehwah?" as he carried her away. I curled up, drunk with fatigue and adoration, content knowing that three rested parents would be taking care of her upstairs. Then I drifted off to sleep with a smile on my lips, thinking about one thing.

My greatest fear of fatherhood hadn't been of illness or sleep deprivation or poop. I knew most babies were healthy and everything would
work itself out. Instead, I'd worried that I just wasn't a baby person. I've
never been drawn to other parents' infants and never needed to hold all
the babies I met. The newborns I took care of in medical school just terrified me a little. So my greatest fear was that while I would certainly be
good to Piper, I wouldn't *feel* enough.

How wrong I turned out to be. Just thinking about Piper's trip to
the NICU fills my eyes with stinging tears. Kissing her tiny foldable
ears, brushing her chubby cheeks with my eyelashes, watching her lust-
ily devour a bottle, and feeling her fingers grip my pinkie—all of these
things make my heart leap like nothing before. My first night with my
daughter bonded us together for life. I can't wait to share adventures with
her, whether that's learning to walk, reading together, graduations, falling
in love, or children of her own (she'd better not wait as long as I did to
have kids, though, because if she does, she'll be diapering me and her kid
at the same time).

Good night, little Piper, I thought, as I fell asleep.
You're perfect.
Daddy loves you.
All *your daddies love you.*

CHAPTER 45

AFTERWORD

finished the last edits to Piper's book just as we celebrated two and a half years with her. She was a superbaby, and she remains a wonderkid, a blue-ribbon child, a legend for the ages. As she weaned from bottles, she ate anything, literally anything, without complaint: all baby foods, plus everything from bland, blenderized greens to Moroccan spiced couscous. She even ate a chunk of serrano pepper Jeremy mistook for bell pepper, mixed into an Eritrean curry with tangy injera bread.

Getting her to sleep was a different matter. To handle all those rough nights of infancy, especially as I took over as the primary daddy on my parental leave, I developed the following fourteen-step process:

1. Place baby in crib.

2. Walk away. The baby is now asleep.

Steps three through fourteen are repeats of steps 1 and 2 for the other six nights of the week. I'm being completely serious. Piper started sleeping through the night at four weeks. As Alan jokes, you get what you pay for. Baby duty during Piper's first year was not a bad gig; you usually got a full night's sleep, and after a morning feed, you could lounge around in bed with a baby cuddled in your arms, watching her smack her lips to a milk dream. Upstairs, the two "off-duty" dads usually got woken up more by our pack of dogs. Any one of the dogs could hear a squirrel down the street—or just have a bad dream—and a second later all four would be shrieking, sprinting across faces or groins, racing for the dog door to investigate.

I had a harder time sleeping than Piper. Even though I never risked cosleeping with her due to the danger of suffocation, I had recurring nightmares that she was smothering in the bed. I'd wake, heart racing, and run my hands through the sheets to find her. Half the time I'd realize she was in her crib safe and sound. Half the time I'd find a fragile, warm little body next to me and spend a second puzzling over why it was so furry, only to realize one of our dogs had wandered down from the master bedroom to slumber with me. It's my terror from the NICU, and it will always be with me.

So I had nightmares—but we also had a ton of help. We had our sequential parental leaves, plus help from Meghan and a rotation of seven grandparents. Piper only cried for food, except for a very few times when she just needed to be walked around the house or strollered around the block to soothe her. Each time frightened us—friends told me they suffered through colic every night for a year, but Piper's bouts were so rare, we'd always check and recheck her temperature, assuming she was dying.

Since then, Piper's grown into a little girl who amazes us every day. Into her twos, she has definitely started testing us, and if she misses a nap, she might have a full Chernobyl meltdown. But she's sweet, and she loves her family. She has an astonishing vocabulary that includes fifty-plus words of sign language and fifty-plus words of Spanish, and she says remarkable things that I jot down in a dedicated notebook:

Running like a maniac: "I'm young again!"

Requesting a hot tub session: "Hey, parents! Hot tub time. Thank you for taking off your clothes!"

To a preschool classmate: "You have two parents. I have *three* parents."

To a jar of applesauce on its side in the fridge: "Sleeping jar! Good night, applesauce!"

Wanting an emphatic kiss: "No! Do it with loud lips."

When I asked her what knitting was: "It's when you take the moon with you."

Out of the blue: "Salmonella! I want to go there." And: "I want to eat hay with the chickens."

Stuffing shirt with underpants: "I want boobies!"

To the universe: "I am a strong, innapenant woman! I am flexing my muscles!"

While potty training: "The poopies are sleeping…in my butt!" (mischievous smile).

But my favorite so far, the one that left me crying out of the blue in the middle of folding the laundry: "Papa! I want you to know!" she said. "Know what?" I asked her, and she said, "That I love you, and you make me happy." And she threw her arms around me and gave me a minute-long hug. I wiped away my happy tears and thought (as Alan has said) that someday I'll get cancer, or kidney failure when I'm too old to bother with dialysis, and I will think of this and smile and I won't be afraid. It will all be okay. What greater gift could a child give?

Piper has been joined by a little brother, Parker Lewis. Delilah bowed out, of course, after that shudder-inducing retained placental fragment, and we found Latisha, Parker's amazing surrogate, through an agency. Latisha has a broad smile and warm personality (when Piper saw the cover of Michelle Obama's book, *Becoming,* she exclaimed, "That Latisha! Latisha on a book!"). Latisha played Parker music and spoke to him through uterine speakers, and all her efforts seem to have paid off. He's developing a curious and sweet personality, just as he's growing his first two teeth. In the last week he's begun crawling at eighty miles an hour. He's as smiley and good-natured and easy to put to sleep as Piper (although he does enjoy a 3:00 a.m. bottle even at eight months). We couldn't dream of better kids.

So both infancies were just . . . easy. Getting there? Earning the right to parent? Quite a lot harder. Now that we're through all the rough patches and all, I've moved on to worrying about the local schools and whatever horrible app will be the Snapchat of our kids' tween years, we've reflected on the journey and reached a few key conclusions.

First, babies are adorable. I could have *said* that before Piper, but only now does thinking about baby squeals and giggles bring tears to my eyes. It's not just me; it's everyone at work who sees Piper, or everyone at the store when she wore her glam, sequined, fortune-teller turban. At least twenty people stopped to sigh over her or tell us she'd made their day the last time we dressed her for shopping. Sharing joy makes the world go round. So get your infant a fascinator.

Second, women are awesome. All of those people who stopped to gawk at Piper? Women. Our kind and trusting embryo donors, who started us on the journey to Piper? Women. Our amazing surrogates? Women. Egg donor and milk angel? Women. Most of our time-donating, gift-giving, blanket-making, babysitting-offering friends? Women. Every single person who has ever offered to help us juggle a baby and her gear at a restaurant or airport? Women. Every last one of them. Women cared for almost everyone on this Earth, and they created the rest. Why they don't run the world is beyond me.

Third, it takes *parents,* but a village sure is helpful. Ultimately, Alan, Jeremy, and I decided to have Piper, and it's our responsibility to give her the best life we can. But we're forever indebted to all the family and friends who've pitched in to assist us. We're indebted to the judge who let us all be parents to her from birth. We're appreciative of the leave policies that let us focus on nurturing Piper instead of worrying about work hassles. Babies deserve attentive parents, and they deserve communities and societies that facilitate raising them, from parental leave policies to well-funded schools to health promotion.

Fourth, *wow,* IVF families are expensive. All told, having Piper cost us $120,000, not counting that baby shower and the failed $23,000 second embryo cycle. We didn't set out to spend that much. We know it is the height of privilege to be able to spend that much to have a family, when so many people can't afford to. Others make the effort and end up with nothing to show for it.

But it doesn't have to be that bad. I give talks on waste in health care, both to medical students and practicing physicians, and while American health care is famous for providing unnecessary services, our biggest problem is that the prices for everything from drugs to procedures are just way too high.[103,104] That's true for hospital care (my field), and fertility medicine is also no exception. We were lucky to find a fantastic specialist in Dr. Blumberg, but fertility treatments should be affordable, not just excellent.

People seeking surrogacy services should press their physicians about cost and insist on disclosure and justification before work is done. Just because you want a baby doesn't mean you don't deserve fair and transparent pricing. Prospective parents should ask why routine ultrasounds and brief office visits generate hefty bills when they're already paying large fees for fertility cycles. No one should have to pay $25,000 for implantation work (and while you might have to, you should at least get clear instructions for your trouble).

No one should get pressured into fee-for-service exams and routine testing that could be done by their regular physician and paid for by their health insurance—IVF doctors commonly perform and bill for these services without telling patients they might be able to get them for free, which I consider unethical and wrong. No one should have to fork over $5,000 for fertility medicines when out-of-country pharmacies can supply them at half that cost. For those who are afraid to use foreign meds for such a crucial endeavor, IVF clinics should at least negotiate bulk-purchasing deals and only dispense what individual clients need, so they don't end up throwing out hundreds of dollars of medicines at the end of the process. And of course, no one should ever pay a ten- to twenty-fold markup on regular vitamins.

Lastly, love is love. The love in a gay family or a poly family is just as good as the love in a traditional *Leave It to Beaver* nuclear family. Kids understand this without effort, even if adults have a hard time. They feel love, and they return it. They don't care if their parents are gay or straight, brown or white, coupled or poly. The fact that Piper has three parents is just not a big deal. I have three parents myself—my mother, father, and stepmother—and no one thinks anything of it. In fact, I hate that word, *stepmother,* because mine helped raise me from an early age and taught me to love books and writing. She's not my stepmother. She's my mother.

I don't see any reason why there should be any fuss about a kid having gay parents or three parents. Why should that inspire hate? Hate isn't natural. Children have to be taught to hate. If someone's got the free time to go around judging other people's parenting, I recommend they go looking for the kids who are starved for affection—or even food—and help *them*. Find the kids who aren't being encouraged to reach their full potential. Find the kids who don't have parents who want them to discover joy and wonder in the world, every day. If they still have time, maybe they could focus on parents who teach children to hate, instead of love. If they deal with all of that, and they're *still* upset that our kid has an extra dad and lives a life full of happiness, music, and laughter in our babyproofed home, I'd be willing to hash it out with them over coffee, just to thank them for helping those kids.

The three of us strongly believe that the law should facilitate, not complicate, the raising of children by loving families. If we had not been determined, well-resourced, nonthreatening "regular" people living in California, we almost certainly could not have received a triple-dad birth certificate for Piper—and that does not sit well with us. To put her birth certificate in perspective, I reached out to our attorney, who told us that our family milestone had been discussed at judicial conferences up and down the West Coast. The issuing of a birth certificate to a loving poly family, he said, has changed the tone of surrogacy discussions in California, which leads the way for the whole nation. We know of one immediate positive impact: when we obtained our family's second poly family birth certificate, for our second child, Parker, we didn't even have to go to court and beg. In fact, we didn't even need to go to court. Our attorney handled the whole thing, which had become, as for two-parent families, a mere formality.

I also checked in with Will Halm, who'd briefly served as the attorney for my sperm-donation contract, and who had spurred us toward legal arrangements that honestly reflected the reality of our three-father family. He and his partner recently celebrated the graduation of their daughter from Yale. She's proud of her two dads and has not been harmed by the publicity that accompanied her trailblazing conception and birth. Their experience helped the three of us decide to share Piper's story. It is only because of people who bravely share the truths of their lives that society has moved from the traditional view that gay people should be vilified, shunned, and kept from contact with children, to one where gay parenting by surrogacy has become unremarkable and inspiring, all within a few short decades.

As for the legal considerations, I learned that Will had been closely following our path through the courts and had already celebrated our success. He knew all the attorneys we'd worked with. So, I asked, as an LA-based reproductive law attorney, did he know of any other poly family birth certificates? No, he said. There were a number of triple-parent families, as I'd learned from my research, but no poly families. He reminded me that court proceedings at this level are not made public. There could be other tri-dad or tri-mom families with joint custody; there could even be a polycule composed of a lesbian and three pansexual people with rotating sleeping arrangements, all of whom were dating a nonbinary Wiccan priest. There was just no way to find out.

What Will *did* know was that no such families had shared their stories. Reproductive law attorneys were discussing only one child with poly parents: ours. "You advanced the frontier of parenting law," he said. Now those attorneys could tell poly clients that *yes,* it is possible for their stable, loving families to be recognized with joint parentage, and for their children to receive all the benefits that come from having a legal relationship to all the adults that rear them. That, after all the stress and expense and trouble we went through to be recognized as Piper's dads, makes it worthwhile. Maybe another family has already benefited from the news or started down the path to recognition. And maybe our experience will nudge American society to be a little more accepting of all the different kinds of families out there, or nudge a few people into listening to their hearts and starting a consensual, honest, and respectful poly relationship. I just wish the law made it a bit easier for them.

The costs and legal irritations never remotely diminished our ocean of love for Piper, who's turning into a "strong innapenant" little woman and melting my heart more and more every day. Nothing besides Piper's joy makes me cry tears of happiness. During our first brunch, Delilah told me that fatherhood would make me a better person, and she was right. Piper helped me set aside screen time for real experiences. She has made me a more loving, giving, empathetic, appreciative person. I now love all the babies and children I meet, even in passing; I am now and will remain a man who offers to help a parent who has their hands full. The gift of our baby taught me to be a better person.

Piper (like her wondrous brother, Parker) is a true blessing. She radiates so much joy I figure she needs three dads, an adoring egg donor, an adoring surrogate, seven grandparents, and a community of friends just to absorb it all.

ACKNOWLEDGMENTS

My deepest gratitude for:

Alan and Jeremy, without whom there would be no baby and no book, for your love and for tolerating my personality defects a combined twenty-six years and counting.

Julie and Stephanie, for trusting us with your embryos and getting us started on our journey. Meghan, for giving us Meggs and giving our children your your love, your smile, and your cheerful disposition. Delilah, for making us a very sturdy baby; sorry about the laceration. Ladies, without your gifts, there would be no Piper. Thanks to Ashley for a year of milk and Latisha for making Piper a brother.

Dr. Blumberg, for getting Piper into Delilah's uterus. Dr. Gordon, for getting her out. The NICU team, for getting her well.

Our attorneys and judge, for our triple-parentage.

My three parents, Hope, David, and Susan, who taught me to love words, with chocolate. Jeremy's parents, Renee and Bob, and Alan's parents, Maddy and Michael, for welcoming us into your families and letting me write about you.

Numerous friends who supported me, gave me feedback on drafts, or let me include their anecdotes in *Three Dads*. Everyone in our book club, for letting me pick my own book and for your feedback, and particularly Neha, for expecting more. Everyone in Jeremy's book club, for your feedback as well.

Jessica Alvarez, my agent. Thank you for your hard work, incisive edits, and especially for believing in this project. Hannah Bennett and Cleis Press, thank you for giving me a voice and a chance to work with an LGBT-friendly publisher, and your edits as well. You elevated my work.

And Steve Shepard, wow. You were briefly my patient, you Googled me, and you offered to edit my first novel. For the love of writing and the payment of perhaps five coffees you offered me a river of red-inked edits and uncountable hours of your time, and taught me more than a year of university. Sheila Kirschenbaum, you generously loaned me your husband Steve for many hours when we didn't know he was running out of time—hours the two of you should have spent together. I miss him, and I'm sorry.

REFERENCES

ENDNOTES

1   "100 most frequently challenged books: 1990–1999," American Library Association http://www.ala.org/advocacy/bbooks/100-most-frequently-challenged-books-1990–1999.

2   "Egg donor costs + fees," ConceiveAbilities, https://www.conceiveabilities.com/parents/egg-donor-cost.

3   "West Coast Surrogacy Costs & Fees," West Cost Surrogacy, https://www.westcoastsurrogacy.com/surrogate-program-for-intended-parents/surrogate-mother-cost.

4   "Baby Gammy: Surrogacy row family cleared of abandoning child with Down syndrome in Thailand," ABC News, April 14, 2016, https://www.abc.net.au/news/2016-04-14/baby-gammy-twin-must-remain-with-family-wa-court-rules/7326196.

5   Lavers, Michael, "Gay couple unable to leave Thailand with daughter," Washington Blade, June 24, 2015, http://www.washingtonblade.com/2015/06/24/gay-couple-unable-to-leave-thailand-with-daughter/.

6   Trachman, Ellen, "Surrogacy in Asia is a Hot Mess," Above the Law, June 7, 2017, https://abovethelaw.com/2017/06/surrogacy-in-asia-is-a-hot-mess/.

7   Barker, Ann, "'Desperate' Australian couples unable to leave Cambodia with surrogate babies," ABC News, February 23, 2017, http://www.abc.net.au/news/2017-02-23/australian-couples-with-surrogate-babies-stuck-in-cambodia/8294810.

8   Healy, Catherine, "Irish dad and Kiwi partner stranded in Mexico with their surrogate babies," Thejournal.ie, March 29, 2016, http://www.thejournal.ie/new-zealand-babies-appeal-2686204-Mar2016/.

9   "The United States Surrogacy Law Map," Creative Family Connections LLC, https://www.creativefamilyconnections.com/us-surrogacy-law-map/.

10   Dobner, Jennifer, "Utah couple heads to state Supreme Court over law that prevents married gay men from having biological children through surrogacy," *Salt Lake Tribune*, September 12, 2017, http://www.sltrib.com/news/2017/09/12/married-gay-couple-challenges-utahs-surrogacy-law-after-court-denies-petition/.

11   Knox, Annie, "Utah high court throws out ban on valid surrogacy contracts for gay couples," Deseret News, August 2, 2019, https://www.deseret.com/2019/8/2/20755888/utah-high-court-throws-out-ban-on-valid-surrogacy-contracts-for-gay-couples.

12   Kaplan, Sarah, "Thousands of scientists issue bleak 'second notice' to humanity," *Washington Post*, November 13, 2017, https://www.washingtonpost.com/news/speaking-of-science/wp/2017/11/13/thousands-of-scientists-issue-bleak-second-notice-to-humanity/?utm_term=.c42d91cd0586.

13   Roser, Max, Hannah Ritchie, and Esteban Ortiz-Ospina, "World Population growth," Our World in Data, https://ourworldindata.org/world-population-growth.

14   Jarvis, Brooke, "The Insect Apocalypse Is Here," *New York Times,* November 27, 2018, https://www.nytimes.com/2018/11/27/magazine/insect-apocalypse.html.

15   Pierre-Louis, Kendra, "Greenhouse Gas Emissions Accelerate Like a 'Speeding Freight Train' in 2018," *New York Times,* December 5, 2018, https://www.nytimes.com/2018/12/05/climate/greenhouse-gas-emissions-2018.html

16   Friedman, Lisa and Glenn Thrush, "U.S. Report Says Humans Cause Climate Change, Contradicting Top Trump Officials," *New York Times,* November 13, 2018, https://www.nytimes.com/2017/11/03/climate/us-climate-report.html?_r=1.

17   Volodzko, David, "Trump's Climate Denial Is a National Security Threat," *Forbes*, August 23, 2018, https://www.forbes.com/sites/davidvolodzko/2019/02/23/manufacturing-climate-denial-is-a-threat-to-manufacturing/#293ee38d21b9.

18   Milman, Oliver, "Scott Pruitt is out but his impact on the environment will be felt for years," The Guardian, April 26, 2018, https://www.theguardian.com/environment/2018/jul/05/scott-pruitt-epa-impact-on-environment-analysis.

19   Gillett, Rachel, "7 Reasons people shouldn't have children, according to science," *Business Insider*, November 27, 2017, http://www.businessinsider.com/why-people-should-not-have-children-2017-11.

20   Brown, Jessica, "Can Friendships Survive Parenthood?" Parents, November 13, 2017, https://www.parents.com/parenting/relationships/friendship/can-friendships-survive-parenthood/.

21   Dick, John, "Hands down, people without kids have better lives—except for this one major thing," Quartz, September 11, 2014, https://qz.com/262645/people-without-kids-live-better-than-parents-on-all-fronts-except-one/.

22   Twenge, Jean M., W. Keith Campbell, and Craig A. Foster, "Parenthood and Marital Satisfaction: A Meta-Analytic Review," *Journal of Marriage and Family* 65, no. 3 (2003): 574–583.

21   Dick, John, "Hands down, people without kids have better lives—except for this one major thing," Quartz, September 11, 2014, https://qz.com/262645/people-without-kids-live-better-than-parents-on-all-fronts-except-one/.

24   Nelson, S. Katherine, Kostadin Kushlev, and Sonja Lyubomirsky, "The pains and pleasures of parenting: When, why, and how is parenthood associated with more or less well-being?" *Psychological Bulletin* 140, no. 3 (2014): 846.

25   Barash, David P., and Judith Eve Lipton. *The Myth of Monogamy: Fidelity and Infidelity in Animals and People*. Macmillan, 2002.

26   Rakoff, David, "The Way We Live Now: 4-22-01: Questions for David Barash and Judith Eve Lipton; Your Cheating Heart," *New York Times Magazine*, April 22, 2001, https://www.nytimes.com/2001/04/22/magazine/way-we-live-now-4-22-01-questions-for-david-barash-judith-eve-lipton-your.html.

27   Barash, David P., and Judith Eve Lipton. *The Myth of Monogamy: Fidelity and Infidelity in Animals and People.* Macmillan, 2002.

28   Stanley, Scott, "What Is the Divorce Rate, Anyway? Around 42 Percent, One Scholar Believes," Institute for Family Studies, January 22, 2015, https://ifstudies. org/blog/what-is-the-divorce-rate-anyway-around-42-percent-one-scholar-believes/.

29   Miller, Claire Cain, "The Divorce Surge is Over, But the Myth Lives On," *New York Times,* December 2, 2014, https://www.nytimes.com/2014/12/02/upshot/the-divorce-surge-is-over-but-the-myth-lives-on.html.

30   "U.S. Divorce Rates and Statistics," DivorceSource.com, https://www. divorcesource.com/ds/main/u-s-divorce-rates-and-statistics-1037.shtml.

31   Bair, Deirdre, "The 40-Year Itch," *New York Times,* June 3, 2010, https://www. nytimes.com/2010/06/04/opinion/04bair.html.

32   Twenge, Jean M., Ryne A. Sherman, and Brooke E. Wells. "Changes in American adults' sexual behavior and attitudes, 1972–2012." *Archives of Sexual Behavior* 44, no. 8 (2015): 2273–2285.

33   Haupert, Mara L., Amanda N. Gesselman, Amy C. Moors, Helen E. Fisher, and Justin R. Garcia. "Prevalence of experiences with consensual nonmonogamous relationships: Findings from two national samples of single Americans." *Journal of Sex & Marital Therapy* 43, no. 5 (2017): 424–440.

34   Sheff, Elisabeth, "How Many Polyamorists Are There in the U.S.?" psychologytoday.com, June 9, 2014, www.psychologytoday.com/us/blog/the-polyamorists-next-door/201405/how-many-polyamorists-are-there-in-the-us.

35   Whisman, Mark A., and Douglas K. Snyder. "Sexual infidelity in a national survey of American women: Differences in prevalence and correlates as a function of method of assessment." *Journal of Family Psychology* 21, no. 2 (2007): 147.

36   Blow, Adrian J., and Kelley Hartnett. "Infidelity in committed relationships: A substantive review." *Journal of Marital and Family Therapy* 31, no. 2 (2005): 217–233.

37   Wiederman, Michael W., and Catherine Hurd. "Extradyadic involvement during dating." *Journal of Social and Personal Relationships* 16, no. 2 (1999): 265–274.

38   Parker-Pope, Tara, "Love, sex and the changing landscape of infidelity," *New York Times,* October 28, 2008, https://www.nytimes.com/2008/10/28/health/28iht-28well.17304096.html.

39   Lehmiller, Justin J. "A comparison of sexual health history and practices among monogamous and consensually nonmonogamous sexual partners." *The Journal of Sexual Medicine* 12, no. 10 (2015): 2022–2028.

40   Swan, D. Joye, and Suzanne C. Thompson. "Monogamy, the protective fallacy: Sexual versus emotional exclusivity and the implication for sexual health risk." *The Journal of Sex Research* 53, no. 1 (2016): 64–73.

41   Anderson, Eric. *The Monogamy Gap: Men, Love, and the Reality of Cheating.* Oxford University Press, 2012.

42   Anderson, Eric, "Five myths about cheating," *Washington Post,* February 13, 2012, https://www.washingtonpost.com/opinions/five-myths-about-cheating/2012/02/08/gIQANGdaBR_story.html.

43   Smith, Tom, "American Sexual Behavior: Trends, Socio-demographic differences, and risk behavior," National Opinion Research Center, GSS Topical Report No. 25, updated March 2006, http://www.norc.org/PDFs/Publications/AmericanSexualBehavior2006.pdf.

44   "The good, the bad, and the dirty: The iVillage 2013 married sex survey results," Today, July 30, 2014, https://www.today.com/health/ivillage-2013-married-sex-survey-results-1D80245229.

45   Weaver, Jane, "Many cheat for a thrill, more stay true for love," NBC News, May 15, 2007, http://www.nbcnews.com/id/17951664/ns/health-sexual_health/t/many-cheat-thrill-more-stay-true-love.

46   Ryan, Christopher, and Jethá, Cacilda. *Sex at Dawn: The Prehistoric Origins of Modern Sexuality.* Harper Perennial, 2010.

47   Najibullah, Farangis, "Polygamy a fact of life in Kazakhstan," Radio Free Europe Radio Liberty, June 21, 2011, https://www.rferl.org/a/polygamy_a_fact_of_life_in_kazakhstan/24242198.html.

48   Gooch, Liz, "Malaysian polygamy club draws criticism," *New York Times,* January 5, 2010, https://www.nytimes.com/2010/01/06/world/asia/06malaysia.html.

49   Ibrahim, Farid, and Holly Robertson, "Inside Indonesia's controversial training seminars preparing Muslims for polygamous marriage," ABC News, April 4, 2019 https://www.abc.net.au/news/2019-04-05/inside-indonesias-polygamy-training-schools/10965646.

50   Ryan, Christopher, and Cacilda Jethá, *Sex at Dawn: The Prehistoric Origins of Modern Sexuality*. Harper Perennial, 2010.

51   Montague, Susan. "Trobriand kinship and the virgin birth controversy." *Man* 6, no. 3 (1971) 353–368.

52   "Same Sex Marriage? Answering the Toughest Questions," National Organization for Marriage, https://nationformarriage.org/uploads/resources/667_Talking_Points_%255BJLG_FINAL%255D.pdf.

53   Regnerus, Mark. "How different are the adult children of parents who have same-sex relationships? Findings from the New Family Structures Study." *Social Science Research* 41, no. 4 (2012): 752–770.

54   Regnerus, Mark, "Queers as Folk," Slate, June 11, 2012, https://slate.com/human-interest/2012/06/gay-parents-are-they-really-no-different.html.

55   Oppenheimer, Mark, "Sociologist's Paper Raises Questions on Role of Faith in Scholarship," *New York Times,* October 13, 2012, https://www.nytimes.com/2012/10/13/us/mark-regnerus-and-the-role-of-faith-in-academics.html.

56   Sprigg, Peter, "Homosexual Parent Study: Summary of Findings," Family Research Council, https://www.frc.org/issuebrief/homosexual-parent-study-summary-of-findings.

57   Stanton, G., "Key findings of Mark Regnerus' Family Structure Study," Focus on the Family, October 6, 2012, https://www.focusonthefamily.com/faith/key-findings-of-mark-regnerus-new-family-structure-study/.

58   Cheng, Simon, and Powell, Brian. "Measurement, methods, and divergent patterns. Reassessing the effects of same-sex parents." *Social Science Research* 52, (2015) 615–626.

59   Carpenter, Dale, "A "reality check for the Regnerus study on gay parenting [UPDATED], *Washington Post*, May 10, 2015, https://www.washingtonpost.com/news/volokh-conspiracy/wp/2015/05/10/new-criticism-of-regnerus-study-on-parenting-study/.

60   Bartlett, Tom, "Controversial Gay-Parenting Study Is Severely Flawed, Journal's Audit Finds," Chronicle.com, accessed April 14, 2018, https://www.chronicle.com/blogs/percolator/controversial-gay-parenting-study-is-severely-flawed-journals-audit-finds/30255.

61   Brodzinsky, Sibylla, "Colombia legally recognises union between three men," The Guardian, July 3, 2017, https://www.theguardian.com/world/2017/jul/03/colombia-three-men-union-alejandro-rodriguez-manuel-bermudez-victor-hugo-prada.

62   Bruni, Frank, "A Small-but-Growing Sorority is Giving Birth to Children for Gay Men," *New York Times,* June 25, 1998, https://www.nytimes.com/1998/06/25/us/a-small-but-growing-sorority-is-giving-birth-to-children-for-gay-men.html.

63   Manson, Bill, "San Diego woman offers herself for Growing Generations, gay surrogacy group," San Diego Reader, July 9, 1998, https://www.sandiegoreader.com/news/1998/jul/09/queen-surrogates/#.

64   Divilbiss, April, "PolyFamily Child Custody Case Ends After 2 Year Battle . . ." The Polyamory Society, http://www.polyamorysociety.org/Divilbiss_Families_Case_Ends.html.

65   Cloud, John, "Henry & Mary & Janet & . . ." *Time*, November 7, 1999, http://content.time.com/time/magazine/article/0,9171,33866-2,00.html.

66   Sheff, Elisabeth, telephone conversation with author, April 2018.

67   Peltz, Jennifer, "Courts and 'Tri-parenting': A State-By-State Look," U.S. News & World Report, June 18, 2017, https://www.usnews.com/news/best-states/louisiana/articles/2017-06-18/courts-and-tri-parenting-a-state-by-state-look.

68   "Checklist for Polyamorous People Contemplating Childhood," Sexual Freedom Defense and Education Fund, http://www.sfldef.org/poly-parent-tips.php.

69   Dobbs, Jared, "Polyamory! Why Not?" Alliance Defending Freedom, October 17, 2017, https://www.adflegal.org/detailspages/blog-details/allianceedge/2017/05/01/polyamory!-why-not.

70   Goldberg, Michelle, "Is a Surrogate a Mother?" Slate, February 15, 2016, http://www.slate.com/articles/double_x/doublex/2016/02/custody_case_over_triplets_in_california_raises_questions_about_surrogacy.html.

71   Vaughn, Rich, "California Court Rules Surrogacy Constitutional," International Fertility Law Group, January 1, 2017, https://www.iflg.net/california-court-rules-surrogacy-constitutional/

72   In re M.C., 195 Cal.App.4th 197 (Cal. Ct. App. 2011)

73   De Jesus, Jason, "When it comes to parents, three's no longer a crowd: California's answer to in re: M.C.," *Loyola of Los Angeles Law Review*, January 1, 2016, https://digitalcommons.lmu.edu/cgi/viewcontent.cgi?article=2982&context=llr.

74   Peltz, Jennifer, "Courts and 'Tri-parenting': A State-By-State Look," U.S. News & World Report, June 18, 2017, https://www.usnews.com/news/best-states/louisiana/articles/2017-06-18/courts-and-tri-parenting-a-state-by-state-look.

75   McNeil Jr., Donald, Romero, Simon, Tavernise, Sabrina, "How a Medical Mystery in Brazil Led Doctors to Zika," *New York Times*, February 7, 2016, https://www.nytimes.com/2016/02/07/health/zika-virus-brazil-how-it-spread-explained.html

76   Belluck, Pam, and McNeil Jr., Donald, "The Zika Virus Grew Deadlier with a Small Mutation, Study Suggests," *New York Times*, September 28, 2017, https://www.nytimes.com/2017/09/28/health/zika-mutation-microcephaly.html.

77   Tavernise, Sabrina, "Zika Virus 'Spreading Explosively' in Americas, W.H.O. Says," *New York Times*, January 29, 2016, https://www.nytimes.com/2016/01/29/health/zika-virus-spreading-explosively-in-americas-who-says.html

78   McNeil Jr., Donald. "Growing Support Among Experts for Zika Advice to Delay Pregnancy," *New York Times*, February 9, 2016, https://www.nytimes.com/2016/02/09/health/zika-virus-women-pregnancy.html.

79   Johansson, Michael A., Luis Mier-y-Teran-Romero, Jennita Reefhuis, Suzanne M. Gilboa, and Susan L. Hills. "Zika and the risk of microcephaly." *New England Journal of Medicine* 375, no. 1 (2016): 1–4.

80   Levine, Hagai, Niels Jørgensen, Anderson Martino-Andrade, Jaime Mendiola, Dan Weksler-Derri, Irina Mindlis, Rachel Pinotti, and Shanna H. Swan. "Temporal trends in sperm count: a systematic review and meta-regression analysis." *Human Reproduction Update* 23, no. 6 (2017): 646–659.

81   Salam, Maya, "Sperm Count in Western Men Has Dropped Over 50 Percent Since 1973, Paper Finds," *New York Times*, August 16, 2017, https://www.nytimes.com/2017/08/16/health/male-sperm-count-problem.html.

82   Lao, Xiang Qian, Zilong Zhang, Alexis KH Lau, Ta-Chien Chan, Yuan Chieh Chuang, Jimmy Chan, Changqing Lin et al. "Exposure to ambient fine particulate matter and semen quality in Taiwan." *Occup Environ Med* 75, no. 2 (2018): 148–154.

83   Møbjerg Kristensen, David, Christèle Desdoits-Lethimonier, Abigail Mackey, et al., "Ibuprofen alters human testicular physiology to produce a state of compensated hypogonadism." *Proceedings of the National Academy of Sciences* 115 (2018) E715-E724.

84   Allen, Joseph, "Stop playing whack-a-mole with hazardous chemicals," *Washington Post*, December 15, 2016, https://www.washingtonpost.com/opinions/stop-playing-whack-a-mole-with-hazardous-chemicals/2016/12/15/9a357090-bb36-11e6-91ee-1adddfe36cbe_story.html

85   Horan, Tegan S., Hannah Pulcastro, Crystal Lawson, Roy Gerona, Spencer Martin, Mary C. Gieske, Caroline V. Sartain, and Patricia A. Hunt. "Replacement bisphenols adversely affect mouse gametogenesis with consequences for subsequent generations." *Current Biology* 28, no. 18 (2018): 2948–2954.

86   Mesnage, Robin, Alexia Phedonos, Matthew Arno, Sucharitha Balu, J. Christopher Corton, and Michael N. Antoniou. "Editor's highlight: transcriptome profiling reveals bisphenol A alternatives activate estrogen receptor alpha in human breast cancer cells." *Toxicological Sciences* 158, no. 2 (2017): 431–443.

87   Mahler, Jess, "Polyamory and Pregnancy: Legal Stuff," Jess Mahler, January 15, 2017, http://polyamoryonpurpose.com/tag/birth-certificates/.

88   WORLD Policy Analysis Center, "Is paid leave available for mothers of infants?" WORLD Policy Analysis Center, https://www.worldpolicycenter.org/policies/is-paid-leave-available-to-mothers-and-fathers-of-infants/is-paid-leave-available-for-mothers-of-infants

89   Kaplan, Karen, "For babies, breastfeeding is still best, even if it doesn't make them smarter (though it might)," *Los Angeles Times*, March 27, 2017, http://www.latimes.com/science/sciencenow/la-sci-sn-breastfeeding-baby-iq-20170327-story.html

90   Deahl, Jessica, "Countries Around the World Beat the U.S. on Paid Parental Leave," NPR, October 6, 2016, http://www.npr.org/2016/10/06/495839588/countries-around-the-world-beat-the-u-s-on-paid-parental-leave.

91   Popovich, Nadja, "The US is still the only developed country that doesn't guarantee paid maternity leave," The Guardian, December 3, 2014, https://www.theguardian.com/us-news/2014/dec/03/-sp-america-only-developed-country-paid-maternity-leave.

92   Academic Personnel Services, "UC San Diego Policy and Procedure Manual," UC San Diego, July 1, 2010, http://adminrecords.ucsd.edu/ppm/docs/230-10.pdf.

93   Wagner, Erich, "Feds at two major agencies would not get paid parental leave under new law," Government Executive, January 6, 2020, https://www.govexec.com/pay-benefits/2020/01/feds-two-major-agencies-would-not-get-paid-parental-leave-under-new-law/162254.

94   United States Office of Personnel Management, *Handbook on Leave and Workplace Flexibilities for Childbirth, Adoption, and Foster Care*, United States Office of Personal Management, https://www.opm.gov/policy-data-oversight/pay-leave/leave-administration/fact-sheets/handbook-on-leave-and-workplace-flexibilities-for-childbirth-adoption-and-foster-care.pdf.

95   Toobin, Jeffrey, "How badly is Neil Gorsuch annoying the other Supreme Court Justices?" *New Yorker*, September 29, 2017, https://www.newyorker.com/news/daily-comment/how-badly-is-neil-gorsuch-annoying-the-other-supreme-court-justices.

96   Associated Press, "Modern Family: More Courts Allowing Three Parents of One Child," NBC News, June 19, 2017, https://www.nbcnews.com/feature/nbc-out/modern-family-more-courts-allowing-three-parents-one-child-n774031.

97   California Code, Family Code - FAM § 7962, Find Law for Legal Professionals, https://codes.findlaw.com/ca/family-code/fam-sect-7962.html.

98   Liu, Shiliang, Robert M. Liston, K. S. Joseph, Maureen Heaman, Reg Sauve, and Michael S. Kramer. "Maternal mortality and severe morbidity associated with low-risk planned cesarean delivery versus planned vaginal delivery at term." *Cmaj* 176, no. 4 (2007): 455–460.

99   "C-Section Complications," American Pregnancy Association, April 25, 2012, https://americanpregnancy.org/labor-and-birth/cesarean-risks/.

100 Wampach, Linda, Anna Heintz-Buschart, Joëlle V. Fritz, Javier Ramiro-Garcia, Janine Habier, Malte Herold, Shaman Narayanasamy et al. "Birth mode is associated with earliest strain-conferred gut microbiome functions and immunostimulatory potential." *Nature Communications* 9, no. 1 (2018): 50–91.

101 Steiner, Anne Z., David Pritchard, Frank Z. Stanczyk, James S. Kesner, Juliana W. Meadows, Amy H. Herring, and Donna D. Baird. "Association between biomarkers of ovarian reserve and infertility among older women of reproductive age." *JAMA* 318, no. 14 (2017): 1367–1376.

102 Mead Johnson Nutrition, Enfamil Enspire product page, Enfamil, https://shop.enfamil.com/enfamil-enspire/.

103 Anderson, Gerard, Peter Hussey, and Varduhi Petrosyan, "It's Still the Prices, Stupid: Why the US Spends So Much on Health Care, and a Tribute to Uwe Reinhardt," Health Affairs, January 2019, https://www.healthaffairs.org/doi/10.1377/hlthaff.2018.05144.

104 Sanger-Katz, Margot, "In the U.S., an Angioplasty Costs $32,000. Elsewhere? Maybe $6,400," *New York Times*, December 27, 2019, https://www.nytimes.com/2019/12/27/upshot/expensive-health-care-world-comparison.html.